I0521771

"A Captivating Crossroads of Cultures and History

Chicken in a Strange Way by Melanie Thomas Armstrong is a fascinating and engaging read, particularly for someone like myself, who grew up in Communist Poland and spent most of my life in the United States. The book offers a unique and personal perspective on a pivotal moment in history—Eastern Europe's transition from communism to a free-market economy.

At just 25, Melanie, a California native, landed a job at one of the world's most prestigious accounting firms in Prague, a city still grappling with the remnants of its communist past. Having previously visited East Berlin before the fall of the Wall, she was well-prepared to navigate the complexities of a society in flux. Her storytelling is richly detailed, bringing to life the cultural contrasts, bureaucratic absurdities, and daily struggles of a country redefining itself.

What makes *Chicken in a Strange Way* particularly compelling for me is how it resonates on a personal level. As someone who experienced this historical shift from the opposite direction—leaving Warsaw for New York—I found Melanie's observations both insightful and nostalgic. Her anecdotes, such as her story describing the unexpected need for a tone dialer in her new office, serve as vivid reminders of a world where past and present collided in sometimes humorous, sometimes frustrating ways.

Beyond being a personal memoir, this book is an important historical snapshot. It offers younger generations an engaging and accessible account of a time when Eastern Europe stood at a crossroads, seen through the eyes of a young professional navigating an unfamiliar yet fascinating world. Thought-provoking and inspiring, *Chicken in a Strange Way* is a must-read for those interested in history, cultural adaptation, and the resilience of human experience."

—SLAWOMIR GRÜNBERG, Emmy Award–winning documentary producer, director, and cameraman; recipient of Guggenheim Fellowship as well as the New York Foundation for the Arts and Soros Justice Media Fellowships

"When you tear down walls and a system of governance, a perfect, shiny new system doesn't just erect itself. Any of us who lived in post-communist Europe and helped to shape new institutions as democracy was forming will laugh with melancholy at Armstrong's memories; the restaurants that only had one dish—*was that gravy?*; the convenience stores with that one beer brand; the baking-hot radiators in winter and summer; and *ALL* the awful stinks. For those who have never, and hopefully will never, see up close what an autocratic regime that commands the economy can do to everyone's sense of normal, here's the one book to read."

—JUD NIRENBERG, prolific author; former resident of Czechia and of Slovakia and Roma civil rights movement leader; guest lecturer on Europe's civil right issues; director of philanthropic fund for Roma nonprofits and advocacy groups; winner of the Romani-American community's Baxt Award

"WOW did I enjoy reading *Chicken in a Strange Way*! Seriously, it was so fun and funny and heartfelt and ultimately helped me understand that culture and the forces that drive it are so much more complex than it ever seems on the surface. What this book offers is a glimpse of a culture in the middle of enormous change, with all the friction that entails— but we see that change through the banal, absurd, everyday interactions that shape real everyday lives. I truly enjoyed this journey."

—EMILY GINDLESPARGER, *Wall Street Journal* bestselling ghostwriter, book coach, and editor; author of the memoir *Please Make Me Love Me*; cofounder of Tell Your Story Memoir Academy

"Having grown up in the Ukrainian Republic during the Soviet Union and later immigrated to the United States in 1996, I read Melanie's book *Chicken in a Strange Way* through a deeply personal lens. For me, that world—gray apartment blocks, ration cards, and the quiet resignation of a people told not to ask questions—was simply reality. I never considered it strange until I arrived in the U.S. and saw that, through the Western prism, much of what I once accepted as normal was anything but.

Reading Melanie's account as a young American woman navigating 'my world' from the other side of the Iron Curtain was riveting. I couldn't put the book down. I laughed, I nodded in recognition, and I was transported back—not just to a place but to a mindset, a rhythm of life that many today cannot imagine.

Melanie doesn't just recount her experiences; she relives them with honesty, nuance, and a rare ability to capture the absurdity and beauty of that world. Her storytelling is vivid and true, and as someone who lived under that system, I can say without hesitation: She got it right! Her writing placed me back on the ground alongside her, and I felt as if I were living those moments all over again.

This book is not just a memoir—it's a bridge between two realities, a testimony to resilience, and a reminder of how deeply systems shape our logic, our habits, and our hearts. Absolutely amazing!"

—MAXIM NAUMENKO, Ukrainian immigrant and American businessman

A *SoCal* BEACH GIRL
TAKES ON COMMUNISM

CHICKEN
in a
Strange
Way

MELANIE THOMAS ARMSTRONG

Ballast Books, LLC
www.ballastbooks.com

Copyright © 2026 by Melanie Thomas Armstrong

ISBN: 978-1-966786-87-0 (Paperback)
ISBN: 978-1-966786-88-7 (Hardcover)
ISBN: 978-1-966786-90-0 (E-book)

Edited by Philip Pendleton Wilson Jr.
Cover design by Katherine Bryja Shady
Interior design by Suzanne Uchytil

Printed in the United States of America

Published by Ballast Books
www.ballastbooks.com

For more information, bulk orders, appearances, or speaking requests, please email info@ballastbooks.com, email melanie@chickeninastrangeway.com, or visit www.chickeninastrangeway.com.

For my children, two of the most amazing people I know.

In loving memory of Josef Pivoňka.

AUTHOR'S NOTE

WHEN I ARRIVED IN PRAGUE IN 1992, I was 25 years old. Young and naïve. A 5´3˝ accounting pit bull—5´4˝ in heels.

The Berlin Wall fell in October 1989 and triggered a domino effect across the Eastern Bloc. Czechoslovakia's Communist Party was ousted in November 1989 and the country split into two on January 1, 1993. The economic transition to capitalism took three years on paper but much longer in the hearts and minds of the people. Those years, 1992 through 1995, were a time of massive upheaval and probably the most dramatic change the country went through. It was the purgatory between the authoritarian government and capitalism. They had a communist party hangover. Things changed daily and I was there for it.

The word "communism" is commonly, and incorrectly, used by the West to describe the political and economic environment in Czechoslovakia, and the Soviet Bloc, at that time. In turn, I will do the same. In reality, the country was ruled by the Communist Party but never achieved true communism. It was an authoritarian regime. The few controlled the many. And the few benefited at the expense of the many. The idea of a "classless and stateless society" was poetic propaganda put forth by the rulers themselves. Make no mistake. This was a one-party dictatorship. The Communist Party seized power in 1948 and kept that power until they were toppled in 1989. The Communist officials dictated every aspect of the economy and society for 40 years. Wealth was not redistributed. There was no equality for all. They never achieved true socialism or communism.

I may not recall every conversation or situation perfectly, but every story in this book is true to the moment. The conversations are from memory and not intended to be word-for-word transcripts. Instead, I have retold them in a way that best conveys the essence of each conversation. In some cases, I have compressed events and conversations in order to better convey the stories of others. Some names and identifying details have been changed to protect the privacy of the organizations and people involved.

This is my story about what I experienced and how I experienced it. About how long it took to understand the environment and what the Czechs had lived through. I share these stories out of love and admiration for the Czechs and others in the Eastern Bloc who adapted to their situation because there was no other choice.

How do you tell a Communist?
Well, it's someone who reads Marx and Lenin.

And how do you tell an anti-Communist?
It's someone who understands Marx and Lenin.

RONALD REAGAN

CONTENTS

THE WALL 1

West Berlin 3
East Berlin 7

ME 14

THE FALL 16

THE OPPORTUNITY 18

The Research 21
The Visit 24
Orientation 26
The Packing 28
The Language 29
Ready to Go? 31

PRAGUE 1993 32

I'm Not in Kansas Anymore 33
Is It Me? 36
Pivo 39
Pizza Pizza 42
First Letter Home 45
They Have Beer 47
Hotel Atom 50
Kava 54
Pencils 58

Letter from Ostrava 61
Best Road Trip Ever 63
Good Help Is Hard to Find 66
Fridays at Pizza Taxi: The
   Beginning 69
Super Bowl 71
Brutalism (or The Weekend They
   Converted the Currency) 73
Blue Margaritas 79
Super Bowl Redux 82
Tomayto, Tomahto 83
Certified Nerd 85
Happy Birthday to Me 87
I Can't Ask That 90
Fridays at Pizza Taxi: Clients 93
Living in a Kafka Novel 97
Chauvinism 100
Spare Parts 102
Crash 110
Fridays at Pizza Taxi: Jamie and the
   Deli Bar 116
Melanie's Guide to Prague 119
Quarterly News of the Weird and
   Wonderful 122
Fiesta Mexicana 125
It's Impossible 131
Just One Native English Speaker . . . 133

CONTENTS

Breakfast Tickets 138

Inventory 140

Fridays at Pizza Taxi: Lost in
Translation 144

X-Games: Grocery Shopping 148

General Ledger 150

The Cementář 156

Stephen and the Two Desserts 158

Letter to Grandma 160

Fridays at Pizza Taxi: Flats and
Landlords 162

Baby Names 165

Nights with Jan Hus 169

Mike and the Shower 171

Subject: Lights 174

X-Games: Shopping Bags 177

Fridays at Pizza Taxi: Sexism 181

Mother's Milk 186

Porphyrophobia 188

*Quarterly News of the Weird and
Wonderful* 191

Thumping 195

Candle Man 197

Slashes 203

Communist Cuisine 205

Fridays at Pizza Taxi: Mike and the
Shower Redux 209

Jo's Bar 211

Are We There Yet? 214

Goodbye, Peter 219

The Stink Talk 221

X-Games: Baskets 225

Absurdism 228

My Kitchen Tried to Kill me 235

Markéta (or No Means Yes) 239

Fridays at Pizza Taxi: A Good Laugh
and a Terrible Cough 245

The Shoebox 250

We Have a Kmart! 252

*Quarterly News of the Weird and
Wonderful* 255

Josef and the Trabant 259

My Škoda 261

Fridays at Pizza Taxi: Škodas 263

Café Slavia 267

Cheers 270

Christmas Shopping (or Nothing
to Buy Here) 273

The Move 275

*Quarterly News of the Weird and
Wonderful* 277

PRAGUE 1994 281

New Flat 282

New Frustration 285

New Office 286

Fridays at Pizza Taxi: Flats and
Landlords Redux 289

Matróna and the Macho Pig 293

Letter Home 301

Chairs and Stools 302

Capitalism? 305

Jason, Therese, the Tram, and the
Coffee Mugs 307

U Šatlavy 310

Andrea and the Baileys 312

Tiles Olomouc 314

Fridays at Pizza Taxi: Socialized
Medicine 316

Healthcare News 320

Hardware Zlín 323

CONTENTS

Čínská Restaurace 325

Quarterly News of the Weird and Wonderful 327

Panels Telč 331

Fridays at Pizza Taxi: Communist Accounting 333

Bricks Mělník 340

Goodbye, Mike 344

The Grift 345

Concrete Brno 347

We Have Music! 354

Where Are All the Cows? 356

Moscow 359

Quarterly News of the Weird and Wonderful 367

Goodbye, Jamie (or Jamie and the Ribs) 370

Cauliflower 373

Wine Caves 375

Fridays at Pizza Taxi: Škoda Redux .. 378

Vašek and the Wedding 381

Quarterly News of the Weird and Wonderful 384

Gossip 388

Ten Twelfths to 1995 392

Game Meat 396

Absinthe 399

Fridays at Pizza Taxi: Communism .. 401

Merry Christmas 405

The New Year 410

Quarterly News of the Weird and Wonderful 411

PRAGUE 1995 415

Uniforms 416

Bribes 418

Quarterly News of the Weird and Wonderful 420

Goodbye, Me 424

Charles Bridge 427

Sweaty Socks 430

USA 1995 432

The Kettle 433

Exulansis 435

PRAGUE REVISITED ... 438

EPILOGUE 451

Notes 457

Acknowledgments 459

THE WALL

BANG! BANG! BANG! BANG! BANG!

EAST GERMAN BORDER GUARD: "PASAPORTE!"

I leapt off the toilet and tried not to pee on myself. There I was, a 5′3″ former band nerd with my acid wash jeans pulled down to my knees. An angry border guard was shouting at me from the other side of the bathroom door. I tried to keep my balance, and my cool, as the train sped through the East German countryside. My heart raced as I tried desperately to pull myself together without touching any of the nasty surfaces in this bathroom.

EAST GERMAN BORDER GUARD: "PASAPORTE!"

ME: "One minute!"

One minute? Really? Like that was gonna help the situation. I nervously rambled a few more things while I hurriedly pulled up and buttoned my jeans. I took a deep, deep breath and nervously opened the door. I had never been so terrified in all my life. A 22-year-old American girl face-to-face with an East German border guard. His anger was clear on his ruddy face, and his disdain for me was palpable. I imagined I could smell the vodka, sweat, and cigarette smoke on him. I knew I had done nothing wrong but trembled at the thought of being in trouble for some manufactured reason. A communist reason. Something ludicrous, silly, and that I would never understand. I may have watched one too many Cold War movies.

I handed over my passport, afraid he would find some flaw with it and wouldn't give it back. I was worried he would drag me off the train at the next station and accuse me of some infraction. He studied my passport like a gemologist studying a rare diamond. Then, he shoved the passport back at me with a huff and walked away with his boots clacking on the train floor.

I quickly turned and hurried back to my seat. It only took one look. Kathy could tell I was rattled.

Kathy and I were exchange students in Scotland for the year. For Easter break, we had visited a friend on the eastern edge of West Germany. Berlin was only a 2½-hour train ride away; this was our chance to visit the city split into two. West Berlin was capitalist and free. East Berlin was communist and closed. It would be so rad. We didn't know anyone who had ever been there. What's more, our guidebook, the ubiquitous *Let's Go Europe*, the so-called Bible of the budget traveler, said it was possible to visit East Berlin for a day. We would be the first people we knew to visit a communist country. We were the only people we knew who wanted to. No Orange Julius? No Benetton? No Hot Dog on a Stick? No way.

We had known before boarding the train that we would have to travel through East Germany since Berlin sat deep inside the communist country. We would be "hostages" on the train until the final destination of West Berlin. We hadn't worried about that too much. Suddenly it seemed like we should have.

Thankfully, the rest of the trip was uneventful. But I didn't dare to go to the bathroom again.

WEST BERLIN

MARCH 1989
EASTER WEEKEND

WHEN WE FINALLY ARRIVED, we emerged from the train station into one of the most vibrant, colorful, neon cities I'd ever seen. It was ALIVE. With traffic and people and lights. In many ways, it was just like other big European cities. Charming cafés, great restaurants, and historical sites. But in West Berlin, there seemed to be more of everything—especially the neon lights. Green. Red. Yellow. Blue. Enormous signs flashing and blinking. The entire city was like a carnival gone mad. It was blinding and disorienting. A huge strobe light that was never turned off.

On our second day, we made our way on foot to Checkpoint Charlie, the most famous border crossing into East Berlin and the world of communism. We walked towards the Wall slowly, as if it could somehow reach out and pull us to the other side. Nothing had prepared us for the reality in front of us. We strolled down Friedrichstraße towards the checkpoint. The street was full of quaint European shops and restaurants. Until the end. Smack in the middle of the street was a white guard booth surrounded by sandbags. Long wooden arms beside the booth were raised and lowered to let the occasional car through. Just past Checkpoint Charlie was the Wall itself. And on the other side: communism.

ME: "There it is."

Master of the obvious.

KATHY: "Wow. Just like in the movies."

The Wall was covered in colorful graffiti, which seemed to fit this neon city perfectly. As we got closer, we began reading the graffiti. Messages of love and hope for the people on the other side. A lot were in German and other languages, but I saw plenty in English. "If you love somebody set them free" was scrawled across the rounded top of the Wall.

Truthfully, we could have spent a long time in West Berlin before coming across the Wall. It wasn't especially tall, and the gray, graffitied cement blended in with the surrounding buildings, lights, and daily life. It was hiding in plain sight. But once we saw it, we would never unsee it.

We took each other's pictures in front of it like good tourists. Then I scanned our surroundings.

ME: "Is that a Checkpoint Charlie museum?"

KATHY: "That's what it says."

ME: "Doesn't that seem weird? Museums are usually about history, but the checkpoint is still here and active."

KATHY: "Weird."

Then things got even weirder. Right next to the Wall was a high wooden platform full of tourists. They were staring over the Wall into the East.

ME: "Do you think we can go up there?"

KATHY: "I don't see why not. Let's go for it."

We climbed the 18 steps up the wooden staircase and joined the others on the platform. What we saw over the Wall took my breath away. There was a wide strip of gravel and dirt between two walls. Crossing over the Wall was much more difficult than I'd ever realized. I had been so naïve.

ME: "Look at those guard towers. They're just like the ones I saw at a concentration camp once. But all of these are still manned by guards with machine guns."

KATHY: "Nobody would make it across the field without being shot."

A random tourist heard us talking and chimed in.

RANDOM TOURIST: "They call the field the 'death strip.' There are guards with dogs that will chase people down if they try to cross. If the dogs don't get them, the machine guns will."

I was absolutely horrified. This was happening right then. In 1989! More than 40 years after the end of WWII.

As we peered over the Wall, it was as if the East Germans were animals in a zoo. A zoo of communism. We were observing them in their natural habitat, just walking down the street. Or holding their guns up in the towers. I hated it. It felt so wrong to be watching them. Human beings held hostage in their own country. I couldn't imagine how anyone could be ok living like that. Trapped in a human cage. But now I knew why they didn't try to leave.

They couldn't easily come to the West, but we could visit them in the East. For a day. Despite how terrifying this suddenly seemed, we stuck with our plan. We were going into East Berlin to see for ourselves what it was like there. American movies made us think everyone wanted out. But maybe it wasn't as bad as we were imagining.

Our *Let's Go* guidebook had just a few pages about visiting East Berlin. Americans could cross into East Berlin for the day but were required to leave the city by midnight. We would each be required to exchange 25 Deutsche Marks for 25 Ostmarks (East German marks) to spend in the East. We wouldn't be permitted to bring any of the money back out. We worked out the cost in our heads. Around $45. Not bad. We figured we'd need that much for food, taxis, and souvenirs, so we weren't concerned. I didn't want to admit I was nervous. But it all seemed so odd. Why couldn't we stay overnight? Were there no hotels? Why were we required to exchange a certain amount of money? Why couldn't I keep some as a souvenir? Would I need more money? Why did this feel like a day at a museum instead of a visit to a foreign city?

We cautiously approached Checkpoint Charlie. The American guards in their drab olive fatigues were friendly but smiled at us quizzically. As if to ask why two American college chicks wanted to go to East Berlin. But they welcomed us into the one-room building. The border guards checked our passports, asked us about our visit, and reminded us to return before midnight. I was certain they were thinking "good luck" and wondering what the heck we were even thinking. We exited the building, and as we passed the infamous "You are leaving the American sector" sign, I stood for a moment in my white Reeboks and stared. The dark and imposing East German border crossing lay ahead.

EAST BERLIN

MARCH 1989
EASTER SUNDAY

KATHY AND I ENTERED THE FIRST ROOM of the border crossing building on the East German side. An armed border guard in gray, somehow an even more drab uniform than the American green, took our passports with a frown and shuttled us one at a time into a long, dark hallway. The guards were on a raised platform behind tinted glass. The light shone behind them as they peered down at me. I felt nauseous. It was like a movie about the Cold War. I felt like one of the characters being interrogated before they were shot. Three armed soldiers in gray uniforms looked at me, looked at my passport photo, talked to each other, and looked back at me again. The talking stopped. And after what felt like a very long time, the door at the other end of the hallway opened, and I emerged from the dark holding cell.

They returned my passport to me and led me into a series of additional rooms for different checkpoints. First, they checked everything in my backpack to see what I was bringing into the country. I really hoped they wouldn't confiscate my camera. I was sure *Let's Go* said I could bring one, but now I was worried. They exchanged my money. The Ostmarks felt like coins from a board game. They were weightless. As if they were worthless. How could this be their real money? I waited anxiously for Kathy to get through the gauntlet of border checks. She entered the last room, and we were "free" to go, both with our cameras and cash.

ME: "Ok, that was intense."

KATHY: "For real."

ME: "It was like that movie *Berlin Tunnel 21*. Same scary guards, a spotlight in my face, the intense scrutiny. I felt the same nervousness, wondering how it would go down."

Then, in an instant, the final door closed behind us. Two American college kids with permed hair and strawberry lip gloss in our pockets were standing on the streets of East Berlin. We were immediately overwhelmed by the nothingness of it all.

ME: "Everything is so gray."

KATHY: "Where are the cars?"

ME: "And the people?"

KATHY: "It's so . . . empty."

It was like a ghost town. The architecture was stark and downright ugly. The streets were empty but for the occasional little gray car driving by. There were no people walking down the street.

ME: "Maybe we went the wrong way."

KATHY: "I don't see how that's possible since the other way is back to West Berlin."

ME: "Maybe we just need to keep going to get to the center of the city."

We walked further and came upon a much larger road—Unter den Linden. We turned right and strolled down this wide street.

ME: "This seems like a major road, but there are no storefronts, nothing is open, and nobody is here . . ."

Wasn't this the capital of East Germany? Shouldn't it be a vibrant metropolis?

We checked our guidebook. We *were* going the right way. And Unter den Linden—which means "under the linden trees"—was described as "the famous grand boulevard of prewar Berlin." It was a lovely, leafy, tree-lined grand boulevard, but it was lifeless. We continued until we came to

Alexanderplatz and the TV Tower. The tower was, by far, the tallest building around. We used it as our compass. Seeing no stores, restaurants, or people, we decided to see the sights recommended by *Let's Go*.[1]

We made our way to the New Synagogue, one of the few synagogues that survived Kristallnacht, the "Night of Broken Glass," when the Nazis torched and ransacked Jewish businesses and temples. As we approached it, we began stepping around rubble. There was debris all around the synagogue and scaffolding covering most of the building. The doors were locked. We cupped our hands around our eyes and peered through the dusty windows. The dome was damaged, and light peered through. I stood back and took in the entire scene. After staring at it in silence for a few minutes, I realized what was really bothering me—more than the history we were learning about.

It looked like nobody had bothered to clear the rubble or repair the synagogue. Like they just left it as it was the morning after Kristallnacht, more than 40 years ago.

ME: "Why does it seem like Kristallnacht just happened yesterday?"

KATHY: "*Let's Go* says it was torched on November 9, 1938, and has never been renovated."

How could this be? That wasn't possible, was it? But it was true, and this stuck with me for the rest of the trip—and maybe much longer. Was this continued hatred of the Jews? Lack of money in the Soviet Bloc? Too few Jews left alive to matter? Simple neglect? I didn't know the answer, but it bothered me to my core. There was a very small sign on the side of the synagogue that said "Never forget this." It seemed like it would be hard to forget given that it appeared as though it had all just happened.

ME: "This bums me out. How can they have left it like this?"

KATHY: "At least they have that sign acknowledging what happened."

ME: "True. But wow. So depressing."

KATHY: "Yeah. I really need to see something more uplifting now."

I checked *Let's Go* to see what was listed.

ME: "How about the Monument to the Victims of Fascism and Militarism?"

She laughed out loud. Funny, not funny, but there wasn't anything that sounded charming or upbeat.

ME: "Ok, how about the Jewish Cemetery?"

KATHY: "That could be cool. Anything showing they know the war ended a long time ago would be better."

We walked to the cemetery on Große Hamburger Straße and discovered that the cemetery had a small park with a memorial called "Jewish Victims of Fascism." It was a beautiful sculpture, about the size of a dining room table, with a dozen eerie figures standing on a platform. They were about a foot tall—gray, stone figures of men, women, and children. Incredibly, this raised our spirits a bit. It was well maintained compared to the synagogue. And it was good to see a more significant remembrance of the horrors of the Holocaust that killed so many.

Having stared at it as long as we could bear, we went to find some lunch.

We wandered around the main square in town searching for a restaurant.

KATHY: "I don't see any obvious restaurants . . . do you?"

ME: "Not one."

Let's Go was of little help except to let us know we would have to stand in line and sit at communal tables. We were pretty much on our own to actually find a restaurant. We wandered around, but there were no restaurant signs. And certainly not the neon lights of West Berlin. We walked in circles for an hour. Then, we saw people—adults and children—heading through the door of a gray building. Seemed unlikely to be an office, so we followed, not at all sure what we were walking into. But it wasn't like we had a better plan.

The room was well lit but undecorated. The walls were completely bare. People carried trays of food and sat at long, communal tables in the middle of the room. It looked like we had found a restaurant of sorts.

KATHY: "Is it just me, or does this feel like a junior high cafeteria?"

I laughed.

ME: "It really does. Can we even eat here?"

KATHY: "I have no idea, but let's get in line and find out."

So we joined the line and each took a metal tray. As we neared the counter, where women in white uniforms and plastic hair coverings were serving food, we realized there was no menu. We didn't speak German, and no one spoke English. I looked around the restaurant and saw that everyone was eating exactly the same thing.

ME: "What do we think they're serving?"

KATHY: "I'm not sure . . ."

The women in white uniforms plopped some food onto plates and pushed them along the countertop. We grabbed the plates and put them on our trays. We took what they were serving; we were starving. We each held out a handful of Ostmarks and let the cashier take what she wanted. We sat down at a long table and ate what might have been chicken with a side of red cabbage. It was bland like the city. But we were happy to have eaten.

As we wandered around town, we encountered a few more people and cars sporadically. And we saw the Wall from "the other side." In the West, the Wall was covered in colorful, wild, serpentine graffiti. In the East, it was painted gray or dingy white. Not a speck of graffiti. Nobody stood or walked near the Wall; it was as if it were radioactive. But even from a distance, we could see the tourists on the platforms looking into the East, just as Kathy and I had done that morning. East Berliners knew they were being observed with fascination by the West. They could easily see them if they looked across the Wall. I wondered whether they were ever tempted to try to talk to the people on the platforms. I wondered if they dared. But maybe they'd grown accustomed to it and just carried on as if it were normal. I wondered what they made of it all.

ME: "*Let's Go* says we should visit the 'powerful' Soviet War Memorial in Treptower Park."

KATHY: "Great. Let's do that. How do we get there?"

ME: "We need to navigate the S-Bahn."

There were no signs in English, but the S-Bahn was pretty simple to figure out. Just like at other subways or metros we'd been to, we bought tickets at a booth and followed people to the tracks. We successfully made our way to Treptower Park Station with no issues. We strolled through a large park, scouring the area for a small memorial like we'd seen for the Jews who'd died. But once we came upon it, we stopped in our tracks. It was hard to process what we were seeing.

We slowed our walk as we headed up a large staircase towards two tall red granite structures we took to be the memorial. They were triangular and maybe 20 feet tall. One was engraved with a hammer and sickle. As we reached the top of the stairs, we realized these triangles were just framing the entrance to the actual memorial. And it took my breath away.

It. Was. Massive.

Peering through the entrance, we saw a football field–sized space with more statues and structures.

ME: "Dude. What are we looking at?"

KATHY: "I'm not sure . . . but it's huge!"

ME: "*Let's Go* says it's the largest Soviet WWII memorial outside the Soviet Union. Dedicated to the 80,000 Russians who died capturing Berlin."

KATHY: "The 80,000 Russians? Not the six million Jews?"

ME: "Nope. Let's see . . . the reliefs and sculptures are celebrating the role the Soviets played in ending the war. The marble used might be from Hitler's offices. Wow. Just wow. Are they honoring Hitler?"

KATHY: "Hopefully they pillaged his offices. Let's walk around the outside."

It was a promenade around a center garden.

ME: "Those granite slabs are engraved with Joseph Stalin quotes."

My skin crawled.

KATHY: "They're celebrating Stalin?! A murderous dictator?!"

ME: "Seems like it . . . I'm glad I can't read German. That enormous sculpture on the end is a soldier destroying a swastika, so that seems better."

KATHY: "This is psycho."

ME: "Totally."

We knew our photos wouldn't do it justice. It was the size of two football fields.

It was the first time I realized that the entire Soviet Bloc might really view the world differently than we did in the West. The disparity between the sizes of the memorials to the Jews and the Russian soldiers was beyond description.

It was getting late. We decided to head back towards the East German side of the checkpoint before it got dark. We needed to spend our Ostmarks, but there were no souvenir stands to speak of. We managed to find a shop with a few black and white postcards. We bought them all and resigned ourselves to simply forfeiting the remainder of our cash.

Going back through was even more unnerving than the first time. As a border guard escorted me into the first room, we walked past another room where an East German soldier was going through little scraps of paper pulled from a man's backpack. They looked like maybe they were phone numbers of people he'd met on his travels. The soldier was clearly questioning him about each scrap. As they rifled through my backpack, I worried that the border guards would "find" something. I held my breath. Would they confiscate my postcards? Or my camera and film? I was on pins and needles until he waved me out of the room to passport control. We left the imposing East German building and walked towards the friendlier American building. It was hard not to run forward to its safety.

Only that night did I realize I still had a pocket full of the almost weightless East German coins. Oh man! I had unwittingly crossed the border with contraband. I couldn't help but wonder what would have happened to me if they'd discovered them.

As we walked through the streets of West Berlin, it seemed the entire city was trying to frenetically overcompensate for the gray lifelessness on the other side of the Wall.

ME

I GREW UP A TRUE CALIFORNIA GIRL. Sand between my toes. Flip-flops and dolphin shorts. Lazy days beside the blue Pacific. I was born and raised in Manhattan Beach, a sleepy surfing town when I lived there but now a haven for the rich and famous. Both of my parents worked office jobs. I walked to school every day and to my friends' houses afterwards. It was always shorts weather, no matter the season. I don't think I ever owned a warm jacket except to go skiing or visit relatives up north. During the summer, my friends and I walked the mile and a half to the beach and hung out all day, slathering ourselves in handfuls of baby oil to fry in the West Coast sun in a way that would horrify parents today. We swam, talked, gossiped, and played cards all day. The only real rule was that I had to be home by dark.

It was something of a paradise. And there was nothing that a teenage girl needed in the world that she couldn't buy at the mall. I listened to Madonna scandalously sing "Like a Virgin" on the radio. I blasted the Bee Gees and ELO from my record player. We wore our Dittos and Jordaches to high school parties. White Reeboks sat in the corner of my room. The movie *The Breakfast Club* was the window to our souls. Then there was *Rocky IV*, where Rocky went up against the evil and brutish Communist menace, Drago. And *WarGames*, where the USA almost accidentally got into a nuclear war with the Soviet Union.

I'm a child of the Cold War. I went to junior high, high school, and college entirely in the 1980s under "the shadow of communism." This shaped me: the music I love, the movies I watch (and later made my kids watch), and my take on the world. The Soviet Union was our nemesis in all things. As far as I could tell, American politics was almost entirely focused on communism being the enemy of the USA. We heard it all the time: *Communism is bad*. I never really knew why. I had very little concept of what it really entailed, what it really was, or why we were taught it was so terrible. America was against the communists, and the Soviet Union was our enemy. And that was that.

Occasionally, I would think about "them." I saw dreary photos of emotionless people in drab clothes and the occasional news story about someone being killed trying to escape to the West. I had to conclude that the Soviet Bloc was a massive, continent-sized prison. Why else would people risk dying trying to leave? Why would the communists prevent people from leaving? And if it was so bad, why didn't anyone make it better? Didn't communists want a better way of life? But the truth was that I didn't know what was going on. None of us did. We just knew something over there was very different than here at home. It was us vs. them. Forever.

My endless fascination beckoned me to visit East Berlin when I had the chance.

THE FALL

I RETURNED TO MY OFF-CAMPUS APARTMENT after a long day of classes to find my roommates gathered around the TV.

ME: "Guys, what's going on?"

I was back at UCLA for my final quarter of college in the fall of 1989 and taking a very full load to knock out all the credits. It had been a long day of classes, and I was simply hoping to relax for a second. I walked up behind them to see what had grabbed their attention. It was the NBC news, of all things, not Thursday night "Must See TV."

I watched with them and was mesmerized. People were tearing apart the Berlin Wall with hammers, chisels, and anything they could get their hands on. They were climbing on top of the Wall and pulling other people up to join them. Tom Brokaw was in Berlin for a story the day before and was broadcasting live from The Wall. The East German government had announced that people could travel freely. (It turned out to be a bureaucratic mistake, but there was no turning back.) East Germans flooded through to the West and celebrated. Tom said, "The people are here to celebrate freedom."

Tears began to stream down my cheeks. I couldn't hold them back. I couldn't get the words out to explain to my roommates why I was crying. But I had connected with the images on the screen. Relief. Joy. Fascination. Jubilation.

I had been standing at the Wall just eight months ago. I had stared into the faces of the East German armed guards who were ready to shoot anyone who came too close to that very wall. Just two years prior, Ronald Reagan had said, "Mr. Gorbachev, tear down this wall!" And now it had happened. Over the next two years, I watched the news of revolutions, governments overthrown, reformers voted into power, democracies established, and, finally, the collapse of the Soviet Union. It went from what I feared was just a one-night fluke to a historic transition. It was real. I was overjoyed for the people who lived there. I thought they must have been thrilled to be free. Thrilled to no longer live in a colorless world. I thought it was particularly cool that the Czechoslovakians elected Václav Havel, a poet and former dissident, as their new president.

On the first day of 1990, he gave a speech to the entire country. He spoke about what they had all been through and what their government had done to them. He spoke about the wasted time and energy spent on producing things nobody needed yet not having the things they did need. He spoke about the people not being able to speak up under the prior regime. And about how this had worn them all down. But he ended with the miracle of their peaceful revolution and his vision for the future.

> "You may ask what kind of republic I dream of. Let me reply: I dream of a republic independent, free, and democratic, of a republic economically prosperous and yet socially just; in short, of a humane republic that serves the individual and that therefore holds the hope that the individual will serve it in turn. Of a republic of well-rounded people, because without such people it is impossible to solve any of our problems—human, economic, ecological, social, or political.
>
> People, your government has returned to you!"[2]

It gave me goosebumps.

THE OPPORTUNITY

AFTER GRADUATING IN DECEMBER 1989, I moved back in with my parents. My degree was in psychology, but I was really more of a math and numbers girl, so I took a leap and applied for accounting jobs. Through sheer gumption, I got a job as an auditor, which required me to become a CPA. I had to take night classes to qualify. The good thing was that I had a job. A *real* job. A *paying* job. It was with Arthur Andersen, then arguably the world's most renowned accounting firm. I was the most junior auditor on numerous clients, mostly in real estate and manufacturing. We dug into their financial records to make sure their financial statements were properly presented. I started out slowly, having taken only two quarters of accounting, but I learned quickly and really enjoyed the work. After a year and a half, I was promoted from "associate" to "senior," and I started leading tasks and supervising associates. My career was off to a good start.

The internet was just dawning, and we didn't have email yet. Just paper. I went to check my mailbox in the office mail room. There was a memo.

TO: Los Angeles Office Seniors
FROM: Robert G. Kralovetz
DATE: 19 June 1992
SUBJECT: Urgent Need for Audit and Business Advisory Seniors in
Central and Eastern European Offices

We have exciting opportunities available in Central and Eastern Europe. The need for partners and managers is beginning to be met, but the need for seniors in these offices has become critical. We are currently experiencing a period of steep growth, which is expected to continue throughout the next several years. In order to be in a position to pursue our development of a strong client base and to ensure that we can properly service their needs, as well as those of our existing worldwide

My visit to East Berlin came flooding back. The grayness. The drabness. The dullness. I couldn't wait to apply! I was intrigued by that world. Could it truly be as gray and sad as it had seemed? I wanted to talk to people and find out what it had really been like. I wanted to know what it was like now.

I wandered around to find out if anyone else had seen the memo. Nobody seemed interested. But I was. This was my chance to finally learn more about life behind the Iron Curtain. I told everyone I knew that I was applying for this. I got the same response every time.

EVERYONE ELSE: "Why would you want to go there?"

ME: "Why WOULDN'T I want to? Why wouldn't YOU want to?"

I couldn't understand everyone's lack of interest. Who could pass up an opportunity like this?

The large accounting firms were setting up shop in the former Eastern Bloc countries starting with Poland, Russia, Czechoslovakia, and Hungary. These countries were transitioning back to capitalism, and the firms were there to support the transition. I had no idea what that entailed, but they needed auditors. I was all in. Applicants couldn't pick a city, but I couldn't have cared less—I would have gone to any of them. I submitted my résumé, crossed my fingers, and went about my daily routine.

A week and a half later, my beige office desk phone rang. It was from Prague! Czechoslovakia!

I had a call with Susan, the office director, in Prague. We talked about the job and what the work would entail. They were very interested in my experience with manufacturing clients, and they had no issue with the fact that I was newly promoted. At the end, she asked me a final question.

SUSAN: "Would you like to see Prague for yourself before you make a decision?"

Was she serious? It sounded so thrilling. Romantic. Exotic. They had that cool "Z" in their name. They had a poet as president. I hadn't been allowed to apply to a specific office, but Prague had *chosen* me. I was psyched. It was my first choice.

ME: "I don't need to. I'm ready to go."

But she insisted. Looking back, there may have been a subtle warning to her insistence. Her way of saying, "You have no idea what you're signing up for," and they wanted to see if I could handle that. So, I prepared to fly to Prague for a long weekend.

THE RESEARCH

AUGUST 1992

I DRAGGED MY MOM TO THE BOOKSTORE at the mall. The tourism section was sizable. Here I would learn everything I needed to know about Czechoslovakia.

ME: "I don't see anything . . . do you?"

MOM: "No . . . nothing at all."

ME: "It's like the country doesn't exist."

We checked the section again and again. Nothing.

ME: "The Wall fell three years ago . . . shouldn't there be something on Eastern Europe by now?"

The salesclerk checked the computer. They didn't have any books in the store, but they found one they could order for me. The *Olympia Guide* to Czechoslovakia. I'd have Czechoslovakia at my fingertips.

When the book arrived, I rushed to the store to pick it up. I read the back cover.

> The guide is enriched with plans, a large amount of photographic material and an index.

Ok . . . I opened it up to the first page.

> Czechoslovakia offers foreign visitors a very rich selection of interesting tourist sights and enough opportunities for everyone to enjoy several days or even weeks of active rest.

Active rest? Enough opportunities for everyone? There were verbal oddities everywhere. I checked the date. 1991. It was current.

The history section began:

> The territory of Czechoslovakia has been settled unceasingly since olden times.

What was this bizarre form of English? Who translated this?

The lodging section was an incredibly dense and impenetrable paragraph on the Czech classification system for hotels. But there was not a single mention—not one—of a particular hotel. And the national tourist board, Čedok, which was supposedly the reservation agent for these theoretical hotels, had no contact information whatsoever. None.

Next up was food. I read the section called "Catering." What we would consider "Dining." Nothing about where to actually eat or how much it would cost, of course, but the writer did try to warn me:

> . . . dishes are usually heavier and richer in calories . . .

> . . . a smaller selection is usually possible when it comes to fresh vegetables . . .

> Not in vain is the typical Czech dish made up of pork, sauerkraut, and dumplings. Lighter kinds of meat are 'improved' in the same sense with, for instance, cream sauce . . .

> . . . beer is consumed to the greatest extent . . . [3]

If I only had paid more attention, I would have realized that someday soon I would go months and months before I saw a piece of fruit, a vegetable, or a salad.

The remainder of the book—more than 200 pages—was a dry recitation of seemingly every historical building in the country. I was so frustrated. I reread it. I still couldn't tell you where to stay or eat, but I'd certainly be able to answer one or two trivia questions about random buildings. I was as ready as I could be for my trip.

Still, I had no clue what to expect.

THE VISIT

AUGUST 1992
PRAGUE

THE SUMMER DAYS WERE BEAUTIFUL, and Prague, the city of a thousand spires, did not disappoint. The streets were packed with tourists, and I could've taken pictures for days. It was stunning. Old buildings, a castle, churches with spires, and beautiful architecture painted in pastel colors. It was nothing like the gray Soviet-style East Berlin I'd seen. It was the original Disneyland. Dark cobblestone streets. Mysterious alleyways. Graceful arches. Red tiled roofs. I was sold. Prague was a fairytale.

I was in Prague for my in-person interview at the Arthur Andersen office. Prague was flooded with young Westerners. I met a lot of people while I was there. Some of the people I'd be working for, a few expatriate colleagues, and some Czech staff. One day, I went to lunch with one of the Arthur Andersen staff, Jana, a Czech my age. We fought the crowds of tourists to get to a restaurant. There were so many people walking on the streets looking up at the buildings that we had to dodge and swerve repeatedly to try to make progress towards the restaurant. I was afraid I would twist an ankle on the cobblestone roads.

Thirty minutes later, we'd gone a few blocks and finally sat down for lunch. Jana helped me place my order, and we talked about the office. About the work, the people, the clients. What I really wanted to know was what it had been like living behind the Iron Curtain, but I wasn't sure how to ask. Finally, I tried.

ME: "So . . . what's different now compared to four years ago?"

JANA: "As soon as we were allowed to leave the country, I took a trip to London. I was amazed by so many things, but I'll never forget the moment I realized just how different it was from Czechoslovakia."

ME: "Oh? What happened?"

JANA: "I went to Harrods. When I walked into the food hall, I stopped and stared. So many different things. So much variety. Such delicious-looking sweets and breads and everything else. I stood there with tears running down my face."

ME: "Tears?"

JANA: "All I could think was, 'Why have they been keeping all this from us?'"

I wondered the same thing. I mean, I knew it had seemed bleak in East Berlin, but Prague was alive and vibrant. I had no reason to believe it had been anything like what I had experienced just four years earlier.

JANA: "Things are changing in Czechoslovakia but very slowly. Things are much different now than before the revolution but nothing at all like London."

I was spellbound. I just had to get this assignment. What was changing? How had it been before? I wanted so badly to hear more of these stories and see it all for myself. To know what this place had been and help it get to wherever it was going.

On my last day in Prague, I was offered the job. I was ecstatic.

ORIENTATION

TEACHER: "You're going to need a tone dialer."

What in the world is a tone dialer?

Arthur Andersen gave me four months to get ready to move to Prague. The first step was expat orientation in Chicago. Camp Pendleton for auditors. We signed paperwork. We learned some basics: dual taxation for expats, shipping goods internationally, things to take, background of the country in which we were to work.

And we learned about tone dialers.

There were no touch-tone phones in Czechoslovakia or the rest of the region. Only rotary phones. *Okie dokie.* To access our office voicemail, we needed the tones of a touch-tone phone. So, there was a handheld device we all needed to get. They sold them at Radio Shack. It had numerical buttons on one side. A speaker on the other. You held the tone dialer up to the receiver and pressed the numbers. And voila—modern voicemail. Who knew?

INSTRUCTOR: "All of you are going to hardship locations."

Really? Hardship? Other than the tone dialer, I was baffled. *Hardship how?*

I wondered. East Germany would have been a hardship, but I hadn't had the same experience or feeling in Prague. Jana had told me a little, but now Prague seemed just like any other big European city I'd been to before.

The instructor passed out a memo that laid out the hardship pay we would get depending on where we were going. I was shocked to see that the only location considered a bigger hardship than Prague was Moscow.

ME: "Ummm . . . why is Prague a hardship? What's hard about it?"

TEACHER: "Well, I haven't been, but the ATM fees are probably high. Things like that."

That didn't sound so hard. I was excited.

We had a little free time after orientation, so I went to explore the city. It was freezing cold! This SoCal woman did not take kindly to the Chicago weather. I realized this was the perfect opportunity to buy a heavy coat—a coat that simply didn't exist in Southern California. I headed to a local department store. They had an entire floor of warm coats! Fake suede coats. Fake fur coats. Neon turquoise ski jackets. I had never seen so many coats. I found a heavy jacket in dark brown and a London Fog raincoat in deep purple. I loved them. I was excited to have found something interesting and fun to wear since I imagined I'd being wearing them a lot through the winters. I might be cold in Prague, but damn if I wasn't going to be stylish.

And I had so much more to do to get ready to move.

THE PACKING

NOVEMBER 1992

Dear Debbie:

Dobrý den! How are you doing? When I visited, you mentioned that if I made a list of everything I ever buy at the grocery store, you could go through it and tell me if those things are available in Prague. Here are some of the key things I'm curious about. Please let me know if these can be found or if I should include them in my shipment.

Crest toothpaste
Suave shampoo
Dry Idea deodorant
Revlon lipstick—in Redwood
Tortilla chips
Peanut butter
Pop-Tarts

Debbie must have laughed when she got my list—nothing on it was available in Prague. I packed my suitcase and shipment full of supplies, including a five-pound container of peanut butter from Costco that would hopefully last me until my first visit home.

THE LANGUAGE

NEXT STEP: LANGUAGE LESSONS.

HELENA: "Hello, my name is Helena. As soon as we start, I won't speak English to you again. We'll meet each day at 8:30 a.m. and go until 5:30 p.m. Do you have any questions before we start?"

ME: "I don't think so."

HELENA: "Dobře."

And that was it. We spent the morning looking at pictures. Helena pointed to each one, telling me the Czech word for every item. We practiced the same words over and over and over. By lunchtime, my brain was swirling. *Finally, a break.*

We walked to a nearby restaurant and sat down. I asked her what I should eat there. Helena rattled off something in Czech. *Ohmigod.* She was only going to speak Czech. Even at lunch. I paused for a moment . . . took a deep breath . . . and started pointing at things myself. Salt—*sůl.* Pepper—*pepř.* Plate—*talíř.* Fork—*vidlička.* Spoon—*lžíce.* Knife—*nůž.* On and on.

All day, every weekday, for three weeks. Only Czech. Not a single word of English.

Not.

One.

Word.

I learned some key things about the language that seemed sure to come in handy.

An S with a butterfly, or háček (ˇ), Š, was the same as our "sh."

A C with a háček, Č, was "ch."

Awesome. I've got this.

Ť was . . . oh wait. That was more like "tj." Or "ty." Or somewhere in the middle. But did they not have the "th" sound?

Ř was downright impossible to pronounce. Something like "rtz?" With a trill. Kind of.

Ň was like "ny." *Ok . . .*

Ž was sort of like "zh"—if we had that sound.

Ď was like the Ť.

So, no hard-and-fast rule for what the butterfly did. Great.

There were lots of accents on vowels . . . I ignored those since the vowels made essentially the same sounds either way—at least to my ears. There was a "Ů" that sounded different, but I couldn't figure out how to make that sound.

At the end of each day, I was completely and utterly brain dead. I was emotionally and mentally exhausted. I couldn't think. Czech sounds and words swirled in my head. So many Zs, not enough vowels, sounds I couldn't pronounce. It was an intense three weeks.

As I headed to Prague, I didn't really remember much. I hoped it would come back to me. But I knew how to say one very important thing.

Zmrzlina. Ice cream. That was enough, right?

READY TO GO?

I WAS READY.

Take CPA exam. *Check.*

Find the mysterious tone dialer. *Check.*

Get guidebooks. *Check?*

Buy a lifetime supply of peanut butter. *Check.*

Stock up on deodorant, tampons, and other hygiene products not available in Prague. *Check.*

Ship personal belongings. *Check.*

Pack suitcase to last me until my shipment from home arrives. *Check.*

Learn Czech. *Eh.*

Yes. I was ready.

PRAGUE
1993

I'M NOT IN KANSAS ANYMORE

I ARRIVED IN A NEW COUNTRY with a new name and a bit of an identity crisis.

A little history. In 1918, after World War I, an independent Czechoslovakia was created from the former Austro-Hungarian Empire. In 1948, after World War II, the Soviet Union took control of the country and turned it into a Marxist-Leninist state. In late November 1989, they had peaceful protests against the Communist government, which became known as the Velvet Revolution. After 40 years, the Communists had been removed from power. For a few years afterwards, the country was known as the Czech and Slovak Federative Republic (ČSFR). A formal separation of sorts. In November 1992, Parliament voted to split the country, a decision known as the Velvet Divorce. On January 1, 1993—just days before I arrived—it split into two countries, the Czech republic and Slovakia, each beginning to move towards democracy and capitalism.

So it was that I arrived in the newly founded *Česká republika*, or Czech republic. (In Czech, the "r" in republika was lower case, so with no official guidance forthcoming, our office decided not to capitalize the "r" in republic either.)

I was picked up at the Prague airport by the office driver, who took me directly to the corporate flat where I would live until I found my own place. The flat was affectionately known by the name of the street it was on: Dušní (pronounced DOO-shni). I entered the flat and looked for the bedroom to start unpacking. Weirdly, I didn't immediately see a bedroom. It wasn't exactly a big place; there couldn't be too many places for a bedroom to hide. I found the living room and the bathroom. As I entered the kitchen, I stopped in my tracks.

There it was. The bed. In the kitchen.

The twin bed was on the far side of the room, just past a small dining table with a few chairs. I really had no idea what to make of this, but I put my suitcase on the bed—in the kitchen—and started unpacking. I took a shower to clean up after my long day of traveling. The water pressure wasn't great, but the water was hot. (I made a mental note to myself to find a flat with good water pressure. And a bedroom.) When I returned to the kitchen/bedroom, I noticed that the sink was full of dirty water. I hadn't seen that earlier. Yuck. It was late, but I decided to call my office contact. I found the rotary dial phone in the sitting room, but when I lifted the receiver, there was nothing but silence. *Great.* No bedroom, the sink was full of dirty water, and the phone didn't work. Welcome to Prague. I realized I wouldn't solve anything that night, so I settled into bed to watch TV because, of course, the TV was also in the kitchen. The only thing I could find in English was CNN, so I watched the news for a bit before drifting off.

When I woke in the morning, the sink was empty of brown water, but the phone still didn't work. I was excited to explore the city, so I got ready to go.

I went to the kitchen to see if there was any food. Someone had kindly stocked some basics: rolls, butter, and a box of milk, all sitting on the counter. I opened the refrigerator, but it was warm and empty inside. No bedroom, no phone, no fridge, and a sink that filled with dirty water. Was this some sort of bizarre hazing ritual? I decided to get food while I was out.

I checked myself in the mirror, and I was horrified! My hair was a disaster. Crumpled and lifeless. Even worse were my bangs. I had a permed '80s hairstyle with big bangs that required serious maintenance. My bangs hadn't been this flat in years. Not a good look. And I had no hairdryer or curling iron. Purchasing those two items was clearly a top priority if I was going to go to the office anytime soon. I sighed, put on a headband to hide my deflated bangs, and ventured out for my first day in Prague.

Later I would learn that the flat was infamous among the company expats for just how "quirky" it was. Everyone had stayed there at least once. It was a rite of passage.

IS IT ME?

THE WINDOWLESS ROOM WAS SET UP like a classroom with tables for two in rows facing a flipchart at the front. It was small and seemed cozy. At first.

My initial week on the job, I had been asked to teach a new staff training class along with several other expats. The class was very similar to the audit class I'd taken when I started my job. Arthur Andersen was known for sending all their staff to the same training so we would perform our work in the same way. Other firms called us androids. I was just excited that my first assignment was something familiar to me.

There were ten students. Four Bulgarians and six Czechs, all friendly and good humored despite the language challenges. All spoke some level of English. Yet many accounting terms were so new to them, even in Czech, that we were teaching both concepts and words. Nobody was afraid to ask questions or try out their English skills. Thank goodness because my Czech skills were practically nonexistent and my one word—*zmrzlina*—was not going to come in handy.

Two students caught my attention. One was named Vašek (pronunced VAH-sheck). He would be working out of town with me for the next five or six weeks. He worked hard and was very intense. The other was named

Josef (like Joseph with a YO). He constantly made fun of himself (and everyone else in the office). He made me laugh every time we talked. I was happy to see him in class.

It was warm in the room and had been getting warmer since midmorning. No windows. No ventilation. Old-school radiators blazing away. As I leaned over to answer someone's question, I got a faint whiff of sweat. I looked around and realized everyone had removed every layer that decorum would allow. Scarves, suit jackets, sweaters. As much as one could. The room's one door was hanging open for fresh air, but it didn't help the situation much.

I had never experienced this before in an office setting in America, where temperature control was just a turn of a dial. But this office was different. Heat was blasting and we couldn't seem to turn it down. There were no more windows or doors to open. By early afternoon, it was *hot* in there. I wasn't sure what to do. I tried standing near the open door as much as possible.

The odor grew stronger and stronger as the afternoon progressed. I couldn't get away from it. Then, it was my turn to teach, and I walked up the aisle to the front of the room. Several questions raced through my mind. *Was it me?! Could it be me?! Did I forget deodorant today? Why would I smell like this?* I worked hard to keep my arms at my sides to prevent the smell from escaping. I was finding it impossible to write on the flipchart without lifting my arms. I began calling on different students to have them write the notes on the chart instead. For the rest of the day, I kept my distance from others as much as I could and tried not to let my face show my horror. I attempted to surreptitiously smell myself, but I wasn't able to figure out if I was the source of the stench. The entire place smelled like a packed locker room. There was no escaping it.

After class, the expats decided to meet up at a pub with other expats from the office. I desperately wanted to go home to take a quick shower and put on some deodorant, but time wouldn't allow it. At the pub, I kept my jacket on and my arms pinned to my sides.

We talked about the standard expat things—where we were from, why we'd come to Prague, and the class we'd just taught. After a few beers, someone said something about the classroom. Finally, someone mentioned the smell.

PETER: "Oh! Right?! What was that? I was afraid it was me, so every time I went to the front of the class, I would try to smell my armpit when I wrote on the flipchart."

ME: "No way. I thought it was me. Was it you?"

PETER: "Nope. After I checked my right armpit, I wrote on the chart with my left hand so I could smell that armpit too. But it wasn't me. I was so relieved!"

I had to laugh. And each person at the table laughed with relief as they realized they weren't the culprit. Finally, Mike, a Texan who'd been in Prague for several months, stated the obvious.

MIKE: "The Czechs seem to have a different perception of body odor than we do. It's everywhere and considered acceptable."

He was right. It was everywhere. On trams. In buses. Pubs. Restaurants. Cabs. Shops. Inescapable.

MIKE: "To be fair, this is pretty common in other parts of Europe."

That was also true. But it was surprising to all of us to experience it at work. Czechs had yet to embrace the impossibly obsessive American-style daily hygiene relentlessly reinforced by Irish Spring TV commercials.

But it was the beginning of a bonding experience for some of us expats—dealing with something so foreign to us as a group was somehow comforting. We made plans to hang out over the weekend.

PIVO

JANUARY 1993

JOSEF: "Who wants a pivo?"

US (in unison): "I do!"

Pivo means beer. PEE-vō. And it might be the most important word in Prague.

The waiter arrived and we tried to order.

ME: "Can I get a Budweiser?"

WAITER: "Neh."

Ok.

ME: "Can I get a Pilsner Urquell?"

WAITER: "Neh."

ME: "Can I get a Velkopopovický Kozel?"

WAITER: "Neh."

What's wrong now?

Why couldn't I just get a beer? This was the freaking Czech republic. Czechs were the world's biggest beer drinkers. Bar none. Czechs could outdrink the second-place country two to one. There was a brewery on every street corner. Czechs invented Pilsner, the world's most popular type of beer. The *Fleet Sheet*[4]—an English-language summary of Czech news stories—confirmed the Czechs' love of beer.

> (MFD/3) Though the average Czech drank 15 fewer liters of beer last year than in 1992, Czechs still remain the world's biggest consumers of the liquid. At around 150 liters per person, Czechs downed eight liters more than their nearest competition, the Germans and the Danes.
>
> (RP/6) According to the six-volume Atlas of Prague Taverns (Atlas pražských hospod), there are 1,311 places in Prague that serve beer. Visitors to the Old Town will have the least trouble finding a place to wet their whistle - there are 79 beer sellers in an area of 1.38 square kilometers.
>
> (LN/12) A recent poll has found that 28% of Prague residents drink at least one beer almost every day.

There were people all around me drinking beer at their tables. *Why can't I manage to order a beer?*

ME: "Can I get a Gambrinus?"

WAITER: "Neh."

ME: "Can I get a Radegast?"

WAITER: "Neh."

ME: "Zubr? Litovel?"

WAITER: "Neh."

I cannot overstate Czechs' love of beer. They drink it morning, noon, and night. Even their breakfast is tailored for beer drinking. Salty meats and cheeses with a bit of bread. "Pivo" is probably the second most spoken word in the country after "ahoj." The "all-American beer" Budweiser is actually taken from a Czech beer. The name and slogan were stolen by a good American capitalist, Adolphus Busch. A beer is to a Czech what a cigarette is to a chain-smoker. A connection that is impossible to break. The Czechs made wine and a variety of hard liquors and liqueurs. But beer was king. And queen, and prince, and princess.

I gave up.

ME: "What beer do you have?"

WAITER: "Staropramen."

I didn't like Staropramen.

ME: "What other beer do you have?"

WAITER: "We have Staropramen."

Sigh.

ME: "I'll have a Beton."

A Beton is a mixed drink made from Becherovka and tonic. Becherovka is a uniquely Czech liquor. It has a mysterious herbal taste with a hint of cinnamon. It tastes like Christmas. Beton also means "concrete" in Czech. I was amused by that since auditing cement factories was to be my life here. I drank many a "concrete" drink in the Czech republic. I giggled a little to myself every time I ordered one.

Finally, Josef explained that every pub was aligned with one brewery and one brewery only. A brewery would pay off an individual pub owner to carry only its beer. An over-the-table bribe, so to speak. It was capitalistic communism in practice. I had no idea if this was true; it didn't sound right. But I was never able to find another answer.

Some breweries made more than one brew, so there might be an option of light (světlé) or dark (tmavé) beer. But otherwise, we were out of luck. From then on, we made sure to choose our pubs based on which beer was on tap. It was the only way to have any sort of say in the matter.

PIZZA PIZZA

JAMIE AND I WERE WALKING AROUND PRAGUE taking pictures. Jamie was a cute guy from Nebraska. He'd been in the Czech republic for several months already and was auditing a cement factory several hours away. He was excited to be back in Prague for the weekend and was showing me around town. The city was absolutely beautiful, and I was snapping photos of random buildings everywhere we walked. We also saw some inexplicable things going on around town.

JAMIE: "Is that man seriously pulling a full side of beef out of the trunk of his Škoda?"

ME: "Ohmigod. And a crate full of cow parts. That does not seem sanitary..."

We didn't discuss the dog obstructing traffic by peeing in the middle of the road. We were just happy the dog made it to the other side of the road where a babička was sweeping the street with a broom made out of twigs. Twigs! Something right out of Hansel and Gretel.

ME: "That can't possibly work, can it?"

Jamie shrugged his shoulders and shook his head in wonder. It seemed futile.

We passed a small house where an older couple was in their yard gardening. I did a double take.

ME: "Is it my imagination, or are they gardening in their underwear?"

I thought my eyes must be deceiving me.

JAMIE: "Yeah, I've noticed that before . . . no idea what that's about."

We decided we should duck into a pizza place to get food and beer before we saw aliens landing. The place was small and bare. Nobody else was there. That should have been a clue. But we were starving.

We ordered a sausage pizza and a few beers. And waited.

The beers arrived first, so we chatted about how much we loved Old Town and about where we should go next. Then we waited for our food. And kept chatting. And waited. And waited.

We ordered a second round of beers. And waited.

ME: "Did they have to go somewhere else to get this pizza?"

JAMIE: "This is nothing . . ."

ME: "Oh dear . . ."

JAMIE: "How do I put this? Service isn't exactly a priority here."

Halfway through our second beers, our pizza finally arrived.

JAMIE: "It's not sliced. Hold on."

He grabbed a fork and knife and tried to cut it. The sauce was thick and kind of went everywhere. After he'd managed to cut a few triangular-ish pieces, we each took one and dug in.

As I chewed, I realized something was off. I wasn't quite sure what it was at first, but then I looked at Jamie. His chewing had slowed to almost a full stop, and his eyes were wide open in alarm. I stopped chewing and had to think about what I was tasting. It was normal and yet not normal at all. Then it hit me.

ME: "Ohmigod. It's KETCHUP!"

Not tomato sauce. Flat-out *ketchup*.

Jamie closed his eyes and swallowed the rest of his bite. I debated spitting it out into a napkin, but there were no napkins to be found. I stopped chewing, swallowed, and gave him a look. We both understood. Ketchup was fine served with French fries or a hot dog. Good even! But NOT ON PIZZA! We sucked down the rest of our beer, trying to cleanse our palates, left 100 Kč (koruna česká or Czech crown) on the table—more than enough to cover our bill—and bolted out the door.

FIRST LETTER HOME

Dear Mom and Dad,

Where do I start?

I actually found a store with curling irons. Ok . . . so they were flat instead of round. And no, they were not straighteners. Worse, there was no way to hold on to your hair. Actually, I bought one that *is* round, but it's a round brush that blows hot air out and onto your hair (from inside the rod), and there's still no way to hold your hair onto it. But it seemed to have more potential than the flat one. I haven't quite gotten the hang of it yet—my bangs don't look good, but at least they aren't totally straight. (I may have to grow them out because this isn't sustainable.)

And I found all of these brushes at an ELECTRONICS STORE. After searching drugstores and beauty supply stores for hours, someone suggested I try electronics. I thought they were nuts, but no. They were there. Honestly, that would never have occurred to me. After that, I noticed that many things are categorized differently here—toilet paper is sold with stationery, and plaster, with soap. Sometimes I can understand the logic, but other times . . . I have no idea. For example, feminine hygiene products are also at the paper goods or stationery store! It's always safer to ask a Czech where to look for something before you set out on your own.

I'm really up on world affairs now because there's nothing else to do other than watch CNN at my temporary flat. I get a few satellite channels, so I have some English language stuff. Right now, I can watch bowling in Czech; *The Cosby Show* in German; MTV, CNN, or the movie *Fame* in English. CNN and MTV are the only English language stations the cable is currently picking up (how *Fame* is in English, I have no idea), although, admittedly, I was tempted to watch the German version of *Studs* earlier. (Amazingly, someone has copied—exactly—that show.) Oh! I just found a German version of *Wheel of Fortune*. Anyway, the selection is pretty poor, so now I'm writing to you. (A much better choice anyway.) The next-door neighbor practices his oboe for three to four hours a day beginning about five minutes after I get home. So, I blast him out with CNN.

The weather was great the day I arrived (the hottest temp ever recorded on that date) but has gotten steadily colder. Today it snowed on me! It was a light snow, and it didn't stick, but, as I told Josef—who claimed it wasn't really snow—if I could see it fall and land, it was snow. I'm much warmer than when I studied in Scotland (it's not as windy, and nobody is without central heating), but just like in Scotland, nobody has figured out how to properly heat a room when it's cold outside. It's always much too hot, and you have to wear spring or summer clothes under your warm coat unless you want to sweat (and I don't have any such clothes with me yet).

Love,

Melanie

THEY HAVE BEER

JANUARY 1993

I NEEDED A FLAT. Ideally with an actual bedroom, working appliances, and properly functioning plumbing. The office had a real estate guy, Roman. He helped all the expats find flats when they arrived. He was part of the family—the husband of a manager in the office. They were from Chicago, but he had Czech parents and spoke the language.

Roman took me around town to look at some options. It was an amazing tour of '60s and '70s décor. Shag carpets. Outrageous colors. Crazy wallpaper. We're talking time travel. I saw lots of orange, mustard, and brown. *Lots* of gaudy furniture. The layouts were sometimes a bit odd, and the bathrooms were made of plastic.

Finally, he showed me a place I really liked. I was overjoyed.

Most people lived about 15 to 30 minutes from the office. Their apartments had three rooms plus a kitchen and a bath. The flat I liked was farther from the center, but it had five rooms plus a kitchen, a bathroom, and a large balcony. It was the top floor and a half of a 3½-story house. Since the house was an A-frame, all the rooms had slanted ceilings. I loved the spiral staircase in the living room that led to the ½-floor with two tiny bedrooms. The main bedroom window overlooked a forest, and the balcony overlooked the backyard. It had snowed the last two days, so the forest was covered in white. The snow didn't stick in the center of town because there was no grass, but out by my flat, it was a winter wonderland. I loved it. My commute was going to be longer than my friends', but I could make it in 30 minutes if I timed it right. I wasn't deterred.

The landlords, Rudolf and Jitka, lived downstairs with their teenage kids. They were great. And though the apartment was only half furnished, they said they would finish furnishing it by Saturday. The furniture already there was beautiful. Ok, beautiful might be kind of strong, but it was IKEA-ish instead of groovy 1970s like in all the other flats. The house was in an area of Prague called Hrdlořezy.

ROMAN: "It's pronounced herd-LO-zhe-zee."

I tried it several times.

ME: "Herrrr-DLOW-zhe-zeeeee. Her-DLOW-zhe-zee. Herd-LO-zhe-zee."

ROMAN: "Good!"

ME: "What does it mean?"

ROMAN: "Oh. Well. It means 'the place where people's throats get cut.'"

Oh God. I didn't know why it was called that, and I was pretty sure I would be better off not knowing. I guessed I would just have to take my chances.

I had found home.

Josef and I had become fast friends, and he helped me move into my new flat. After the last bag was brought upstairs, we headed to a small local store to buy groceries. I filled my basket with a few basics: yogurt, water, and bread. Josef was on the other side of the five-aisle store to see what else they had.

JOSEF: "Do you want beer?"

ME: "What kind do they have?"

JOSEF: "They have . . . beer."

ME: "What do you mean?"

JOSEF: "I mean, they have beer."

Oh, right . . . this store still had communist selections. Some of the larger grocery stores were beginning to stock more variety, but not the small stores outside the center of Prague. They still stocked inventory the way they had for decades. One kind of yogurt. Chunks of lard. One type of bread.

I laughed.

ME: "Ok then. I'll have beer."

JOSEF: "See how easy it is to shop here?"

He wasn't wrong.

HOTEL ATOM

MY FIRST ASSIGNMENT WAS IN the industrial city of Ostrava. I packed a bag, locked my flat, and headed out into the cold winter air. Like a soldier—a 5´3˝ accounting mercenary—marching off to the battlefield.

It was really, really early. Too early. And it was cooold. So cold for a girl from Los Angeles. I put on as many clothes as I could wear while still being able to walk and headed out into the darkness. The ground was covered with snow, and I was dragging my suitcase, leaving a trail of parted snow behind me. After 20 minutes of huffing and puffing, I finally arrived at the bus stop.

I hadn't seen a single person on my walk. Yet the bus was packed. People were hanging onto the poles, bars, and loops to prevent themselves from falling. It was so packed that I don't think I could have fallen if I'd wanted to. And it was *hot*. Every bus, train, and building was too warm for people wearing heavy winter coats, scarves, and hats. There wasn't enough space to remove my coat or other layers, but the ride was, thankfully, brief.

Unfortunately, I hadn't taken into account the fact that in this sort of heat, with everyone still in their winter coats and packed together, everyone would be sweating. Profusely. I couldn't escape it. Nobody else seemed to notice. The tall man next to me raised his arm to hold onto the loop. I'm only 5′3″, so my face was directly in his armpit. People were on all sides of me. I couldn't even turn around. My eyes watered and I held my breath, praying for the bus to arrive at its destination. At least this time I knew it wasn't me. I was starting to grow accustomed to this aspect of life here.

After the longest short bus ride of my life, I got onto a slightly less crowded tram to the train station: Masarykovo nádraží.

Masarykovo nádraží was much smaller than the main train station. It is the oldest train station in Prague—active since 1845—and has a beautiful facade. I was surprised by the green metal overhang that looked like it belonged on a gingerbread house, an architectural gem in the midst of so many bland communist buildings.

I quickly found Vašek and Jan. Vašek took my bags, and we headed to the train car. We entered our compartment and Vašek put all our bags up top for the trip. I was thrilled to finally be able to remove my winter gear. I settled onto the worn, burgundy velvet seats next to the window and prayed there would be coffee.

I stared out the window and realized, from the looks of things, I was going to continue to be very, very cold. It was only one hour into the four-hour train ride, and it already looked like how I imagined Siberia looked. Nothing but snow out these windows. Almost a complete whiteout.

On the train, I got to know the guys. The approach taken by the accounting firms was to hire English-speaking foreigners for all supervisory roles and English-speaking Czechs for entry-level roles. As the Czechs got promoted and took over all roles, the foreigners would leave. As we all chatted, I learned that they knew very little about accounting or auditing. English seemed to have been the #1 criteria for being hired. I hadn't known a lot either when I'd started as a new staff member in Los Angeles, especially since I'd been a psychology major. They would learn on the job as I had. I just hoped I would have some idea how to guide them.

A woman came with a snack cart—no coffee. *How in the world can there be a snack cart at this hour of the morning that doesn't serve coffee?* Sigh. A small juice box would have to do. Vašek, Jan ("Honza" to his friends and now me), and I chatted every second of the way. I shared my background and learned about theirs. I always felt like Vašek's eyes were boring holes into me. I couldn't tell if he was just super interested in what I had to say or if he was analyzing me. It was a little unnerving. Honza didn't take anything seriously and just made us both laugh and laugh again. Something told me that as long as Honza was there, we would have fun working together. But the jury was out about how well Vašek and I would get along. I couldn't read him at all.

OSTRAVA

Our first stop was the Hotel Atom. It was as grim as it sounded. Industrial and unwelcoming, with the warmth of a factory floor. Gray, dingy architecture and communist service. The lobby was chilly and bare. The receptionist was icy and clearly unhappy she had to check us in. But we got our room assignments and our breakfast tickets for the remainder of the week. My room was sparsely furnished. More like a college dorm room than a hotel. It had a single bed, desk, and TV. Thin carpet, old curtains. Pretty sure the last time the décor was updated was never. But it was clean.

After dropping our bags, we drove around Ostrava to get our bearings. We passed the cement factory so we knew where to go early the next morning. I had done some background reading to prepare for our kickoff meeting the next morning. Still, I had no idea what to expect. And it's probably best that nobody warned me—I don't think I would have believed them.

The cement business started early, so I woke before dawn—again. A morning person I am not. I turned on the only English-language TV channel . . . MTV. At least I had music. Tasmin Archer's "Sleeping Satellite" kept me company as I got ready for work. Every morning, she blamed me for the moon lighting the sky and for killing her dreams. But she said it so nicely that I sang along. I would hear it at the same time the next morning. And the next morning after that. It was like Groundhog Day. MTV was on some sort of loop. That song remains an earworm to this day and always takes me back to dark, early mornings at the Hotel Atom.

Breakfast was coffee, ham, cheese, and rohlíky (the ubiquitous Czech bread roll). I was in desperate need of a coffee refill, but the waitresses were huddled in a corner with their backs to us. Dressed in their white blouses, dark skirts, thick tights, and white terrycloth slippers. They were chatting and smoking, doing their best to ignore us. And why not? Here, and at every pub and restaurant I'd been to since I arrived, the waitstaff seemed to keep their jobs regardless of how well they did them. Or perhaps ignoring the customers was the goal. Our version of customer service was an unknown concept. Customer satisfaction? Not a thing. The customer is always right? Are you kidding?

We tried everything. We took turns saying "Prosim?" loudly to try to get their attention. *Please? Prosim?* No. I waved a hand. I waved both hands. All of us waved at the same time. I was starting to think we were invisible. We flailed our arms wildly. I joked that we might need to send up a flare. Vašek and Honza looked at me quizzically. They were used to this. The communist system had no performance incentives or performance management system like we were used to in the West. It was enough to show up and pretend to do the job. As much as it frustrated me, I could hardly blame them. I finally got someone's attention when I rose from the table and walked towards the coffee pot to serve myself. Apparently, *THAT* was not allowed. That was *their* job, not mine. Weird given how much they didn't want to serve us. One of the waitresses sighed and put out her cigarette. She shuffled over in her house slippers with a pot of coffee. I held my breath as she raised her arm to pour.

Ahhh . . . sweet, glorious, super strong but thankfully caffeinated coffee.

As soon as we finished breakfast, we made our way to the cement factory for our kick-off meeting with the client. Let the games begin.

KAVA

JANUARY 1993
OSTRAVA

I TOOK A BIG SIP OF MY THIRD CUP of coffee and immediately knew something was wrong. Like, *really* wrong.

It was 7 a.m., and I was now sitting at a small conference table. The managing director, pan Balej (pronounced bAH-lay), was 30 minutes into his welcoming speech at our first big meeting. His assistant shuffled imperviously around the table, serving coffee to everyone.

And I had a huge problem.

My mouth was full of coffee grounds! Why in the world were there so many grounds in my coffee? It was a thick, gravelly, brown paste. And my mouth was full of it.

I'd been relieved to see coffee served at this early hour, but my relief was immediately overtaken by panic. *What do I do?* I looked around the table to see what others were doing, but no one else had lifted their cup yet.

The drive to Cemos had been dreary. It was cold and the outskirts of the city were covered in snow. We'd arrived at a small, squat office building. It was gray and blended in with the gray sky behind it. We walked down a hallway with no carpet, no pictures on the walls, and closed door after closed door with no signage of any kind. I didn't see a single person until we arrived at the managing director's office, where I now sat with my mouth full of coffee grounds.

Do I leave the room so I can spit these out? Where would I go if I did? I didn't know where the restroom was, and it certainly wasn't identifiable—just one of those closed doors—and I couldn't ask anyone while my mouth was full of coffee grounds.

This was the first time that Cemos had been the subject of an international audit. We needed to review everything on their balance sheet. What they owned and how much it was worth. Inventory, property, equipment. Most of their stuff was two or three decades old. We weren't sure how we would value anything because it was unclear whether they had any records, and everything was certain to be obsolete by Western standards. But I digress.

Ugh. Do I spit them out? That seemed rude for a client meeting—especially my very first one. (As if it would be ok at the third meeting . . .) I sat there with a mouthful of grounds for what seemed like an eternity.

I tried hard to focus on what was being said and act as if nothing was wrong. I was really, really distracted by my current predicament. Everything they discussed—cement production, cement distribution, Czech accounting—flew right by me.

Do I swallow them? That seemed like a horrible idea.

The managing director, pan Balej, droned on and on. In Czech, "pan" means "mister." I'd studied Spanish for six years, and in Spanish, "pan" means "bread." He was a short, doughy man. Rotund body, rotund fingers, rotund face. Like a bread roll. Like the lovechild of the Pillsbury Doughboy and Danny DeVito. I stifled a giggle every time someone called him bread Balej.

The coffee grounds were now becoming impossible to deal with. I was working hard not to laugh and spit the grounds out on the table. *Think, Melanie. Think!* Eventually, I decided I needed to get the grounds out of my mouth as subtly as I could. I lifted my cup and pretended to have another sip while gently dripping the grounds back into the cup. I tried to hide it, but I felt certain the others knew. Was this a prank they played on all the new expats?

I took several fake sips to release the grounds back into the cup, but I could tell I still had grounds in my teeth. How bad was it? I had no idea. I was afraid to open my mouth. I sat silently while pretending to understand what was happening in the meeting, but I was consumed with my continuing dilemma.

Now what do I do?

At some point, pan Balej's assistant returned with a pitcher of water and glasses. *Thank God.* How subtly could I gargle? Or swirl water around my mouth? I tried to slowly rinse my teeth and swallow the remaining coffee grounds. I drank several glasses of water, and I felt every sandy grain of coffee grounds slide down my throat. I was so relieved.

Around 8:30 a.m., the assistant was back with a bottle of clear liquid and a bunch of small crystal shot glasses. *What fresh hell is this? Shots? At a business meeting? At 8:30 in the morning?* She poured a glass for each of us and passed them around. I was horrified but didn't want to offend. Nobody explained what was happening as they all lifted their glasses and drank together. I raised my glass and tried to sip it, but that wasn't how this was done. So I shot it. Liquid fire. It was all I could do not to spit it across the table. But I'd survived the coffee grounds; surely, I could survive one shot of this lighter fluid. I just hoped, *prayed*, this wasn't an everyday ritual.

It turned out to be slivovice. Slivovice is plum brandy, and it is *not* smooth. A lot of Czech families made homemade slivovice. Really, it was the Moravians—the people in the eastern part of the country. The Bohemians occupied the western part of the country and had different cultures, languages, and traditions. Slivovice is basically Moravian moonshine. Adults had a shot each morning because it was believed to kill bacteria and be good for digestion. I could believe it killed everything in its path. The Czechs also believed it was good to drink it after eating fatty or greasy food, but since this included pretty much all the food I'd eaten to date, I felt certain this was a rationalization.

We went back to the meeting agenda and alternated between Czech and the broken English translations of information that, at this point, was still gobbledygook to me. And now I needed to pee. I had drunk glass after glass of water trying to clean my teeth. But the meeting kept going. Did nobody else need a break?

Around 9:30 a.m., the assistant brought a tray of snacks called chlebíčky. "Chleba" means bread. Chlebíčky means "little breads." They were traditional open-faced sandwiches. The Czechs adored them. Foreigners loved them too. Chlebíčky were slathered with a thick, gooey layer of mayonnaise, sometimes with horseradish included, and topped with a meat (ham, salami, beef), a slice of cheese, and a small nod to a vegetable for show. Maybe a gherkin, a small slice of tomato or cucumber, some parsley. And often a dollop of cream or butter. They were always cute, pretty, well-dressed sandwiches. But they were *slathered* with mayonnaise. I will eat almost anything once, but I cannot stand mayonnaise.

I took one because I didn't want to be rude. I tried a bite. Yep. Just as mayonnaise-y as I feared. Everyone else was on their third chlebíčky when someone asked me what was wrong with mine. I lied and said I wasn't hungry. But I was. I proceeded to eat the "veggies" and cheese off the top because I was desperate. I'd pushed through the coffee grounds and the booze for breakfast, but I was done. My mouth and my stomach were in desperate need of something familiar and appropriate to ingest before noon. I was like a thirsty woman on an island surrounded by salt water.

Somehow, I survived my first meeting. The coffee grounds. The slivovice. The chlebíčky. Two very long hours. Mercifully, I found a restroom, but lunch wasn't for a little while longer. I'd have to tough it out.

Time to get to work.

PENCILS

JANUARY 1993

WE SETTLED IN THAT WEEK to begin auditing. I was very quickly confused.

ME: "Why does a cement factory have a 50-year supply of pencils in their inventory?"

The Czechs looked at me as if they didn't understand what I'd asked. I repeated the question. Still nothing.

ACCOUNTING LESSON 1: "Inventory" should consist of the things a company sells. Why were there boxes upon boxes upon boxes of pencils in inventory? Was the cement factory selling pencils too? I didn't think so. But I guessed I would find out.

ACCOUNTING LESSON 2: Nobody should have a 50-year supply of anything . . . that's called "excess," and excess anything is generally written off the books. Would these pencils even be good in 50 years? Or the preferred writing instrument? Who knew?

ACCOUNTING LESSON 3: Inventory should have value. Of some kind. To someone.

I asked my staff again.

ME: "Why does a cement factory have 50-years' worth of pencils in their inventory?"

Jan and Vašek stared at me blankly.

I tried a different question. "Does Cemos sell pencils?"

JAN: "No. Of course not. They sell cement."

ME: "Ok, good. Do they use . . . like . . . an extraordinary number of pencils here?"

VAŠEK: "No. Just normal."

ME: "Ok, good. So why do they have so many pencils? And why are they in inventory?"

More blank stares. I realized they truly didn't understand my questions. So I tried one at a time.

ME: "Why do they have so many pencils?"

Blank stares.

ME: "Ok . . . why are the pencils in inventory if they don't sell pencils?"

VAŠEK: "Because they own them."

We were getting nowhere.

ME: "But why do they own them?"

They stared at me. Ok. No "why" questions. The question "why" seemed to have no reasonable meaning or answer here.

I tried a different approach.

ME: "How did they get them?"

VAŠEK: "They bought them from the pencil factory."

ME: "Ok . . . because they needed a ton of pencils?"

VAŠEK: "Because that was the plan."

ME: "Whose plan?"

VAŠEK: "The plan."

ME: "THE plan?"

What in the world were we talking about? *Ohhhhhhh.* Eureka! A "holy sh*t" moment.

The plan. THE PLAN! (In my mind, I said this just like Tattoo at the beginning of each episode of *Fantasy Island.* "De plane! De plane!") Under Czechoslovakia's planned or command economy, the cement factory was required to buy products from other companies, and those companies were required to buy cement from Cemos. Because that's the way it was. If I were auditing the pencil factory, I suspected would find a massive supply of cement they didn't need.

And it seemed that in this Czech world, everything a company owned was viewed as having value. Everything. Lots of random things showed up in inventory. I suppose it helped make their companies look like they were actually thriving businesses—instead of fronts pretending to do actual business, micromanaged by the communist government. I also learned that until 1993, the Federal Ministry of Finance didn't allow companies to reduce the value of the things they owned, even if they were obsolete, excessive, uncollectible, or otherwise useless and without value. Every single item appeared as an asset of the company. Forever.

Compounding these problems was the fact that the state-owned companies had been required to take out loans from the government (read: themselves) to pay for these purchases. So in addition to a lot of "inventory" they didn't need, they had a lot of debt they couldn't repay. It was a massive shell game. Holy crapola. How would we ever straighten this out?

Sigh. And this was week one.

LETTER FROM OSTRAVA

JANUARY 1993

Dear Mom and Dad,

I am assigned to work on the audits of two cement factories: Cemos Ostrava and Cement Hranice. These companies are being invested in by a foreign cement company. We will audit the books and convert the financial statements from Czech accounting standards to International Accounting Standards. I know nothing about cement, Czech accounting, or International Accounting Standards . . . nothing like being thrown into the deep end! But I've learned a little about the situation here. "The theory of Communists may be summed up in the single sentence: Abolition of private property." —Karl Marx, *The Communist Manifesto*

And they were serious about that. When the Communist Party took over 40 years ago, they abolished private property. They seized all the assets and wealth, leaving the people with nothing and the government with everything. Every house. Every company. All the land. Everything. Now that the country is transitioning back to capitalism, all the property needs to be given back. There are several pieces to that. The restitution program is returning land, homes, shops, and other assets to private citizens from whom the property was originally taken. The privatization efforts are shifting government-owned businesses to the people through foreign investment and a voucher program allowing individuals to buy voucher booklets and use the vouchers to buy shares in companies. The first wave was last year before I arrived. We're here to help with the second and final wave. It's one of the largest property transfers in history! Crazy.

The team and I went by train Monday at 6:15 a.m. We went to Ostrava (about 3 ½ hours away) near the border with Poland. Their inventory records and accounting are a mess (right up my alley), but the clients don't really respect women and have never met an American! So between Vašek and the interpreter, I hope I can get them to cooperate with me!

The workpapers are in Kč. Some transactions are converted from DM (German Deutsch Marks). The other senior is Australian, so he thinks in Australian dollars, and I can think in British sterling or US dollars. I have little side notes sometimes of four or five different currencies! I just don't know how many I can think in at one time!

The whole job is daunting, but I'm excited for the challenge!

Love,

Melanie

BEST ROAD TRIP EVER

JANUARY 1993
BUDAPEST, HUNGARY

BUDAPEST HAD A DUNKIN' DONUTS?!

I'd heard the rumor and hadn't believed it could possibly be true. Glazed donuts? Boston Cream donuts? Old-fashioned donuts? And MUNCH-KINS too? But it was true!

The expats from the office decided to go to Budapest for the weekend to get donuts.

Instead of returning to Prague, I took a train directly from Ostrava to Budapest to meet everyone. A long 5 ½ hours, but I longed for the taste of something familiar. Something overly sweet. Overly fried. Overly salted. Something American. Anything American.

Budapest was beautiful and had a similar layout to Prague. A river running through the center and a castle towering over the city. The architecture was gorgeous but mostly stone gray. Budapest felt somehow darker than Prague. More masculine to Prague's pastel-colored feminine. Budapest had amazing coffee, good nightlife, delicious goulash (guláš in Czech; gulyás in Hungarian), and . . . Dunkin' Donuts! Never had a fried circle of dough tasted so good.

Budapest also had KFC. And Burger King. And McDonald's. Only McDonald's had reached Prague so far. I decided they had been right about Prague. It *was* a hardship location.

I ate too many donuts and took a few with me for the trip back to Ostrava. Everyone else bought a dozen donuts and took them back to Prague. They told me they froze really well and that we could enjoy them for weeks. They promised to share when I was back in Prague. I couldn't wait for the first donut party.

On the train ride back to Ostrava early Monday morning, I had to change trains in Břeclav, the first stop after crossing into the Czech republic. The train station was small and dingy. I was in business clothes—a skirt, a blouse, nylons, and high heels—and I stood out like a sore thumb. Everyone else was in Eastern European factory garb. Overalls, dark coats, boots. Sleepwalking to work. It felt Orwellian.

I'd been awake for hours and was in desperate need of coffee. Mercifully, there was a small food counter in the station. I ordered *kávu s mlékem* (coffee with milk), one of the few very necessary things I now knew how to say in Czech. The man handed it to me in a tiny plastic cup that was never intended to hold hot beverages. It was like a shot of coffee. But it was too hot to touch, and the cup seemed to be melting. I grabbed some napkins to use like a potholder and stood alone at a small table. As soon as it was cool enough, I drank it in one gulp. Like a shot of tequila.

Huge. Mistake.

Melanie, how stupid could you be? I fell for it again. My mouth was full of coffee grounds.

I had asked the other expats about this while we were in Budapest. There were no drip coffee machines in the Czech republic. No coffee filters. They did it like they always had. They just poured the boiling water over the grounds and waited until the grounds settled at the bottom of the cup before drinking it. I was stunned. How was this the plan? But it explained why nobody else had been drinking their coffee yet when I got a mouth full of grounds at Cemos. I knew this now. And yet I made this mistake again. I would have to get better at this.

I looked around to see if anyone had noticed what I'd done. Nobody even glanced my way. They were immersed in their own worlds. It was mostly men standing around tall round tables, drinking beer before work and chatting. I saw a large trash can and made my way to it. I spit the grounds into the trash. The coffee went with it. I paid a small fortune for a bottle of water to rinse my mouth out. I probably should have just bought the cheaper drink, beer, since I was spitting it out anyway.

Time to board my next train. I prayed they had some sort of caffeinated beverage on board. Without grounds.

GOOD HELP IS HARD TO FIND

ME: "Vašek, please go ask paní Smékalová for all the bank statements."

VAŠEK: "No."

ME: "Excuse me?"

I was shocked by his "in your face" refusal to do what I'd asked.

VAŠEK: "No. No. No."

ME: "What???"

VAŠEK: "I will go."

Oh, right. "No" means "yes" in Czech. The real word is "ano" (AH-no), but they shorten it to "no." This was going to take a while to get used to.

Auditing in the U.S. was prescriptive. A logical, straightforward, step-by-step process. If I was auditing cash, I grabbed the "cash work program" and followed the steps. It listed the documents I needed. Described what to look at. Told me what to do. If I was auditing property, I grabbed the "property work program." And followed along. Like a cookie recipe. Step one of the cash work program was "get the bank statements." Easy, right?

Nope.

I sent Vašek to get the bank statements from the client. But he was back by my side again much sooner than he should have been.

ME: "You got them?"

VAŠEK: "Neh. She said she's too exhausted to help me right now."

ME: "Ummm . . . what? It's 10 a.m., and we can't do any work on cash until she gives us the bank statements."

VAŠEK: "She said she's too exhausted to get them for me."

ME: "But we can't do any work on cash without them. Please go ask her again."

Vašek gave me a "please don't make me" look. The head accountant for Cemos was an angry woman. Unhelpful. Frustrated. Resentful. Suspicious. Just the way one imagined any good communist bureaucrat to be. The name of this nemesis of Western accounting practices was paní Smékalová, the company's accounting clerk.

Vašek returned empty-handed again. Fine. We'd have to work on something else first. I had the team move to the next audit section. We would try again later.

The next morning, I sent Vašek back. Miraculously, he returned with the bank statements. Finally, we could start auditing cash. I was delighted.

ME: "Great! So she's not 'exhausted' today?"

Vašek chuckled and demonstrated what had happened when he'd asked her for the statements this morning. Paní Smékalová had let out a huge, exasperated sigh as if Vašek had been asking the impossible. She'd stood up from her desk, turned to the wall behind her, grabbed three binders off the shelf, and handed them to Vašek. "Here," she had said with a huff.

ME: "That was it? They were on the shelf . . . RIGHT BEHIND HER . . . the WHOLE TIME?"

Vašek nodded, somewhat chagrined.

I was frustrated. Vašek was annoyed. Why was everyone so unhelpful? Why did everything take so long? How was I going to explain to my manager it took days to do something that should have taken 3½ minutes?

We went round and round with paní Smékalová all week. Struggling to get the information we needed because we didn't ask the right question or didn't know what to ask. We were stonewalled at every turn. And as I would soon discover, sometimes the document we wanted wasn't actually available. Sometimes it took ages to get hold of, and even if we got it, it didn't always have the information we expected and needed.

We all had to learn how to get from the beginning to the end without any of the documents we were accustomed to having and without being able to perform any of the steps we'd been taught. It was incredibly frustrating, but we all became much better auditors because of it.

But at the time, I wondered if I was just terrible at my job because I couldn't seem to get anything done.

FRIDAYS AT PIZZA TAXI: THE BEGINNING

JANUARY 1993
PRAGUE (AKA PRAHA)

EVERY FRIDAY AFTERNOON, the Arthur Andersen expats and Czech staff made our way back to Prague from wherever we had each worked that week. We were spread across the country. Peter audited nuclear power plants. Mike audited coal power plants and banks. Laurent audited some client with livestock. Jamie and I audited cement factories. Eva was in the tax department and worked in Prague. She took charge of leaving handwritten notes on our desks in the office to let us know where we should all meet on Friday night. One week, she chose a restaurant called Pizza Taxi. The wine and beer flowed at Pizza Taxi, and we'd heard the pizza wasn't bad. As long as there was no ketchup involved, I was happy.

"You won't believe what happened to me this week," we said in unison as we sat down. Glasses of Frankovka (a drinkable Czech red wine that invariably caused the most insane hangovers no matter how little one might drink) were passed around the table.

I made a lot of friends in the first two weeks, but seven of us really came together. We were becoming a crew. The seven of us were the only unmarried expats in the office. We became somewhat inseparable.

There was Eva from London. She was a kick in the pants and always buying another round of drinks no matter how much we protested.

Mike from Houston was very funny and ripped on me. Always in good fun.

Jamie from Nebraska was a big guy with garage band hair longer than Arthur Andersen usually allowed. Quiet and shy most of the time, Jamie would come out of his shell after a beer or two (or three).

Peter was a very nice guy. A real cutie with an infectious laugh, he was always up for a night at the pub. And he never failed to tell us that he was from the country music capital of Australia.

Laurent and Thierry were from France. They spoke perfect English, but we sometimes struggled with their very French accents.

If Eva was the social director, Mike was the post-party host. His apartment was near our favorite club, so we frequently crashed at his flat because the Prague Metro stopped at midnight.

I settled into the expat life quickly. Quirks and all. We had several important goals here. One was to build a practice staffed with local personnel. We had been encouraged by the managing partner to be sure to pass on our knowledge of auditing as well as Arthur Andersen's culture. That was going to be a heavy lift. But we were all up for the challenge. We had each other to lean on as we navigated through it.

We'd been drinking beer at the pubs for weeks and wanted a change. One night, we decided what we really craved was margaritas. Those didn't exist here, so I invited everyone to a party at my flat the following weekend. Kind of a housewarming party. The others would find the ingredients. I needed to find a blender. This time, I knew to start at the electronics store. *Margaritaville, here we come!*

SUPER BOWL

FEBRUARY 1993

TO: U.S. Expatriates
FROM: Managing Partner
DATE: 2 February 1993
SUBJECT: Super Bowl—Chili Party

I am sure some of us are still suffering from not being able to enjoy our typical U.S. Super Bowl Sunday on 31 January. Because of obvious time differences and lack of understanding of schedules and how to video tape such important events, we have rescheduled our "delayed broadcast" of the 1993 Super Bowl to a more normal time. It will now be shown at the more civilized time of 4 p.m. on Sunday, February 7, at our home. We will be serving a modified Texas/Czech chili supper at half time, or the end of the game, based on majority vote of those present. Of course the cook does have the final say.

Also please note the time of this event has been scheduled in an effort to maximize our office productivity for the expatriates so you can still get in a good day's work before the game.

Fun! Fun! A party to go to, and a Super Bowl party at that. America's celebration of sanctioned violence, consumer culture, and crass commercialization. It sounded like a blast. And after only a one-week delay seemed impressive. We all tried not to learn who had won, which wasn't difficult as long as we avoided CNN for a week. But I hoped he was kidding about the day's work on Sunday. I don't think he was . . .

BRUTALISM
(OR THE WEEKEND THEY
CONVERTED THE CURRENCY)

4-7 FEBRUARY 1993

THE MARGARITA PARTY WAS ONLY A FEW DAYS AWAY. I just needed a few things first. A tape player and a blender. It seemed so simple . . .

Shopping here was a weirdly challenging experience for the expats. Between the language barrier, the store atmosphere, and the communist mentality, it was almost not worth it. There were only three department stores that I knew of, and they were all sparse or confusing. The stores were only open on weekdays until around 6 p.m. and Saturday until around noon—not really convenient for someone working an office job. Given that I worked from 8:30 a.m. to at least 5:30 p.m. every day, I had to shop quickly or go on Saturday.

Thursday night, Jamie and I went to look at "stereos." I use the term loosely, but that was the English translation at the electronics store. Really, they were boomboxes. And the prices were OUTRAGEOUS. The store wasn't open, but through the window, I saw one that I liked and decided to return Friday at lunchtime to buy it. It cost 9,990 Kčs or $350 USD. (The equivalent of about $1,000 today). Insanity. But I wanted music, so this was my only option.

On Friday, I pointed at the one I wanted. The salesperson took it off the shelf and plugged it in. He inserted a tape and pressed play. Ok ... yep. That played music. I wanted it. He pointed me to the cashier's desk.

I left him with the stereo and tried to hand the cashier my credit card. He shook his finger at me and then waved me away. They didn't take credit cards. Crap. I should have known that. Ok. I tried to signal that I would be right back.

Off to the bank I went to get cash. I got 10,000 Kč in cash and returned to the store. I'd been gone for twenty minutes, but now there was a "Reserved" sign on it. What? Maybe it was reserved for me because they realized I was coming back.

I pointed at the "stereo" and then at myself to try to signal my question: *Is that reserved for me?*

CLERK: "Je to rezervováno."

ME: "Ano. Ano. For me?" I pointed at myself.

The clerk shook his finger at me. No. Not for me.

Crap again. It was the last one of that style, and they were holding it for someone else until 4 p.m. So now I had all this cash and no stereo. I had to get back to work but decided I would go back to the shop at 4 p.m. to see if it had been sold or was available for me to buy. If it wasn't available, I'd buy my second choice.

And then I realized I might have a bigger problem. I had all this Czechoslovak cash but after Saturday, it would be WORTHLESS! From Thursday through Saturday, everyone in the entire country had to exchange all their Czechoslovak currency for the new Czech currency. They weren't disbursing the new money until Thursday and after Saturday, the Czechoslovakian currency would be worthless. (Yes, that's right, three days for EVERY PERSON in the Czech republic and Slovakia—more than 15 million people!—to go to a bank or a post office and exchange their money.)

I had to spend or exchange this money on Friday or Saturday one way or another. Frustrated, I kept working until 4 p.m.

I went back to the shop. The reserved sign was gone! Excellent. I pointed at the "stereo" for the third time.

CLERK: "Je to rezervováno."

ME: "Co? What? There's no reserved sign."

CLERK: "Je to rezervováno."

Was he messing with me? The sign was gone, but it was still reserved? We went back and forth, but, of course, I was getting nowhere.

Fine. I looked for my second choice. But it was gone! CRAP! It must have been a hot shopping day for CD and tape players. There was no third option. While I was away, it seemed they'd sold the only two boomboxes in stock while I was at the cash machine. I was out of luck.

I left empty-handed—except, of course, for my 10,000 CZECHOSLOVAK CROWNS. I had to try again on Saturday morning before the stores closed.

I got up early on Saturday because I needed to be done shopping by noon, and I knew this could take hours. I decided to go to a large department store. I planned to buy any tape and CD player I could find and then some sort of blender to make margaritas that night. Both of these items were hard to find in Prague, but I was certain I had seen them BOTH at Kotva. My plan was to buy them both at one store, thus only subjecting myself to shopping one time.

Kotva was a dark and menacing department store hulking between fragile, fairytale-like buildings in Prague. Built in the '70s, Kotva was made of concrete and glass and brutalism. Brutalist architecture was actually defined as being intentionally plain, crude, and stark. It had lots of windows on one side and not enough on another. The concrete had turned a foreboding dark gray from all the coal pollution. It was surreally surrounded by medieval and art deco buildings. It was the communist idea of progress.

The stores were always packed, but Saturdays were worse. There were so many people that day, I was literally herded up the escalator and couldn't have escaped if I had tried. The crowd thinned out a bit after each floor, so I was able to slip away unscathed on the electronics and appliance floor. I was stoked to discover that the CD player and blender were on the same floor. Electronics.

It was cold outside, -9 degrees Celsius (16 degrees Fahrenheit), so everyone was bundled up in sweaters, jackets, and scarves. I would have taken my outerwear off and carried it but that didn't seem to be the norm, so I wandered around fully bundled up like everyone else.

I went to the electronics counter, where I discovered that in order to get service, I had to wait in a line of about ten people while the two salesgirls demonstrated EVERY product that EACH customer was interested in. Absolutely everything was behind the counter. Nothing was on open shelves like back in the States. We weren't allowed to look at them ourselves.

So I waited. And waited. In my heavy jacket. It was getting warmer. I took off my hat and gloves. Then my jacket and scarf. I swear you could feel the temperature rise with every single degree. The room got warmer. The people got warmer. They were sweating. I was sweating. And we all waited.

A man several people ahead of me asked to see a tape player. The clerk retrieved it, plugged it in, and turned it on. The man asked to see another one. And another. Each time, the clerk slowly shuffled into the back room to get the item and slowly strolled back. When the customer finally decided which one he wanted to buy, she disappeared for an extraordinarily long time and came back with one in a box. Good news. The line would move along.

But no. Now she took that one—the exact same model—out of the box and demonstrated it. He nodded his agreement. Now she had to package it up properly. I don't know where she went to find padding and string, but it couldn't have been nearby. The man walked away while she was doing this. Had he abandoned his purchase? Once it was properly packaged, she tied string around the box so that it could be more easily carried. This actually seemed pretty helpful. Just in time, the man returned with a slip of paper and traded it for his tape player. Finally.

The air was hot and stifling. I wasn't sure how much longer I could stand there. I had removed all the clothing I could. I watched this process repeatedly until an hour later, it was my turn.

I pointed, yet again, at a CD player I liked. It was a Sony, played CDs AND tapes (not an easy thing to come by), and cost less than 10,000 Kč ($350). I would take it. It was the only one with all the features I wanted.

The salesgirl casually strolled over to get it. Strolled back. Plugged it in. Turned it on. And showed me how it worked. Great. I gave her a thumbs up.

She put the display model back on the shelf and disappeared into the back room to get a new one. When she finally returned, she signaled that I would need to buy the floor model because it was the last one. Fine with me. She handed me a piece of paper and waved her hand towards the far wall. What? She pointed. Ohhh. On the other side of the room, there was a cashier stand. Must have been where the man had gone. I went to the cashier and got into another line. Once it was my turn, I handed over most of my cash (thank God) and received a carbon copy of a handwritten receipt. I returned to the pick-up counter and was—at long last—able to get my stereo. Hallelujah.

Now the blender.

Of course, I was a seasoned shopper now, so I thought I could handle anything. This line wasn't as long, but there was only one person working. In this department, each customer ahead of me wanted to see two or three different items. And the saleswoman had to go find them all from around the department. Then, she demonstrated each one. *Grrrzzz. Grrrzzz. Grrrzzz.* Every appliance made a really loud noise. Each time, it drew a crowd, and people crushed up against each other to see the demonstration. Once the show was over, they were on their way. It was as if they'd never seen a mixer or a blender or a coffeemaker before. Maybe they hadn't. I wasn't sure.

At last, it was my turn. I pointed to a blender, and the clerk retrieved one from the back. As she set it down on the counter, I tried to skip the demo and simply take it. Not gonna happen. I tried to signal that she didn't need to demonstrate it. I knew how a blender worked. But she plugged it in and tried to demonstrate. It didn't work. I couldn't believe it. She set it aside and went into the back to get another one. This one worked. After the demonstration ended, I hurriedly indicated that I would take it. Instead of the blender, she gave me a paper ticket. *WHAT IS THIS?* Someone kindly pointed out the cashier's desk. Right. I was to prepay before actually receiving the item. So, I went over to the cashier. And got in another line.

The department store was becoming the living embodiment of Dante's

Inferno. I was hot, sweaty, frustrated, infuriated, bored, confused. I'd been there for hours. How could this possibly be the way things were done?

Eventually, I was able to pay. In cash, of course. Plastic credit cards were years away. I took my receipt back to the appliance desk and had to wait my turn—again—to pick up my purchase. The clerk gave me the very same blender she had demonstrated. That was the way the world worked here. You bought the exact item that was demonstrated for you. While standing in all these lines, it dawned on me. In the land of the customer is always wrong, there was probably no such thing as "returns." The product was demonstrated to work when you bought it. After that, you were on your own. It was brilliant, in a way.

At last. Many hours later, I was the proud owner of a Sony CD/tape player and a Tefal "multi-mixer." I hurried home from Kotva to get ready for the party.

BLUE MARGARITAS

I WAS EXCITED TO HAVE MY FRIENDS over to my new flat. Party time! I only had a few cassettes that I brought from home to play on my new "stereo." Prague did not have a single music store. Naked Eyes would play in an endless loop for the rest of the night. I mean, we had to flip the tape and hit play repeatedly, but we always had tunes. We would need to drive to Germany soon to buy current music.

Jamie arrived before the others. He brought ice! My refrigerator had no freezer to speak of, so he managed to make a couple trays of ice cubes at his place and transport them via Tupperware from Strašnice to Hrdlořezy—about a 30- to 40-minute walk. It was below freezing, so the ice cubes were fine even if Jamie was shivering.

I began setting up my new "blender" only to discover four important things:

1) It was very small (not anywhere near the size of a blender back home)—I would have to make just a few drinks at a time.

2) It was insanely loud—industrially loud (seriously—like "I can't f*cking hear you" loud).

3) The only outlet in the kitchen was near the floor.

4) The cord was no more than six inches long. Way too short to plug in and have the mixer sit on the counter.

Oh, come on!

I took a deep breath. Regrouped. Composed myself. After all I had been through at Kotva, I was damn well going to have a margarita. The solution was readily apparent. I would have to sit on the floor, cross-legged, to make the margaritas. Maybe it wasn't going to be that weird. Everyone was going to have to sit on the floor anyway since I had almost no furniture. We could all take turns sitting on my tiny sofa, which was more like a love seat.

My friends arrived in a group: Peter, Eva, Anna, Mike, Barb, and Roman. They came bearing housewarming gifts: one bottle of champagne, two bottles of wine, one bottle of Becherovka, and 12 bottles of beer. I would be well-stocked for quite a while.

I started making margaritas in small batches.

Tequila. *Check.*

Lime juice. *Check.* It was something of a miracle that we found limes in a country with almost no fruits or vegetables.

Triple sec. *No.*

Cointreau. *No.*

Blue Curacao. *Why, yes!* We could find no triple sec or Cointreau anywhere for a traditional margarita. Blue Curacao was close enough—it was an orange-based liquor, at least—and would have to do.

We sat on the thinly carpeted floor in a circle in my living room, with our strange, glowing, bright blue margaritas in hand. Eighties music "blaring" on the "stereo." We were chatting and laughing and excitedly talking over each other. Sharing stories of workweeks and our latest discoveries about living in the Czech republic.

We quickly went through all the ice cubes, but the party developed a rhythm. I warned everyone before turning on the blender. And my friends plugged their ears with each batch. We sat again in a circle and resumed talking. It was quite a sight.

ME: "Ok, everyone. We need to make a toast. To the fact that through hard work and insane perseverance, we managed to have a bizarro margarita party out here in the middle of Hrdlořezy."

EVERYONE: "Nádraží!" we all said with laughter as we raised our glasses.

This was an inside joke. The traditional Czech toast was "Na zdraví," or "To your health." But in the beginning, we always messed it up by saying "Nádraží!" (Train station!) instead. Our toast was silly. A little goofy. But it was a nod to our burgeoning understanding of the different ways needed to survive here.

The next morning, blue lime slices were strewn around my flat. Everywhere. Dirty glasses stood in the sink. My hangover was severe. I had a Super Bowl party to recover for, and thoughts of my pending assignment in Ostrava were the furthest thing from my mind.

SUPER BOWL REDUX

7 FEBRUARY 1993

MOST OF THE EXPATS SHOWED UP at the partner's embassy house for the Super Bowl showing. Not sure they all cared about the Super Bowl, but we knew we'd be fed well. I hadn't totally understood the invitation memo until I spoke to my manager, Stephen, at the Super Bowl get-together.

It seemed the managing partner had someone at home tape the game and DHL it for the weekend event. He sat down to preview it on Thursday night to find, to his disbelief, the Sunday night movie special! But the partner didn't give up. An emergency call to the U.S. to track down another person who taped the game necessitated a second DHL package. But this time, it arrived on Saturday at 10 p.m., which required special customs processing involving a Delta agent, a DHL representative, a customs agent, the managing partner, his wife, a translator and, of course, a "yes" answer to the question of the "life-saving" nature of the package. Hilarious.

All the effort was worth it as we sat in the managing partner's massive living room (pretty sure his house used to be some country's embassy) with new friends, a bowl of Texas chili, football players bashing the hell out of each other, Troy Aikman from my alma mater, Dallas Cowboys cheerleaders, American TV commercials, and Michael Jackson moonwalking across the stage at halftime.

We feasted on the smorgasbord of Americana. We would be back to the office soon enough.

TOMAYTO, TOMAHTO

RECEPTIONIST: "You do not have a reservation," she said as she handed me back my passport.

Vašek and I were checking into the Hotel Atom for our weekly visit to Cemos Ostrava. He gave them his passport and told them his name: Vašek Pavlů. The receptionist flipped through the handwritten reservations list, found his name, and promptly gave him his key and breakfast tickets for the week.

I handed them my passport and said my name: Melanie Thomas. The receptionist once more flipped through the list and looked up at me.

RECEPTIONIST: "You do not have a reservation."

ME: "Yes, I do. Melanie Thomas. With Arthur Andersen."

The receptionist flipped through again and looked up.

RECEPTIONIST: "No. You do not have a reservation."

ME: "That can't be. Arthur Andersen made reservations for both of us just like last week."

RECEPTIONIST: "You do not have one."

ME: "But I do."

RECEPTIONIST: "You do not."

After several more rounds of this, Vašek took matters into his own hands.

VAŠEK: "[Czech Czech Czech] . . . Me-LAH-ni-ay To-ma-so-VA . . . [Czech Czech Czech] . . ."

RECEPTIONIST: "Ohhhh. Melánie Thomasová? Yes. We have a reservation for her."

ME: "What the hell?"

VAŠEK: "She thought Melanie Thomas was a man."

Argh. For time immemorial, Czechs have put -ova at the end of women's names. A man is "Tomáš." A woman is "Tomášová." It is literally Czech law. Well, here I am. A woman. Named Thomas. The receptionist couldn't even conceive of such a thing. So I became Thomasová.

This exchange took an extraordinarily long time. Finally, she gave me my key and breakfast tickets. We dropped our bags and hurried to the client site to get started.

CERTIFIED NERD

FEBRUARY 1993

"PROSÍM! PROSÍM! PROSÍM!"

The ritual coffee dance at the hotel restaurant began once more. We waved our arms. Made faces. Practically yelled "Please! We beg you!" Still, the hotel waitresses huddled in the corner in their strange combination of skin-tight mini-skirts and cloth house slippers. Smoking their cigarettes with their backs to us, trying to do anything in the world other than bring us coffee.

In the morning darkness, I had called my mom to find out my CPA exam results. I'd passed all four parts! This was a huge deal for any auditor. But it also meant I didn't need to fly home to take the exam again. I had rushed to breakfast to share the news with my team. But first, coffee.

ME: "How long do you think we'll have to wait today?"

MARTIN: "This is normal."

ME: "But why?"

MARTIN: "You know the phrase, don't you?"

ME: "What phrase?"

MARTIN: "We pretend to work; they pretend to pay us."

He smiled when he said it. Then we both laughed. That explained a lot about my clients thus far.

The servers didn't like my "stand up and go get it myself" routine, so we waited, and eventually, someone brought us coffee. Trying not to lose my mind over coffee (or rather, the absence of it), I told the team I'd passed the entire CPA exam. They stared at me silently. I assured them it was a big deal. They clearly didn't understand. That was ok.

I was thrilled.

Ostrava was not a foodie's paradise.

We went to dinner as a team—as we always did—because there really weren't a lot of options. This wasn't a cosmopolitan European city where we could walk to local restaurants near the hotel, find a food court, or easily take a cab into town. We drove the rental car to whatever restaurant happened to be nearby.

This night's *restaurace* was dark with lots of mirrors on the walls. The tables were placed before couches—not chairs—and they were covered in a '70s pastel tweed. Martin ordered the trout. TROUT! We were in a land-locked place, and I'd seen too much questionable food to feel comfortable ordering fish anywhere. But the trout was the only thing that distracted me from the very strange feeling that we were sitting in a '70s airport lounge inside a disco ball.

I suppose it was more interesting than the other restaurace in town that had bare white walls, white linoleum floors, and threadbare white tablecloths. It felt like someone had set up tables in the lobby of an office building. They served Czech food, just like every place else.

But this night, in the disco from hell, Stephen—who was in town to visit the client—raised a glass and toasted me for passing the CPA exam. The Czechs remained unimpressed, but Stephen emphasized what a great accomplishment it was. I appreciated that so much. I was in such a strange environment, far from home, always wondering why nothing made sense to me. In that small moment, I felt like someone got me.

HAPPY BIRTHDAY TO ME

13 FEBRUARY 1993

I OPENED THE GIFT, and it was a small, used compact. The mirror inside was broken. *What should I say?*

I'd been in the Czech republic for almost a month, and it was the week of my 26th birthday. I'd spent a lot of time with my staff, so we knew each other pretty well given that I'd only been there for a few weeks. After a long day of craziness at the cement factory, the team decided to go the artfully named Čínská restaurace, which literally translates to "Chinese Restaurant," for dinner.

After we ordered (always the kung pao kuře [chicken] for me), Markéta R., Martin, Jana, and Vašek pulled out small, wrapped packages. Oh wow. Everyone on the team had brought me a gift! I teared up a little bit. I was surprised and touched.

Each gift I opened was a little stranger than the previous one. Silver earrings hanging from the ears of a small stuffed Soldier Švejk doll from Markéta R. The earrings, I understood. The doll, not so much. He was a comical soldier dressed in a gray, dated uniform. Later, I would read an English copy of *The Good Soldier Švejk* to better understand why so many Czechs loved him. Soldier Švejk was like a Czech Gomer Pyle. But with an edge. A Czech simpleton who undermined the authorities around him, a send-up of the time Czechs spent under the rule of the Austrian-Hungarian Empire. He embodied the happy-go-lucky subversiveness that lurks in the Czech soul.

Martin's gift was an amber pin in the shape of a sailboat. Was it real amber? Amber was a big thing in nearby Poland. Maybe. I wasn't at all sure. But no matter. I was more confused by the fact that it was a sailboat. The entire county is landlocked. Funny enough, the Czech word for hello is "ahoj," pronounced like "ahoy, mateys!" Go figure.

I unwrapped the gift from Honza. A three-inch-tall ceramic backpack. An orange clay with a white glaze. It looked like it was covered in frosting. I was wholly unsure what one does with such a thing. Vašek gave me a chipped ceramic pig. At this, I couldn't hide my confusion. They all laughed and explained that pigs are considered lucky—so this was a lucky charm. And it was a well-worn lucky charm being bequeathed to me. I held the pig closely and smiled. What a sweet gesture.

I saved Josef's gift for last. He was on Jamie's audit, not this one, but he had sent it with Martin. It was an old, used, empty compact. I opened it to find that the mirror was cracked. I really had no idea how to react to this—I didn't understand it at all—so I just smiled and said I loved it and would thank him later. As I inspected it that night, I realized how old and beautiful it really was. I didn't understand it or the gifts, but I didn't need to. I treasured all of them. The Czechs had begun letting me into their world. I slept well that night knowing I was accepted by my teammates, who would now be my friends.

I would come to understand that there was almost nothing to buy in this country. I would struggle to find souvenirs and Christmas gifts to take back home. The more I realized how sparse the shops were, the more I appreciated the gifts my team gave me that day. The compact Josef gave me came from an antique shop. All Czechs had at the time was their past. I didn't know how old the compact was, but I could see that it was at one time beautiful and shiny and probably a symbol of beauty, wealth, or success to its original owner. And it had been well-loved. Like Josef, I took to scouring antique shops—and there were many—for unique gifts for my family and friends. My favorite was the one on Betlémské Náměstí, not far from a Czech restaurant we liked called the Konvikt Klub. Room after room of fascinating signs, posters, dishes, jewelry, and trinkets. And a sweet old man who loved to show me his new wares.

With these small gestures, my staff made me feel welcome in a very strange environment where I knew nobody and understood little of what went on around me. I carried the compact for years.

I CAN'T ASK THAT

MARCH 1993

ME: "Honza, please go ask paní Smékalová for the loan payment schedule."

HONZA: "No. No. No."

ME: "What?"

He was pushing away from the desk and standing up to head out of the room.

ME: "Oh, right. Thanks."

How long would it take for me to remember that "no" means "yes"?

A few minutes later, he returned with the loan payment schedule. But it was clearly not finished and not done correctly. The columns were mislabeled and a lot of numbers were missing. Nothing added up correctly.

ME: "Honza, please go ask paní Smékalová to correct this."

HONZA: "I can't ask that."

ME: "Why not?"

HONZA: "I can't ask that."

ME: "Well, I can. Let's go together."

We went to see paní Smékalová. I asked Honza to translate.

ME: "Ahoj, paní Smékalová. This schedule is missing some information. Can you please fill it in?"

HONZA: "I can't say that."

Paní Smékalová watched in silence as she knew not a word of English.

ME: "But we need to have her fix it."

HONZA: "But I can't say that."

ME: "But why not?"

HONZA: "It would be rude."

Sigh. I'd hit the wall. I couldn't ask him to be rude. Back home, none of this would have been a big deal. I tried a different approach.

ME: "Ok . . . we need her to fix this document. What can we ask her?"

Honza stared at me. He didn't have any suggestions. He clearly wanted to avoid the entire conversation.

ME: "Can we ask her to explain the schedule? Or how she got these numbers? Or how it adds up?"

Nope.

Honza was not about to ask her anything that would make it evident she hadn't done it correctly.

I tried again.

ME: "Can you please finish this document?"

Honza translated to Czech, although I had no way of knowing what he actually said to her.

PANÍ SMÉKALOVÁ: "Neh."

HONZA: "Smékalová said no."

ME: "Yeah, I got that. What did she say no to exactly?"

HONZA: "She won't do any more work on the schedule."

Well, there you had it. She was flat-out refusing to do her job. The clients were responsible for preparing documents for the auditors. There's a reason they were called prepared by client (PBC) documents. But at this point, I couldn't spend any more time trying to get Honza to ask for what we needed or getting paní Smékalová to do what we needed her to do.

ME: "Fine. I give. Can you ask her for all the supporting documents?"

Honza agreed.

She angrily handed us a stack of documents and turned her back to us.

Honza and I went back to the conference room and prepared it ourselves.

At the end of each week, the team and I would make a list of notes to give to our manager, Stephen, when we returned to Prague. This day's notes were like no other notes I'd ever written.

Notes for Stephen:

Smékalová gave Vašek and Honza the runaround ALL DAY, and they never got any of the reports or information they had been seeking. We ended up doing the work ourselves.

At 4:40 p.m., we ran out of things we could productively work on.

FRIDAYS AT PIZZA TAXI: CLIENTS

MARCH 1993
PRAGUE

EVERYONE TALKED AT ONCE. Each couldn't wait to tell his or her "unbelievable story." Everyone wanted to share their story, but first, I had a question.

ME: "What in the world is a Pizza Taxi anyway?"

Everyone laughed.

ME: "Or is 'pizza' now an adjective?"

JAMIE: "What does it even mean?"

MIKE: "Does taxi mean something else we don't know about?"

PETER: "Is it a taxi made of pizza?"

JAMIE: "Could it possibly be that they have pizza delivery here?"

We all laughed because that made the most sense and yet was hard to believe given the attitude towards service here.

ME: "Is it just bad English and—as always—if they'd had JUST ONE native English speaker review it, they would have changed it to something that makes more sense?"

We never did find out for sure, but at some point, it was rumored that Pizza Taxi may have actually delivered pizza. Maybe that was always the plan? Maybe? It remained a mystery.

Having exhausted all our theories about the origins of the name "Pizza Taxi," we went back to everyone's "unbelievable story."

PETER: "This week, I got a tour of the nuclear power plant. We drove around to see all the buildings, the cooling towers, and the grounds. We passed a field strewn with what looked like huge pieces of scrap metal. I asked them what it was."

MIKE: "That seems sketchy."

ME: "It really does."

JAMIE: "Well? What was it?"

We were a little afraid of the answer. And rightfully so . . .

PETER: "They said there had been an issue with part of the plant. They took it apart to identify and fix the problem, and when they put it back together, these pieces were leftover . . ."

JAMIE: "WHAT?! Like when you take apart the vacuum cleaner and have some parts leftover that seem like maybe they weren't critical?"

ME: "At a nuclear power plant???"

MIKE: "RUN!!!!!"

PETER: "I tried to hightail it out of there as fast as I could!"

Everyone laughed and drank more wine. That story was truly disturbing.

LAURENT: "We were doing a mid-year inventory this week. We had to 'count' cows and manure. At home when we do inventory of livestock, a plane flies over and takes a photo so we can count the cows."

ME: "I'm gonna go out on a limb and assume there was no plane involved here . . ."

Not a chance.

LAURENT: "No. No. Last week, I was given a bucket of red paint and a paintbrush . . . I had to run around the field in my business suit and swipe each cow's ass after I'd counted it."

We couldn't stop laughing. The image of our coiffed French friend, a true vaniteux, running around chasing cows with a paintbrush was just too much.

LAURENT: "But wait . . . we had to calculate the size of a pile of cow dung since they use it as fertilizer. But before we did, the client reached down and grabbed a huge chunk with his bare hands!"

MIKE: "But why???"

LAURENT: "To show us the quality, I think."

More laughter.

ME: "Please tell me you didn't have to pick up the dung . . ."

LAURENT: "No! Thank goodness. I cannot tell you my relief when I found out they would weigh it for us. We just had to witness it."

Whew. We were all relieved for him.

ME: "Honza flat-out refused to ask the client to actually do her job and prepare a document. So we had to do it ourselves."

PETER: "Why would he refuse to ask?"

ME: "He said it was rude. Rude to ask her to do her job. I gave up and just did the work."

JAMIE: "Wow. The audit will take forever if you have to do their work AND your own."

ME: "The same client said she was too exhausted to help us get binders off the shelf behind her! Literally two feet away from her desk. We had to wait a freaking day to get them."

Everyone shook their heads. We ordered another bottle of Frankovka—hangover be damned.

JAMIE: "You know how American companies do their year-end inventory by counting sometime in the last quarter and then calculating what the value should be on the last day of the year? Because that makes more sense than everyone in the entire country counting inventory at midnight on New Year's Eve?"

We all nodded. We'd all counted inventory many times. Laurent had just been doing a mid-year count.

JAMIE: "Well. Not here. Year-end inventory is done at midnight on December 31st. Last year, I was high up on a tower, peering in to see how much limestone there was, putting a stick in to measure the depth.

All in the freezing cold wind at midnight on New Year's Eve! Happy New Year to me."

The laughter came so easily. It was a relief to bond over our shared experiences.

MIKE: "We did mid-year inventory last week and had to measure piles of coal to determine how much the power plant had on hand."

JAMIE: "That sounds normal . . ."

ME: "What's the punchline?"

MIKE: "One pile seemed a little too big. We insisted on inspecting it closely even though they objected."

We waited with bated breath.

MIKE: "There was a truck underneath it!"

EVERYONE (in unison): "What the f*ck?!"

MIKE: "They didn't think the pile was big enough and they didn't want to get in trouble. So they tried to fake it."

Wow. Just wow. We were mind-blown. We couldn't imagine being that afraid of there being missing inventory. Or of making a mistake. Or getting in trouble for something we had no control over.

And on and on.

We shared our stories, each outdoing the last. Our Friday nights were much-needed therapy from the surprises, craziness, and frustrations of just trying to get through each week with our sanity. We bonded over obstinate clients, situations that seemed illogical, terrible customer service, too much pork, no fresh produce, language barriers, and ridiculous scenarios we couldn't come close to understanding.

The otherness of it all.

It is something you discover when you become an expat. You are surrounded by others, but you are not them. And you can never become them. You cannot relive your life as them. It is theirs and theirs alone. We were a small tribe in someone else's universe.

LIVING IN A KAFKA NOVEL

NOW THAT I WAS BACK IN PRAGUE, I had to go get my Czech ID card. I was told to go to a certain government building, provide a copy of my passport and some documents from the firm, have my photo taken, and get my card. It seemed straightforward. But didn't everything at first?

I entered the building and went to the third floor as instructed. There was no information booth. No receptionist. Just a hallway of closed, unmarked doors that seemed to go on forever. It was like looking into an infinity mirror. There were long lines of people waiting outside each door. I was clueless about which line to join, and I couldn't figure out how any of *them* knew which line to be in.

I went person to person asking for help. I showed a man my documents. He stared blankly at me and turned away. I asked the next person, an older woman.

ME: "I'm here to get an identification card. Where do I go?"

She pointed down the hallway. Well, that was vague. I worked my way down the line of people, showing them my documents and asking, albeit in English.

ME: "Does anyone know where I go to get my identification card?"

Nothing. Either they didn't speak English or they just refused to. I could believe either. After 20 minutes of this, I gave up and got into the shortest line.

Periodically, someone would exit one of the rooms and the person working behind the door would summon the next person in. About an hour later, it was my turn. I went from the stark hallway with linoleum floors and fake wooden doors into a Soviet-style office that held a desk, two chairs, and a filing cabinet. No curtains, no plants, no nothing.

I handed the woman my paperwork. She glanced at it and said something in Czech. Loudly, angrily. She pointed to the door and shooed me away with the back of her hand. I tried frantically—pointing this way and that—to get her to show me which line to wait in. She just turned to the next person in line as if I were no longer there. It was truly Kafkaesque.

Franz Kafka is probably the Czech republic's most famous writer. He wrote about how bureaucracy was more than an annoyance; he wrote of how it could control and even crush lives. Where people "just doing their jobs" were agents of evil and suppression. That bureaucracy was frustrating, illogical, labyrinthine, and more. From what I was seeing, the man definitely knew what he was talking about.

Once again, I stared down the hallway at all the people patiently waiting in their different lines. What the hell did I do now? I took a deep breath, picked a new line, and tried to stay sane. Thankfully, I had brought a book. So I read. And waited.

I was sent away from three more doors. I was truly flummoxed by why nobody else seemed perturbed. Did they all have information I didn't have? Did they magically know what was behind each door? Were there more instructions that had been withheld from me? Did they just love standing in line? Or had they just given up a long time ago? Did they stop expecting things to make sense? Or be straightforward? Had they come to accept that logic and customer service had escaped the country while they were stuck behind the Iron Curtain? Had they caved to the craziness long before I arrived and expected things to change?

After nearly finishing my book, I finally happened upon the correct line.

I'd waited my turn in each and was repeatedly turned away and sent to the next line. By the seventh attempt, I wasn't sent away. And by some miracle, I left with my ID card.

Now, pivo.

CHAUVINISM

MARCH 1993
OSTRAVA

ME: "Vašek, why do you insist on carrying everything?"

VAŠEK: "Because you are a—how do you say?—a weak woman."

I stopped in my tracks.

Every week as we walked to the train, to the taxi, to the hotel—anywhere, really—Vašek insisted on carrying both of our suitcases and both of our audit bags (smaller than a suitcase; bigger than a briefcase).

When Vašek first took my bags at the train station several weeks previously, I had initially objected. But he had been insistent and I was new to the culture, so I let him take them.

During the third week, he grabbed my bags in addition to carrying his own. Watching him juggle our bags as I walked with nothing but my purse, I finally asked him why. His response stunned me. A weak woman????

Really???

I stopped in my tracks.

Vašek kept walking until he realized I was no longer by his side.

He turned to find me.

ME: "Vašek. It is bad enough that you think that . . . but you should NEVER say that to an American woman again."

VAŠEK: "But . . ."

ME: "It's sexist, chauvinistic, misogynistic, and so many other things."

VAŠEK: "But . . ."

ME: "It's rude, offensive, condescending, and demeaning."

VAŠEK: "But . . ."

ME: "It's machismo bullsh*t."

VAŠEK: "But . . ."

ME: "No."

VAŠEK: "But . . ."

ME: "Just no."

I took my bags back and never let him carry them again.

SPARE PARTS

MARCH 1993

ME: "So . . . why does the cement factory have 50 million Kč ($2 million) worth of spare parts on the books? Doesn't that sound like a lot?"

(Never mind the fact that the spare parts were classified as inventory, even though Cemos didn't sell spare parts. But that could wait. I was familiar with that game.)

Blank stares.

I asked again: "Any idea why they would have so many spare parts?"

Nobody knew. No one had given it a second thought. We reviewed a bunch of documents the client had prepared for us, but none of them provided any insight at all.

Time to play detective.

We spoke to a lot of people to try to figure it out: the engineer, the managing director, the warehouse guy, anyone that might have a clue. Each person seemed to know a different bit of information. And we began putting it all together, piece by piece. We already knew the cement factory machinery used at Cemos was old. More than 85 percent had been purchased before 1980 and made somewhere behind the Iron Curtain. And it might not have been the most modern, even when it was new. But we needed to know about these spare parts. We sat down with Inženýr (Ing.) Volák, the chief of fixed assets. He went by Rocky.

ME: "Tell us about all these spare parts."

ROCKY: "Our machinery is no longer produced or sold anywhere."

ME: "Anywhere in the Czech republic?"

ROCKY: "Anywhere at all."

ME: "Anywhere in Eastern Europe?"

ROCKY: "Anywhere in the world."

Wow. Ok . . . so by our definition, all of the machinery was obsolete. The entire cement plant. We were off to a rolling start.

ME: "Ok. So why all the spare parts for out-of-date machinery?"

ROCKY: "Well. It breaks down a lot because it's so old."

Great.

ROCKY: "If the machinery breaks down, we cannot produce any cement. We need to be able to get spare parts quickly. So, we keep them here."

Oh wow.

Rocky was clearly irritated by having to explain this to us. His voice was getting louder as we continued the conversation.

ROCKY: "If we do find someone who can provide the spare part we need, we have trouble getting it for several reasons. Delivery is so slow it can take up to a year to receive the part once it's been ordered."

A year?

ROCKY: "Also, some suppliers will only produce the parts in large quantities, so we have to buy in bulk or not at all."

I didn't have any idea what question to ask next. I was entirely perplexed by this situation. All the parts were obsolete because the entire factory was obsolete . . . I relied on Vašek and Honza to keep the conversation going.

VAŠEK: "Who is responsible for keeping the machines working?"

ROCKY: "When we have a breakdown, I tell Inženýr Pavlů, the chief engineer, what parts we need."

HONZA: "And Ing. Pavlů gets it out of the spare parts you have here?"

ROCKY: "Yes. And if we're running low, he starts the search to find somewhere to buy more."

Rocky was annoyed at what he believed were our stupid questions.

Vašek and the client spoke in Czech for a while. I waited for Vašek to tell me what crazy new thing he'd learned. The client's voice got louder and louder. Honza started chiming in—presumably to smooth things over with the client. Soon the client was yelling at them.

In a nutshell, here's where we were. If the machines broke down, production would stop. If production stopped, Ing. Pavlů would feel the heat. Thus, it was Ing. Pavlů's policy to always purchase whatever Ing. Volák requested, thus ensuring that Ing. Pavlů would not be questioned. And the machines would keep running.

No one considered whether these decisions made any business sense—or were cost-effective—whatsoever. They simply did everything they could to make sure production never stopped. (Right! *Note to self: Production is king in a planned economy.*) Modernizing the machinery wasn't even on the table. That would stop production for some amount of time. Their goal was to make sure they were never asked by the boss to defend their actions and possibly be held responsible. Profit or loss? Efficiencies? Just-in-time manufacturing? Whatever. As long as they were producing, everyone was good.

But I saw some issues in their future. At risk of further angering Rocky, I had to ask some more questions.

ME: "Is it possible that a certain replacement part will become unavailable forever, because the part is, after all, obsolete?"

ROCKY: "Yes."

ME: "If a replacement part is no longer made, can you reengineer the machines to accommodate the new replacement part that is available?"

ROCKY: "No."

ME: "Would reengineering the machine, with the new replacement part, create a domino effect where other parts of the machinery become obsolete as well? Oh wait. You said no. Hm."

They all stared at me. Neither Rocky nor my staff saw the situation the way I did. That this was a great big house of cards ready to fall at any moment. But it was Ing. Pavlů's belief that ALL spare parts on hand would be used over time. It could be tomorrow, or it could be ten years from now, but he believed that all the parts were necessary to have on hand. They were of zero value to anyone else, but they were the lifeblood of Cemos.

I actually understood that. I still thought it was going to come crashing down, but until then, these parts were everything to them. It made sense that they would have millions of dollars of worthless, obsolete machinery parts on hand. They needed to produce. They wanted to avoid ever being questioned. They did what they had to do to achieve those two goals. Communist logic. But I was starting to get it. That scared me a little.

Talk about a Catch-22.

So, I moved the parts out of inventory but kept them on the books with more value than they would have anywhere else in the world. I wrote a long, detailed memo to explain this wild deviation from standard accounting practices. It wouldn't be the last time I had to do that. We affectionately called them "strategic parts" for a while because, in a weird way, that's what they were.

My brain hurt. I needed a break. I headed out of the conference room to find the bathroom and clear my head. I found myself in what felt like a construction zone. There were wires hanging from the ceiling. There was rubble on the floor. I was instantly covered in a fine layer of dust. I had to navigate numerous obstacles—in high heels—to get to the bathroom where, of course, there was no toilet paper.

I went back to the conference room, looking for a solution of some kind. I found that rolls of toilet paper had been provided for us to take to the bathroom each trip. Martin informed me that we were not to leave them in the bathroom itself. They were to be promptly returned to the conference room. I had no idea why. We weren't allowed to share the toilet paper with others? Was there a toilet paper thief in the building? Did they keep track of the rolls in their inventory accounting?

I navigated the corridor for the third time only to discover that the light switch in the bathroom did nothing. Mercifully, there was a window. A little gray light shone through. But the dust and rubble everywhere made me feel as though washing my hands didn't do much good. I headed back and dutifully returned the toilet paper to where it belonged. In the conference room.

MARTIN: "Why are you eating something so unhealthy for lunch?"

ME: "What? You're eating pure fat."

It was lunchtime at the cement factory. Probably 10:30 a.m. The work day started early here. I went to the kantýna (cantina) to see what was being served. The kantýna always had a layer of cement dust on everything. The tables were old, wooden, and covered with waxy, plastic, dingy white tablecloths. The chairs were uncomfortable. In them sat old men eating their lunches slowly. I feared they weren't as old as they looked.

Life under communism was hard and had aged a lot of people before their time. I had been told that the babičkas (the grandmothers) sweeping the streets with brooms made of twigs or collecting change at every restroom weren't nearly as old as they looked. I thought 60s or 70s. But some were in their 40s. HOW WAS THAT POSSIBLE? It blew me away how people had aged so quickly under the communist system. (Perhaps because they had been made to sweep the streets clean with twigs . . .)

Most of the men were sipping some sort of broth-like soup that did not look appetizing. In fact, it didn't look like it had much in it at all. I was pretty sure it was dršťková polévka (tripe soup). Blech. I was not eating soup made from a cow's stomach lining. No way. I declined and bought the only thing that I was certain about: a yogurt.

As I walked into the conference room, Martin was eating a rohlíky (hard roll) with slices of cheese and fat. Martin called it salami, but all I could see was fat. The meat was almost completely white. The fat-to-meat ratio was maybe 80:20.

MARTIN: "It's salami. It's very good for you."

ME: "But it's almost all fat!"

MARTIN: "And it's delicious. I love fat."

ME: "What did you say?"

MARTIN: "Fat is so good."

ME: "You're kidding, right?"

I came from a world where a low-fat diet was all the rage. It seemed like every item in the grocery store had low-fat or no-fat options. Fat was out. Sugar substitutes were in. This was the new definition of "healthy" in America.

Martin loved fat. But I had to share something I'd found shocking and was sure he would too. I told Martin that I'd heard from the expats in Budapest that in Hungary they put fat chunks on a stick, heated them over a fire, and dripped it onto bread.

MARTIN: "That's an amazing idea!"

ME: . . .

Gnarly.

This was another conversation I wasn't going to win.

There was a restaurant in Prague where you could order slices of fat on salad. Pure fat slices . . . on salad. Other than šopský salát—a salad made with tomatoes, cucumbers, and a Bulgarian feta-style cheese—it was the only salad I ever saw on a menu here. Not a chance I would ever order the fat salad.

Later that afternoon, we were working away in the conference room, and I flipped the light switch. Nothing happened. I tried again. Still nothing.

No lights.

It was late afternoon and the room was getting dark. I simply wanted to turn on the lights so I could read the work papers. But the lights weren't coming on.

I peered down the hallway. I couldn't see lights anywhere. *What in the world?!*

I knew the bathroom light didn't work, but all of them? Was there an outage today? Would the lights come on after dark? I had noticed Czechs didn't like having the lights on during the day. Quirky, but whatever. As the sun started setting—around 4 p.m. in the winter—I was struggling to read the documents.

ME: "Does anyone know why the lights don't work?"

MARTIN: "Because the electricity is off."

ME: "Is there an outage?"

MARTIN: "No."

ME: "It's off on purpose? Why would they turn off the electricity?"

MARTIN: "There are no lights in the building after lunchtime."

ME: "What? How can that be?"

MARTIN: "Actually, there is no electricity at all after lunch."

ME: "Am I understanding correctly? There's electricity in the morning when nobody needs the lights on. But no electricity in late afternoon or nighttime when it's dark?"

Martin shrugged.

ME: "And that means they can only use their computers before lunch? Which is at 10:30 a.m.?"

I did NOT understand. I wasn't sure I believed it. I went to other rooms in the building and tried the switches. But there were no lights to be turned on. Anywhere. I was stunned. The Czechs didn't seem to think it was strange, but they couldn't explain it to me.

I made an executive decision.

ME: "Ok, everyone, let's pack up and go back to the hotel."

CZECHS: "What? Why? We have work to do."

ME: "I know. We'll work at the hotel."

CZECHS: "But why?" They clearly thought this was a bizarre idea.

ME: "Because I can't see."

CZECHS: "We can see."

ME: "Well, I require light. I can't read any of these documents. So let's go. We'll work at the hotel."

And so we did. Every day around 3:30 p.m. or 4 p.m. Off to the hotel.

I'm sure they thought I was some batsh*t crazy American. But my poor Western eyes couldn't see in the dark. I like to see when I read. Sorry.

Notes for Stephen:

Ing. Pavlů didn't understand our request about spare parts. Rather than ask us about it, he spent a lot of time preparing information we had not requested. Then he yelled at Vašek twice and both of us once. I still don't know why.

No electricity after lunch forced us to work at the hotel from 4 p.m. on.

CRASH

MARCH 1993
PRAGUE

TECHNICALLY, IT WAS MY FAULT. It was raining. The car was jammed with new IKEA furniture and furnishings. Jamie sat in the passenger's seat, his lap full of packages. There were no signs or signals at the intersection. What was that about? It never even occurred to me to look right or left. Back home, I'd never seen an intersection with no signs—if I didn't have one, the other direction should—so I drove on through. And then BOOM! Hit by a Nissan.

I'd been driving around Prague and the Czech republic for several weeks. The car had become our preferred way to get to the cement factories. I didn't know the rules of the road, and nobody was concerned enough to tell me. Then again, no one seemed to tell the Czech drivers either. It seemed like a free-for-all. Everyone just took their chances. In L.A., there were no trams, trains, car-sized potholes, dogs peeing in the road, elderly crossing in the middle of the street, or intersections with no stop signs or lights. Yet I'd survived. For weeks, my staff and I had driven all over the countryside and throughout Prague at record-breaking speeds. I actually hit 150 kilometers (km) per hour once. (That's about 90 miles per hour [mph].) The dashboard was shaking so hard and making so much noise that Vašek actually got a little bit nervous, and I had to slow down before the car rebelled or he grabbed the wheel.

The noise from the crash brought out all the locals onto this neighborhood street in Prague. In my experience, the Czechs were not a very curious people, but this was a car wreck. One teenage boy, Tomáš, came out to see what the noise was. Tomáš had the complete misfortune of knowing a little bit of English and tried to help. He called the police. Two officers arrived and then a third. I was ready to give my statement and have the insurance company take care of the rest. The police had different ideas.

I was truly in shock when Jamie and I were waved over and had to cram ourselves into the back of a police car. We were to be taken to the police station. For a fender bender. There were no casualties. No injuries. Not even a scratch. But now we would view Prague from the back of a police car.

We arrived at the station and were put into a holding cell. The situation had gone from annoying to perplexing to *what the f*ck?*

Jamie and I sat in a 10-foot-by-10-foot space on a hard, backless wooden bench up against a wall with a locked door to our right, bars to our left, a bare cement wall in front of us, and NOBODY in sight. And even if there were somebody, no one would speak English. Our Czech was limited to "pivo" (beer) and "vepřová s knedlíkem" (pork with dumplings). In their eyes, we were foreigners. Make that "stupid foreigners." No, make that "stupid, rich foreigners" willing and able to pay an exorbitant fine (aka "bribe") in order to get out of this former communist police station. The power was all theirs.

We were petrified.

After forever, we were led into another room. Standing there were Tomáš and the driver of the Nissan. Tomáš had been brought down to help translate for the police. As it turned out, the driver of the Nissan spoke perfect English, but no one had bothered to ask him.

The room was similar to the holding cell but with furniture. That was it. Bigger . . . with furniture. There was a bare light bulb hanging down from the ceiling, a table with a bench in the corner, and a desk and chair against one wall. Smack in the center of the room were two straight-backed wooden chairs facing the desk. Nefariously, the interrogator faced the wall behind the desk, where he had a small table with a typewriter. So, he wouldn't be facing the witnesses as he questioned them. They might as well have had electrodes and arm straps attached to the chairs. We were relieved to be allowed to sit on the bench for the next three hours while they filled out the paperwork.

The police officer taking my statement was old—we're talking childhood friend of Stalin old. The poor man had to type everything on the oldest typewriter I've ever seen. The kind you see in antique shops or museums. You know, black with the really tall keys. *Kthunk, kthunk, kthunk.* And of course, he was making three copies of everything by slipping carbon paper between paper sheets in the typewriter. No different than in the 1920s. Under communism, labor was cheap and electrical goods/appliances were expensive. A copy machine probably cost more than they would pay two men in a year. So they labored on.

First, he filled out the informational sheet. The names, addresses, and ID numbers of both drivers and any witnesses. Tomáš translated the entire conversation.

He handed me the paper to review. Somehow, the elderly policeman had neglected to put Jamie's name on this sheet.

I pointed at Jamie and said, "What about Jamie? He should be listed on this sheet."

The policeman looked at me as if I were crazy.

POLICEMAN: "You want him listed as a witness?"

ME: "Yes. He was in the car with me. He should be listed."

The policeman furrowed his brow. Probably thinking exactly what I was thinking—that I'd just increased the length of this visit by a good 30 or 40 minutes.

But I was learning how things worked here. I was certain that if at any time in the future I EVER wanted to say that Jamie had been in the car with me, I needed his name on that paper. If his name wasn't there, the Czech insurance, the Czech car rental agency, the Czech police, and any other interested parties would never accept he had been in the car. I would have gotten "No, that's impossible. If he had been there, his name would be on this paper." Guaranteed.

The policeman pulled the sheet out of the typewriter and gave it to me to sign. It was an official-looking document with a big empty section and a place for a signature at the bottom. Below the signature line was some Czech legalese. I asked what it meant.

TOMÁŠ: "It says, 'This is my statement, given freely, in my words, under no duress.'"

ME: "But I haven't given a statement yet."

TOMÁŠ: "He'll type it after you sign."

WHAT?!

I found that terrifying. The policeman insisted I sign it before we could move to the next step. I pushed back but to no avail. I clearly didn't have a choice here. It was a standoff. I knew I couldn't win, so I nervously signed and prayed he would type up my statement as I gave it.

ME: "I was driving about 20 kilometers per hour . . ."

POLICEMAN: "We don't care how fast you were driving."

I just signed something saying that this was my statement "in my words."

ME: "But that's what happened . . ."

POLICEMAN: "Go on."

ME: "When I came to the intersection I kept driving. I couldn't see his car because of the garden wall, and I didn't know that I was supposed to stop."

POLICEMAN: "I'll write that you sped into the intersection and hit the other car . . ."

ME: "NO!!! I was only going 20 kilometers per hour! I wasn't speeding, I didn't accelerate . . . I just didn't stop! AND he hit me; I didn't hit him!"

Whose statement was this again? And what did I really sign?

POLICEMAN: "We don't care how fast you were driving. Instead, I'll write . . ."

ME: "NO! That's it! That's the end of my statement!"

The policeman made a few more suggestions for a conclusion sentence that I rejected.

ME: "I don't have anything else to add."

POLICEMAN: "Ok. I'll write 'There is nothing more that I can say.'"

ME: "Fine."

Next up, Jamie.

JAMIE: "My statement is the same as hers."

The policeman narrowed his eyes at Jamie.

POLICEMAN: "WHAT? It's the same? How can it be the same?"

JAMIE: "Well, I was in the same car, had the same view, and, not surprisingly, saw the same thing."

The policeman shrugged as if he still didn't understand but would write it anyway. But then, just as he began to type, he had a revelation. He turned back around with a smug look on his face. He'd figured out our plot.

POLICEMAN: "Aha! Your statement can't be the same . . . you weren't driving!"

Brilliant. A communist Inspector Clouseau.

Jamie laughed as he spoke because at this point if we didn't laugh, we'd cry!

JAMIE: "You're right—you got me . . . put down that I was RIDING in the car with her, and THEN I saw the same thing."

Of course, the policeman again wrestled with the fact that it was all Jamie had to say. Jamie's statement ended the same as mine had: "And there is nothing more that I can say."

Of course, we had no idea if that's what he wrote.

Amazingly, the Nissan driver didn't appear to have any problems with his statement. Bing. Bang. Boom. And done. Either he was a former member of the Communist Party or the policeman made something up later. We couldn't understand a word they said, but it was quick.

We'd been there for so long by this time, I felt like we were becoming a blended family. Right out of a Thursday night sitcom. I thought of pulling out my camera for a group shot. Then, one picture of the policeman with his typewriter. One of the carbon paper. One of the light bulb. Finally, one of Jamie and me in the interrogation chairs. My friends would get a kick out of that. But no. The wizened expat returned. It simply was far too risky a venture in a country where crimes are loosely defined and punishments are random and discretionary.

While we waited for the final paperwork to be sorted, filed, and signed, I glanced out the single window in the room. During the four hours we were there, inches and inches of snow had fallen. The ground and buildings and trees were covered in a gentle white. I was sure that by the time I got paroled, it would be sunny and the snow would be long gone. But I was wrong. They were setting us free.

There was one last thing. Pay the fine. The man said that he could charge me anywhere from 1,000 Kč ($35) to 7,000 Kč for breaking the law. He mulled it over. He said he was only going to fine me 1,000 Kč because I was a foreigner and he didn't want me to have any trouble with the authorities. It seemed like an extraordinarily high fine, $35, so I asked for a receipt. They only had dingy, white, pre-printed receipts in the amount of 50 Kč each, proving my theory that 1,000 Kč must be a special fine for foreigners. He tore one after the other after the other off a pad. I left the station into the snow 1,000 Kč lighter with 20 crumpled paper souvenirs.

FRIDAYS AT PIZZA TAXI: JAMIE AND THE DELI BAR

MARCH 1993

JAMIE: "This language is the worst."

He didn't need to explain any further. This was a land where "no" meant "yes." Indecipherable words with unpronounceable letters reigned supreme. We'd all taken hours and hours of Czech lessons and still struggled to actually receive what we tried to order off a menu. Yes, there were a handful of easy words that we used daily. "Pivo" meant "beer." "Co?" meant "What?" "Dobrý den" meant "Good day" (said in a sing-song manner). "Prosím" meant "please." Beyond that, good luck.

JAMIE: "Markéta and I went to the cement factory kantýna to get a snack. I wanted chocolate, so I asked for a Deli bar. They keep them behind the counter because, you know, someone might steal a candy bar worth one cent, and it's an easy word to pronounce."

We laughed. We'd all been there. Trying to say a difficult Czech word and pointing like crazy people at something behind the counter. But "Deli" is pronounced in Czech just like it is in English. Nothing mysterious. No strange letters. No difficult sounds. No special enunciation.

JAMIE: "So, I said 'Deli, prosím.'"

WOMAN BEHIND THE COUNTER: "Co?" (What?)

JAMIE: "Deli."

WOMAN: "Co?"

JAMIE, pointing at the bin full of Deli candy bars: "Deli."

WOMAN: "Co???"

JAMIE, now waving two hands at the bin full of Deli candy bars: "Deli! Deli! Deli!"

WOMAN: "Co???"

ME: "So, what happened?"

Markéta finished the story.

MARKÉTA: "I tried to help and said to her 'Deli, prosím?'"

WOMAN: "Ahhhhhh, Deli!!!!!"

MARKÉTA: "And she handed me the Deli bar."

All jaws around the table at Pizza Taxi dropped open.

PETER: "What?!"

JAMIE: "Yep. She said exactly what I had been saying. Markéta shook her head and assured me I had been saying it correctly."

MARKÉTA: "It's true. You were saying it exactly right, Jamie. I don't know why she didn't understand."

We discussed this little mystery for a bit. Maybe she just didn't expect an American to speak Czech? Maybe she just didn't like foreigners? Maybe she was just too tired to be helpful? No idea.

MIKE: "Pivo! More pivo for the table."

ME: "That's truly depressing that we aren't even understood when we say the easy words. There are so many words that are impossible to pronounce."

PETER: "Did you know that even little kids have to practice the 'ř' sound?"

The ř was impossible. Something like "rzh" but with the roll of the tongue and super fast. We all struggled.

MARKÉTA: "It's true."

ME: "Seriously? If the language has a sound that even kids have to practice, maybe it should be eliminated from the alphabet."

MARKÉTA: "Ř is classified as a raised alveolar non-sonorant trill."

ME: "I think that says it all."

PETER: "Clears it right up!"

MIKE: "Does the President Václav Havel struggle with it too?"

MARKÉTA: "Yo, yo. We get a good laugh when he says it on TV."

EVA: "Maybe they leave it in the language as a way to shame people."

We laughed. That sounded plausible.

MELANIE'S GUIDE TO PRAGUE

23 MARCH 1993

JAMIE: "Will this work day never end?"

It was 2 p.m. and Jamie was antsy. A friend had sent him a VHS tape of the recent Nebraska Cornhuskers–Oklahoma football game. He was a die-hard Nebraska fan, so despite the game happening five months ago and knowing that Nebraska solidly beat Oklahoma, he couldn't wait to watch it. But we had a lot of other things we needed to get done. He had letters to write, and while he watched the game I planned to make my own Prague guidebook. People were planning to visit and there still weren't any decent guides to Prague available.

It had been more than six months since I'd first tried to buy a guidebook and things hadn't improved much. Things were changing on a daily basis, so even if there were a decent guidebook it would have quickly been out of date. I'd been saving copies of the two English-language newspapers—*Prognosis* and *The Prague Post*—both of which had restaurant reviews, art show listings, and other articles about the latest happenings in the country. (Thank God for these papers or we would never have any idea what was happening here.) I planned to start clipping our favorite information to share with visitors, thereby creating something resembling a travel guide.

I wanted it to be a fun night for Jamie but we had a lot to do in a place where speed and service were not really a thing. I decided to try to lay out a schedule with lots of room for delays we couldn't possibly see coming. Hoping to make him laugh, even if things went horribly wrong and his viewing was delayed, I wrote a memo and left it on his desk.

Jamie and Melanie
Schedule of Events

5:30pm   Leave the office

5:31pm   Be on Václavské Náměstí

5:45pm   Walk to the square to hail a taxi. The walk to the taxi stand will take 15 minutes because we need to navigate around the Bolivian flute players, the Krishnas, the construction, the taxis, and the tourists, just outside the office.

5:45pm   Risk our lives by getting into a taxi. (The things we'll do for clean underwear are amazing.)

6:10pm   Pick up laundry. It will take 25 minutes to get there because, WITHOUT QUESTION, something wildly unexpected will happen on the way there. Maybe we'll get stuck waiting for a slow-moving train which is still 5 miles down the track. Who knows?

6:30pm   Leave the Laundry King (hopefully not empty-handed) where we could spend 20 minutes while they look for our laundry.

6:45pm   Get dropped off at home and immediately begin writing those seven outstanding letters so you can let yourself watch the game. I'll head back to my place to change.

7:00pm   Finish the first letter (for which I have allowed you 15 minutes because I realize that sometimes it's difficult to get into that speed-writing mode.)

7:10pm   Finish the second letter

7:20pm   Finish the third letter

7:30pm   Finish the last four letters very quickly because by this time you'll be sick of trying to write something different to each person so you can just copy the third letter over four more times! (Be sure to save letters to five people who don't know each other for last so these people don't compare letters.) Alternatively, you could just send postcards to these people, thus saving time by limiting your writing space. Or you can try just WRITING BIG!

7:31pm   I'll return to your flat casually-dressed and with all my newspapers in tow, ready to cut and paste articles into a homemade guidebook to Prague.

7:32pm   Leave flat to pick-up čínské jídlo (Chinese food)—the best choice for dinner given the alternatives of my cooking or your cooking with the available ingredients. Optimistically, this should only take 30 minutes.

8:05pm   Settle in with dva piva (two beers), start the Nebraska slaughter of Oklahoma, clip newspapers, and eat Czecho-Chinese food.

Surprise! Nebraska won. And I made a guidebook. It was a good night.

Quarterly News

of the

WEIRD AND WONDERFUL

JANUARY–MARCH 1993

OUR OFFICE SUBSCRIBED to the *Fleet Sheet*. I *looooved* the *Fleet Sheet*. Every day, American Erik Best and his team read through the Czech newspapers, translated the highlights into English, and created a one-page summary. They faxed this sheet to businesses who paid for the service. Our office put a copy in each expat's mail file. Each entry had an abbreviation for the newspaper from which it had come.[5] The sheet covered business, politics, social stories, and even the comic strips. I couldn't wait to get my stack when I came back to town each week. My first few months here yielded some real gems that helped me better understand the upheaval and confusion we were all going through.

(MFD/Thur/6) Tomáš Marek writes that you would think we're back in socialist times judging from the number of owners of private businesses who have simply closed down shop for days on end while they figure out the new tax system. Do they not realize how much this disregard for the customer is costing them, he asks?

Ha. Customer service was not at the forefront of anyone's mind except the expats'.

Ummm. They aren't communist but want to be called communist. Not at all suspicious . . .

(MFD/2) A Jiránek cartoon pictures Communist Party Chairman Jiří Svoboda explaining to a reporter why he was unable to push through a name change for his party: "Some of the old comrades have a strong attachment to the name. You must understand that these are extraordinarily sensitive and emotional people."

(MFD/2) A Jiránek cartoon pictures Communist Party Chairman Jiří Svoboda deeply absorbed in thought. "Don't bother me now, comrade," he tells a co-worker. "Whenever I sit back and think about all the things our party has perpetrated, I'm always deeply moved."

Comrade! Wow. I hadn't really believed that people actually called each other "comrade." Never mind the rest of this entry . . .

This just made me laugh. Where, indeed?

(MD/2) A cartoon pictures a group of diplomats and military officers gathered around a map of Europe. "It's already clear that the world cannot exist without the Iron Curtain," says one of them. "Just one technical question remains: Where to put it?"

(Úspěch/27) Vratislav Šlajer, director of Consus consulting, says that Western consulting companies are not capable of giving good advice given the current state of the local economy and of local management. Their advice is often of little use here, he says, because it does not fit the environment.

This was so, so accurate. Everything we tried to suggest didn't make sense here. I felt validated.

(MS/4/50) Hoping to attract business by letting Austrian travelers know that his rest room is open to the public, the owner of a restaurant in a Czech border town hung the sign "Closed" on the entrance door. It seems that his Czech pronunciation - which calls for devoicing of certain consonants at the end of words - led him astray. He thought the sign read "Klozet."

Ha. Ha. Ha.

(MFD/1) A proposed law under preparation in Parliament would require would-be prostitutes to gain certification as an independent entrepreneur before practicing the trade. A medical examination would be required. Persons engaging in prostitution without the appropriate business license would be prosecuted specifically for not having a licence. Prostitution would be allowed in public places, in private dwellings and in brothels.

Uhhh . . . so what's left? Where is it illegal???

It's clearly gonna take a while for the economy to stabilize!

(MS/4) Asked in an informal survey if anything seems too cheap now that prices have gone up, up, up, one 47-year-old office worker responds wryly, "Yes, manpower."

(MFD/Sat/1) A Prague firearms dealer, Jiří Otta, says that 80% of his customers don't know anything about guns. But neither he nor the police has authority to test the customer's proficiency, he complains.

Oh dear God, that's concerning.

FIESTA MEXICANA

2 APRIL 1993

Hola!!!

You are cordially invited to an intimate dinner party on Friday, April 2, 1993, on the balcony (weather permitting) at Pod Strašnickou Vinicí 4/37, Praha 10, Strašnice. For your dining pleasure, we will have a Mexican feast complete with margaritas, tortillas, guacamole, chips, and queso!!! The cooking and drinking will begin directly after work (schedules permitting) and dinner will be served shortly thereafter. Please bring your assigned ingredients, and we'll see you at 7 p.m.

MENU • JÍDELNÍ LÍSTEK • LISTA DE PLATOS

PŘEDKRMY • HORS D'OUEVRES • BOCADILLOS

imported tortilla chips, salsa, and queso

(skillfully prepared by Mike)

NÁPOJE • BEVERAGES • BEBIDAS

blue margaritas

cerveza/pivo *(albeit Czech, not Mexican)*

HLAVNÍ CHOD • ENTRÉES • PLATOS

chicken and beef fajitas

chicken and beef burritos

(the chicken and beef will be marinated and grilled,
provided that charcoal can be found somewhere in Prague)

PŘÍLOHY • SIDE DISHES • ENTREMÉS

homemade tortillas

homemade refried beans

Mexican rice

guacamole

AND FOR THOSE WHO DON'T MAKE IT HOME FRIDAY EVENING:

SNÍDANĚ • BREAKFAST • DESAYUNO

huevos rancheros

(assuming we don't demolish all the Mexican fixings on Friday night!)

Hasta la vista!!!

I arrived for the party and found Jamie sitting on the ground on his deck in the freezing cold.

ME: "Ummmm . . . whatchya doin'?"

He gave me a look. The "the answer is so ridiculous, I can't say it out loud" look. He was trying to start a charcoal fire in a grill—and I use the term "grill" very loosely. It was about a foot wide and an inch off the ground. He had bought it at Ikea; it was the only one available. Match after match fell between the black coals. His condensated breath hovered above the grill. He had the intensity of a watchmaker.

I laughed and breezed past on my way inside to sit on the floor and make margaritas. I knew the fire would eventually light—or that we would come up with another way to light it. That's the thing about the expat life. You develop a "nothing in this damn place will stop me" attitude. If you want it, somehow, someway, it is gonna happen.

Oh man, I missed Mexican food. There was only one restaurant trying to serve it: Buffalo Bill's. Where do I start? The chips were stale; the margaritas, sickly sweet; the beans, wrong; and some of the ingredients should never have been anywhere near Mexican food. I can only describe it as a spaghetti or pizza with ketchup situation.

Jamie had a moment of inspiration. We would to try to make our own Mexican meal. Jamie said he would host, and he organized the get-together, assigning each person one or two food items to track down and bring to his flat that night. Some ingredients were easy enough to find but others not so much. I was responsible for margaritas since I had somehow managed this before. First hurdle: finding limes again.

Produce of any kind was in short supply in this country. I decided to redouble my efforts to find limes. I went to small corner shops and large grocery stores. Limes generally didn't exist here. It was a miracle we'd found them the one time. I had to go to five, six, seven different stores before I found a solution. Clementines. Small oranges. Incredible. Clementine margaritas. Blue clementine margaritas. Had to be an original.

So, I had packed up my "blender" with the insanely short cord, tequila, blue curacao, and clementines to make something. Wasn't sure what. I figured if it had tequila, it was a margarita. If it had rum, it was a daquiri.

When I went into the kitchen, I discovered that Jamie had brought strawberry margarita mix back with him from the States.

ME: "Oh, thank God!"

PETER: "I agree! Thank God you're here. We need margaritas."

ME: "I'm just glad we don't have to juice all these clementines."

BRENDA: "I'll cut them up for garnish."

ME: "Perfect. Let me find an outlet near the floor and I'll start blending."

PETER: "We also have pivo if anyone wants some."

We had a lot of beer. Jamie's neighbor sold beer from a tap out of her back door. (Did everyone have a keg in their house?) All you had to do was bring your own container. It cost us 10 Kč (maybe 25 cents) to fill a large pitcher. She was the type of neighbor everyone needed. The beer was cheap, convenient, and delicious.

Jamie came inside to get warm and have a much-needed and well-deserved drink.

JAMIE: "Is Anna here?? We can't make tortillas until she shows up with the eggs."

BRENDA: "Why didn't we just buy tortillas?" She said with a smirk.

Everyone laughed. Fat chance.

PETER: "She's not here yet. But when do we want to start grilling?"

JAMIE: "Not until we make the tortillas."

PETER: "Oh good. Because we have some work to do before we can start grilling . . ."

We were puzzled until he pulled the chicken out of the bag. It was a whole chicken, and it still had some feathers on it! It was truly disheveled and not anywhere near being ready to grill.

We stared in horror. Not one of us had ever plucked a chicken before. We grabbed our drinks and dove into the task at hand. We defeathered and deboned the chicken while snacking on tortilla chips and queso, courtesy of Mike. He always had a supply. I'm certain that every time Mike returned from visiting the U.S., his suitcase had no clothes. Instead, it was filled with RO*TEL, chips, and Velveeta. And for those who looked down on Velveeta, shame on them. It was a delicacy. Yum.

There was a knock on the door. Anna!

We offered her a margarita as she set her backpack down.

JAMIE: "Did you get the eggs?"

ANNA: "Yes. They're right here."

ME: "Right where?"

I was dying to see how she'd managed to get them here.

ANNA: "Here."

She pulled a small brown paper bag out of her backpack.

Seriously? THAT was the plan? I was sure I'd been missing some secret egg transportation plan and was excited to finally find out what it was. But there was no secret plan. Anna had somehow managed to transport six eggs in a brown paper bag, in her backpack, through 12 stops on the metro and a 10-minute walk to the flat—and only one broke! I was in awe. I don't think I would have made it with any eggs at all. *Note to self: Do not buy eggs.*

None of us had a tortilla recipe, and there certainly wasn't a way to find one here. We would have to wing it. Making tortilla dough was simple enough. Ok, we made some kind of dough. Water, flour, eggs, a pinch of salt (we were guessing, and incorrectly). Flattening them into tortillas proved to be a challenge.

ME: "How are we going to do this?"

JAMIE: "With this!"

Unbelievably, Jamie had packed a tortilla press in his shipment from home. He was committed. We gave it a whirl.

JAMIE: "Hell. The dough is too tough or thick or something. This won't work."

We looked around his kitchen for anything we could use. We tried a rolling pin, a meat cleaver, and several other things. The only thing that worked was to put the dough between two cookie sheets and stand on them. We took turns standing on the cookie sheets until we had enough tortillas for everyone. They were still several times thicker than they should have been.

And a little more like bread than tortillas. But they would do. *Note to self: Bring back tortillas next time I go to America.*

Margaritas. *Check.*

Chips and queso. *Check.*

Wheatables? *Check?* Someone had brought ranch-flavored Wheatable crackers from the States. Not sure how or why, but they worked well.

Tortillas. *Check?*

Guacamole? *Neh.* As if we could have found an avocado.

We cut the chicken into strips and bundled up to grill it by flashlight.

Finally finished cooking, we sat down to eat our hard-earned meal. It was a ridiculous combination of the fresh ingredients available in Prague, food brought from home, and our memories of what Mexican food actually tasted like. We had fought our way through the traumatic grocery shopping experiences and MacGyvered a way to make dinner with weird ingredients and basic appliances. And it was fabulous. And yes, it was probably better for how hard we'd worked than how it actually tasted. But it would always be memorable.

IT'S IMPOSSIBLE

APRIL 1993

JAMIE WAS STARTING TO WONDER if he was the crazy one.

An hour earlier, we'd been in the office. He told me he was taking a quick break to run down the street to the tailor. He'd bought some new suits on his trip home, and he needed the pants hemmed. He'd gone to the same tailor before, and they'd done a nice job.

He went back to the same building on Na Příkopě, just a five-minute walk from the office and a place we passed every day. He told the tailor he had more pants to be hemmed and asked if he had time right now.

TAILOR: "I'm sorry. We don't hem pants. We only make suits."

JAMIE: "But you hemmed pants for me a few weeks ago."

TAILOR: "I'm sorry, sir. It's impossible. We don't hem pants."

JAMIE: "Wait. I remember you. Don't you remember me?"

TAILOR: "No, sir. We don't hem pants."

Jamie looked around. He was sure he'd been there before. Did this man have a twin? Was there an identical tailor shop next door? No. That couldn't be. He was certain he was in the right place.

JAMIE: "Sir. You hemmed my pants before. I was here. I spoke to you. I remember you."

TAILOR: "It's impossible. You were never here."

And with that, Jamie left. Somehow simultaneously certain he'd had his pants hemmed there and also certain he was losing his mind and had imagined the entire thing.

It reminded me of George Orwell's 1984, which I'd actually read in 1984 during my junior year of high school.

> *The party told you to reject the evidence of your eyes and ears. It was their final, most essential command.*
>
> GEORGE ORWELL, *1984*

George wrote about it. I experienced it. I called it the Communist Mindf*ck.

Deny so completely that your subject begins to doubt their own sanity and stops questioning anything because they know they can never win.

It got to the point where we didn't even have to say it. When something that seemed ridiculous was happening, we would silently glance at each other. We knew the look. "The Communist Mindf*ck." No words required.

JUST ONE NATIVE ENGLISH SPEAKER

APRIL 1993
EASTER SUNDAY
KARLOVY VARY

JAMIE: "Hi. We'd like to go to the spa."

SPA RECEPTIONIST: "Do you have a doctor's note?"

JAMIE: "What? No. We just want to go sit in the hot springs."

SPA RECEPTIONIST: "You need a doctor's note."

JAMIE: "For what?"

SPA RECEPTIONIST: "To say you need this medical treatment."

JAMIE: "We don't need medical treatment. We just want to sit in the hot water."

SPA RECEPTIONIST: "It's impossible. You need a note."

Jamie and I had rented a car for Easter weekend and headed west to the Czech republic's most famous spa town, Karlovy Vary, better known elsewhere by its German name, Carlsbad.

Our destination was the Grandhotel Pupp. It was pronounced "poop," which made every American giggle. The hotel was later featured in a Queen Latifah movie, *The Last Holiday*, and she laughs at the same thing. When we walked into the lobby, we were in awe. The ceilings were two stories high.

The hotel had red carpets, baroque carvings on the walls, and beautiful chandeliers. It was stunning. The town was equally beautiful. A river running through the center. Steep mountains looming on both sides. Gorgeous architecture. Beautiful greenery. We had dropped off our bags and gone in search of these famous hot spring baths everyone had told us about.

ME: "But why do we need a note?"

SPA RECEPTIONIST: "Because you need a note."

JAMIE: "But WHY? What harm will it do if we sit in the water?"

SPA RECEPTIONIST: "You need a doctor's note."

Czechs took their spas seriously. And there were many spread throughout the country. Back home, it was a relaxing weekend. Here, it was serious medicine. There were no water jets, no mood lights, no New Age music. Just a steel tub, institutional lighting, and beige tiles on the walls. Sitting in the lukewarm water for 20 minutes. That was it. And for this, only a prescription would do.

We tried different spas. It was the same conversation every time. So, we decided upon a different plan.

The Hotel Thermal.

This hotel was the one building in town that wasn't beautiful, baroque, or otherwise charming. It can only be described as a spaceship parked next to a Soviet panelák. It was a monstrosity. One building was a round, cement disc. The other was a 15-story cement block. We hated to frequent this communist blight on the town, but we were desperate.

The lobby was even more Soviet than the exterior. It was dead silent in the cavernous space with a long reception desk on the left and a massive coat check on the right. It could have held hundreds of coats, but it was empty now. Before asking about the thermal springs, we were drawn towards a carpeted area by the window packed with insanely high-backed red leather chairs, in groups of four, around low tables. They looked like thrones for Communist Party leaders. I couldn't imagine anyone else actually sitting in them. So, of course, we had to. We sat across from each other and felt simultaneously ridiculous and like we'd stepped back in time. They were fantastic.

Eventually, we went in search of a hot springs experience. This was the final attempt. The hotel had a swimming pool sourced from the hot springs. We went to the pool to check it out, and it was full of people. And I mean FULL. Probably because this was the only option for those of us without doctors' notes. We had no interest in jockeying for space in an enormous pool with a hundred other people.

We gave up our goal of sitting in tepid, carbonated water and decided to drink it instead. We headed off in the direction of Karlovy Vary's famous colonnades. The colonnades were long, covered walkways that each led to a spring. We would get the medical benefits internally instead of externally. And they couldn't stop us.

As we walked towards one of the larger colonnades, we saw several teenage boys on bikes and skateboards heading towards us. We stepped to the side to get out of their way. As they whisked by, I felt a sharp sting on my butt.

SMACK!

I whirled around.

SMACK!

Another sting. The boys were laughing and waving pomlázky in the air. We had heard about this. It certainly sounded crazy. And we hadn't believed it was true. We were stunned. But the tradition was alive and well.

ME: "Ohmigod! I can't believe that happened."

JAMIE: "I thought that was just a joke when people told us about this."

ME: "So did I."

Every Easter, teenage boys made whips—pomlázky—out of intertwined willow branches with cute little ribbons tied to the end. On Easter Monday, the young men of every village walked about town knocking on household doors. The women came to the door to be whipped—a reminder not to be "lazy" in the spring and summer. "Hody, hody doprovody," the young men sang. For the reward of being whipped, the women gave the men a shot of slivovice or a painted egg in return. The most sexist man on earth couldn't dream up a better holiday.

Vašek had given me a homemade pomlázka the week before. A very sweet gesture despite the sexist nature of it. And still, I hadn't believed him about this tradition. What Western woman would? The whole thing sounded ridiculous and was completely sexist, and nobody could explain why or how this had become a tradition. But here I was, getting my butt whipped on Easter Monday.

We finally made it to the colonnade. There, we saw people walking around a small fountain with these strange, little, ornate cups. You can only describe them as beautiful porcelain pitchers that have been shrunk by a ray gun. Occasionally, someone would drink from the elephantine spout. The pretty little pitchers were called pohárky.

We looked at the displays of roses and other things that had been left in the water and completely mineralized. That didn't make me want to drink the water, but I bought a flower as proof of what this water was like. The steam was rising from the water as people strolled along arm in arm, sipping from their little cups. We dipped our new pohárky into the water. It was steaming hot, so we let it cool a bit before we tried it. I wrinkled my nose—the water smelled awful—and tried to swallow quickly. The taste was salty and minerally; the aftertaste, gritty.

We went to several different colonnades, trying the different springs. They were different temperatures, but they all tasted pretty similar. I wasn't going back for seconds. But we'd done it. Check that off the bucket list.

We returned to the Pupp hoping for something tastier. There was a fancy restaurant. They even had a wine list. We read the English descriptions.

CHARDONNAY: Fancy, white floral smell and fragrant mineral in the nose. Mixed up red berries, tastes like dirt, complemented by undertones of wormwood with crispy flavor, acid, and hard end.

SAUVIGNON BLANC: The smelly aroma comes with green melon, lemon zest, and rich elemental ingredients enhanced by the taste of the pushy lemon and its longevity.

SYRAH: Strong wine with mountain fruits, delicious aroma of tobacco and delicious aroma of sand with fruits.

The chardonnay tastes like dirt? The Sauvignon blanc tastes of pushy lemons? The Syrah has the delicious aroma of sand? Let's order! This was the best wine list ever. We laughed and giggled at every description. Fortunately, the wine was better than the descriptions. We went to bed that night with clean palates.

But how hard is it to find just one native English speaker to proofread your menu or sign? You couldn't swing a cat in Prague without hitting two backpackers and an English teacher. This was clearly a no-brainer business opportunity. On the other hand, perhaps customer service was so unimportant that nobody would bother paying to have their menus proofread. We just kept enjoying the terrible but funny translations. Sometimes, we could even tell what they meant.

BREAKFAST TICKETS

APRIL 1993
OSTRAVA

RECEPTIONIST TO VAŠEK: "You do not get breakfast tickets."

VAŠEK: "Why not?"

RECEPTIONIST: "You are Czech."

We were at the Hotel Atom. The receptionist now knew that Melanie Thomas was not a man. But there was a new hiccup.

As usual, I had been given five little slips of paper—redeemable for breakfast each morning. I was always worried I would lose those damn little scraps of paper and have to ask for replacements. I was confident that wouldn't have gone well.

Vašek reminded the receptionist that he needed his tickets.

RECEPTIONIST: "You do not get breakfast tickets."

VAŠEK: "What do you mean?"

RECEPTIONIST: "You do not get tickets."

VAŠEK: "But Melanie got hers."

RECEPTIONIST: "But you do not get tickets."

VAŠEK: "But I've been given breakfast tickets every day for the last several weeks."

RECEPTIONIST: "No."

VAŠEK: "I've eaten breakfast right over there every day."

ME: "He always gets breakfast tickets."

RECEPTIONIST: "Czechs don't get breakfast."

Vašek grew more frustrated.

VAŠEK: "You've seen me. They've all seen me. They've taken my tickets every day."

RECEPTIONIST: "It's impossible. Czechs don't get tickets."

Oh sh*t. Once she said, "It's impossible," he was doomed. The Czechs never backed down. Ever. It's one more bizarre legacy of communism. Their way of revising history on the spot. Creating a false, new reality in an instant. You cannot win. "It's impossible." The only good thing I could see at this moment was that it wasn't just something they did to the expats. They did this to each other too.

Vašek tried reasoning with her with his evidence once more . . . but we both realized we had hit the wall.

RECEPTIONIST: "It's impossible. You never had breakfast tickets."

We left empty-handed and acquiesced to pay for his breakfast every morning.

Over coffee, Vašek told me there were two room prices. One for foreigners and one for Czechs. Foreigners paid the equivalent of $100 a night; Czechs paid $10. Foreigners got breakfast; Czechs didn't. The hotel had obviously erred over the previous several weeks by giving him tickets. But why pretend it had never happened? Why the lie? What was it? The Communist Golden Rule? Lie unto others as you would have them lie to you? It never failed to amaze me.

INVENTORY

APRIL 1993

THE NEXT MORNING, MARTIN CLIMBED through the hatchback of the Škoda, over the back seat, and got into the driver's seat. But of course.

The Škoda Favorit was a boxy little thing. With a large rear window that sloped at a sharp angle. This car was all Czech. Very little horsepower, but somehow it got the job done. The name Škoda is something of an inside joke to Czechs. It was named for its founder, Emil von Škoda, but it also means pity, broken, or shame. That was quite a marketing plan.

This week, we had driven to Ostrava in our "pitiful" car. No train. This made it much easier to get around in the snow and ice. We carried our audit bags from the hotel to the car. I carried my own, as Vašek was no longer allowed to do so. Martin inserted the key into the driver's side door. The doors unlocked. We all reached in unison to open the doors. Nothing. They didn't budge a centimeter. They all were stuck. They had frozen shut overnight.

We tried prying them open. Tried jiggling them. Tried brute force. The car was so lightweight that it rocked with each attempt. There was only one thing to do. We tried the trunk. Miraculously, it opened! We nominated Martin to climb into the car through the hatchback. It wasn't pretty, but he somehow tumbled to the driver's seat. Vašek and I stood outside in the cold while we waited for the heat to unfreeze the door handles. Finally, the handles moved. Hallelujah. We wouldn't all have to climb through the back.

As Vašek and I opened our doors to get in, the car started rolling backwards. Martin already had the car in reverse.

VAŠEK: "Martine!"

Martin hit the brakes. Vašek hesitated and bent down, checking his foot. The Škoda had rolled right over his black business shoe. But the Škoda was like a golf cart, so no harm done to Vašek's foot or shoe. We all got in and slowly "sped" off to Cemos.

VAŠEK: "The warehouse manager wants to speak to you."

ME: "Ok. Why?"

Vašek shrugged as if he didn't know. But he did.

Earlier, we'd spoken with the inventory manager, pan Kratochvil, about their inventory counts.

ME: "How do you record the inventory differences?"

KRATOCHVIL: "There is no difference."

Ok, what? In the Western world, when you counted your inventory, there were always differences.

ME: "What do you mean?"

KRATOCHVIL: "There is no difference."

ME: "So when you count the inventory and then compare it to the records, they're the same amount?"

KRATOCHVIL: "No." (Yes.)

That just wasn't possible. Was it?

ME: "Ever?"

KRATOCHVIL: "Never. There is never a difference."

Shrinkage/shoplifting, miscounts, other mistakes. You counted the inventory, compared what you counted to what the records said you should have, and recorded an adjustment to the books accordingly. So, either the

Czechs had perfected inventory management or something was up. And my gut told me that, of all things, the communists hadn't mastered inventory management over the rest of the world.

We needed more information. Despite the Czechs not finding this at all unusual, I'd sent Vašek to speak with the warehouse manager to learn more. He returned quickly and said the warehouse manager wanted to speak to me.

VAŠEK: "I told the warehouse manager you wanted information about how they actually count inventory. He said, 'Ahhhh. Your boss is a woman? Let me talk to her . . . I'll let her know she really doesn't need this sort of information.'"

What? He said this as if this were totally normal and not at all disturbing or inappropriate or offensive.

I was fired up.

ME: "Oh, hell no. Because I'm a woman, he thinks he can scam me? Charm me? Does he really? Let's go."

Warwick, the senior auditor from Australia, was livid.

WARWICK: "Vašek. You should never put Melanie in that sort of situation. That's just not acceptable."

Warwick was being protective. I wanted to light the warehouse guy up and show him that I was no pushover. Vašek didn't understand the problem. The three of us discussed this at length. Warwick and I tried to explain to Vašek why this wasn't ok. I'm not sure he ever understood where we were coming from. We couldn't send him back to the warehouse manager, as we were pretty sure he would simply conspire with him.

Warwick won. *He* went to see the warehouse manager. When he returned, he shared an eye-popping revelation.

In the Czech republic—and dare I assume the entire Soviet Bloc—they printed the inventory list of record and took it with them when they counted the inventory. So, if it said they should have 10 forks, then they made sure they had what looked like 10 forks by whatever means necessary. If a shipment came in with, say, three extra forks, they would hide those forks for a rainy day. When the spoons came up two short, they put two forks at the bottom of the pile so nobody would notice there were two spoons missing. The warehouse manager would be held personally responsible if anything came up short. Consequently, they made sure there was never a reported inventory shortage. A mistake was simply never made. Or admitted to. Ever. Communism may not have mastered the truth, but they certainly learned to fake it with confidence.

FRIDAYS AT PIZZA TAXI: LOST IN TRANSLATION

APRIL 1993
PRAGUE

JAMIE: "Does anyone have trouble distinguishing between the words 'dívka' and 'děvka?'"

ME: "They sound almost exactly the same to me."

PETER: "Even when I think I'm saying them differently, the Czechs NEVER agree."

JAMIE: "And of course, they couldn't be like 'bad' and 'bed,' the harmless words the Czechs can't pronounce distinctly."

MARKÉTA: "Oh yes. Those are very difficult. Bad. Bed. They sound the same to me."

ME: "Yeah, but 'dívka' and 'děvka' mean 'little girl' and 'whore.' It's like a sick joke you guys play on us."

PETER: "Pronouncing them correctly wouldn't help me since I never remember which is which."

MIKE: "'Objet' and 'oběd.' It's slightly less embarrassing to mix up embrace and lunch."

ME: "'Nikdy' and 'někdy!'"

JAMIE: "That one is cruel, just like dívka and děvka. They sound the same, but they're opposites."

MIKE: "I don't know those ones. What do they mean?"

MARKÉTA: "Never and sometimes."

We roared with laughter. How would we ever learn this language?

ME: "I had the most ridiculous conversation with Vašek the other day. I asked him what 'páva' means. He told me 'páva' wasn't a word. I assured him it was. He said it a few times and reiterated that it's not a Czech word."

JAMIE: "But there's a hotel called U páva . . ."

ME: "That's exactly what I said! Then Vašek said, 'Ohhh! U páva. That means peacock.'"

JAMIE: "What in the world?"

ME: "Without the 'U' in front of it, he didn't know I was saying the word for peacock, which is 'páv.'"

PETER: "Oh wow. That's wild."

ME: "I can't even wrap my brain around why that would be a stretch. I studied Spanish and Portuguese for years. They are so much easier. Czech has seven declensions for each noun and adjective, with different ones for singular and plural. I cannot keep them all straight."

MIKE: "Nobody can."

ME: "They even decline people's names. How can someone's name change?"

PETER: "That's true. When we talk to Vašek, he's Vašku. When we talk to you, Markéta, you're Markéto. I have no idea what the rules are."

MARKÉTA: "Yo, yo, yo."

"No" meant yes, but so did "yo." So much easier to understand.

MARKÉTA: "When they talk about you, it's Melanii Thomasové. For example, 'I have heard about Melanie Thomas' is 'Slyšel jsem o Melanii Thomasové.'"

ME: "Wait. So, when I'm the object of the sentence, it's Melanii Thomasové? When is it Melanii Thomasovou?"

MARKÉTA: "Well, you're the object in both cases. The difference is in the grammatical case. Thomasovou is accusative; Thomasové is locative."

My brain exploded a little bit.

ME: "Any more cases we should know about?"

MARKÉTA: "Let's take the partner at work, Ken Hobbs. If I'm 'with' Ken, it's Kenem Hobbsem,' and it's instrumental. 'I gave a present to Ken' is 'dal jsem dárek Kenu Hobbsovi,' and it's dative."

Jamie burst out laughing and shook his head.

ME: "That's crazy. Even crazier, I read that in English, there are the words 'Czech' and 'Czechs.' Two words. But that in the Czech language, there are more than 100 variations of those words. Can that POSSIBLY be true?"

MARKÉTA: "Yo, yo, yo, Mel. It's true."

I hung my head.

ME: "And this is why we will never learn Czech."

We roared with laughter. And ordered another round of Frankovka.

ME: "Someone told me there are some Czech verbs that have no present tense."

JAMIE: "Come on."

ME: "I don't know if it's true! Does anyone know?"

PETER: "I haven't heard that, but honestly, this language is just difficult enough that I could believe it."

MARKÉTA: "Yo, yo. This is also true. Czech verbs only have three tenses: present, past, and future. But only imperfective verbs have a present tense. Perfective verbs express the finality of a process, so they cannot be present tense."

We learned stranger things every day.

ME: "That hurts my head. And it blows my mind that you know all the terms for these cases. I definitely don't know all of that for English."

EVA: "Have you lot heard the tongue twisters?"

JAMIE: "Oh. Those are insane."

EVA: "My favorite is 'strč prst skrz krk' because it doesn't have any vowels."

MIKE: "Holy crap. What does it mean?"

MARCELA: "Stick your finger through your throat."

MIKE: "In your throat? Down your throat?"

MARCELA: "No. *Through* your throat. As if you were poking a hole from front to back."

We all tried it, saying the words over and over.

ME: "Stirtch, purst, skirz, kirk."

I swear the more beer we drank, the better our pronunciation. We actually started getting them right. At least in our own minds.

MARCELA: "Here's another one: 'Strýc Šusta sušil šustky v Sušici.' It means pan Šusta dried the dresses in the town of Sušice."

We tried it. We sounded like lisping snakes.

MARCELA: "Last one: 'Tři sta třicet tři stříbrných křepelek přeletělo přes tři sta třicet tři stříbrných střech.'"

We doubled over with laughter.

MARCELA: "Three hundred thirty-three silver sparrows flew over three hundred thirty-three silver roofs."

No. There wasn't enough beer in the world for that one.

ME: "I read a quote in a magazine that is spot on: '*Czech—a language so difficult, it is said, that even the Czechs don't speak it correctly.*'"

Everyone burst out laughing with relief. It wasn't just us!

MIKE: "Na zdraví!"

We all shook our heads and toasted to our incompetence at the language. Markéta just sipped her pivo and laughed at us. We were beyond help.

X-GAMES: GROCERY SHOPPING

APRIL 1993

BACK IN PRAGUE, EVERYDAY LIFE CONTINUED. Work. Nights out. And grocery shopping, which was practically an extreme sport.

I needed food in my flat. Eating out was cheap and easy for the expats, but a girl can only eat so many plates of pork and dumplings. There was a small grocery store near my flat. My list was simple—bread, butter, fruit, and maybe some less perishable things. Easy enough.

I grabbed a cart and entered the store. The woman at the counter already looked annoyed. No point in trying to ask her for help.

I saw a refrigerator case and some cabbage in the corner, but the store was predominantly shelves of cans and boxes. I decided to see what was available here. I started in canned goods.

Most of the cans had very little information on the labels. Like everything was "plain wrap"—the generic products sold at American grocery stores in the '70s. I scanned the shelves looking for anything that might give me a clue as to what was inside. Some expats just bought random cans and hoped for the best. Finally, I saw a can with a picture of a cow on it. Canned beef, possibly? Not my thing. I found tuna, or some other fish, as evidenced by the picture of a fish on the can. And pickled vegetables.

It seemed that any vegetable that entered the country had to be pickled. I loved pickles, though, so I figured I would try to find those.

I stopped in my tracks and did a double take. In the midst of the cans with a cow, a fish, and vegetables on the labels, there was a can with a picture of a baby on it. Canned baby? I breathed slowly and processed it. It had to be baby food. Right? RIGHT?!

As I looked through the different cans, I realized something even more concerning. How old was this food? The shelves were sparsely stocked, making it seem like the inventory must sell out and be restocked frequently. But a lot of the cans were covered in dust. I picked up a can to look at the expiration date. Finding none, I grabbed another can. And another. Was that corned beef made in 1972? Who knew? Now it seemed like everything stayed on the shelf or on a rack until it was sold. Outdated. Out of fashion. No matter.

I decided to skip the groceries altogether. I was traumatized by the canned baby. I returned the basket and left the shop. I went out for pork and dumplings.

GENERAL LEDGER

MAY 1993
HRANICE NA MORAVĚ (HRANICE)

NEXT UP WAS HRANICE NA MORAVĚ. We'd finished up the preliminary work at Ostrava the week before. Now we were headed to Hranice, near the border with Poland, to audit the other cement factory. The city was at the far end of the Czech republic. Smaller than Ostrava. With even fewer hotel and restaurant options.

We checked into the hotel, the Hotel Cementář, which means "man who works at the cement factory." The name pretty much summed up our accommodations. It was a big, pink, cement block. A few star levels below a Motel 6. At reception, we were greeted by an unfriendly receptionist, just like at the Hotel Atom. But Martin was so friendly as to be disarming to Czechs and expats alike. He got us checked in without any discernible problems, so everything seemed to be on a good path. We left our suitcases with the receptionist and headed to work.

The name of the company was straightforward enough: Cement Hranice. And, just as in Ostrava, we were led to the small conference room where we would do our audit work. Small, sparsely furnished, bare walls. Drab and cold like the factory itself. The only thing in the room that served no utilitarian purpose were the books on three shelves. I picked one up. And then another. And another. They were all by Marx, Engels, and Lenin. Communism had fallen, yet these books remained. This was 1993, after all. Four years after the fall of the Wall. To be fair, the Czechs had removed all the Lenin and Stalin statues. I hadn't seen a single one since I'd been here and never would. But these books remained. Relics of a bygone era? Memorabilia from a curious past? Or was it that no one thought a thing about them? When I tried to ask the Czechs about them, they shrugged.

8:40 A.M.

ME: "Vašek, please ask the economic director for a copy of the interim general ledger. The G/L."

Vašek returned too soon. This was becoming a pattern.

VAŠEK: "He said there is no interim G/L."

ME: "What do you mean?"

VAŠEK: "He said there isn't one."

ME: "How can there not be one?"

VAŠEK: "He said it doesn't exist."

The G/L is the means for keeping records of a company's total financial accounts. It's the entire shebang. Without it, there is nothing. No accounting. Just random numbers. The G/L is run at month-end and year-end. The interim G/L is a version produced mid-month that can change daily as transactions occur.

ME: "Ok, let's go talk to pan Langr."

Let the games begin.

VAŠEK: "Just Langr."

ME: "What do you mean?"

VAŠEK: "We just say Langr, no pan."

Hmmm . . . no 'mister' before the last name? I chewed on this for a few minutes. I mean, I guess the person's sex was obvious by the last name. If it had an -ova it was a woman. And maybe they didn't care if she was married or not? A woman was either a pani (Mrs. or missus) or a slečna (miss). There was no Ms. that I was aware of. (And slečna sounded awful to me in English—it always jarred me when people yelled "slečnou" at me when I was in trouble for something mysterious.) But why just their last name? I didn't ask. I decided it must be a holdover for calling everyone comrade. Comrade Pavlu. Comrade Langr. At least they'd dropped the "comrade."

Langr had never met an American before. Even stranger, he'd never been to Prague. He said it was too far away . . . and yet, we'd come on the morning train. I was pretty sure this town only existed because there was a limestone quarry here. So, life in Hranice na Moravě was pretty secluded. I had a feeling working together was going to be an eye-opening cultural experience for both of us.

Vašek and I returned to Langr's office together. We asked him for the interim G/L. He told me the same thing he had told Vašek previously. There was no interim G/L. As happened so many times, I thought perhaps I just wasn't asking the right question. *Let me try something else,* I thought. Vašek translated.

ME: "Do you have a month-end general ledger?"

LANGR: "Yes."

Great. So far, so good.

ME: "So in the middle of the month, what report do you look at to see what's going on?"

LANGR: "I don't get a report."

ME: "Ok . . . so, do you look at something on the computer to know what transactions have happened?"

LANGR: "No."

ME: "Ok . . . you're the economic director. . . what do you do with your time all month before you get the G/L?"

VAŠEK: "I can't ask that."

ME: "Why not?"

VAŠEK: "I just can't ask that."

ME: "But we need to know that."

VAŠEK: "But I can't ask him that."

Sigh. I'd been here before. Some questions were just too direct for my Czech staff. They simply wouldn't ask them. I got it. Sort of. I tried rewording the question. Vašek wouldn't budge.

Ok—Plan B.

We left and went in search of accountants, IT staff, or anyone else who might have been able to show us what data was available before month-end. We asked the IT guy to show us on the computer what we could see. We asked the accountants what information they used to process transactions, analyze data, book entries, do anything.

Nada. Nothing. Ziperoonee.

We did this all day. Nobody had anything helpful to add. Everyone told us the same thing: There was no way to see any accounting information before the end of the month. No transactions, no debits and credits, no balances, nothing. At this point, I really had no idea what they did at work all day.

At around 5 p.m., I returned to the economic director's office. I was extremely frustrated. We had spent the entire workday trying to get information that should have taken two minutes to get. I walked into the office and stood near the small conference table. I don't know what got into me. I told him I did not understand what he and his team did all day. I could not have cared less what Vašek was translating. I slapped my hand down on the table, only it wasn't the particleboard tabletop. It was a huge computer printout—the old, dated, green bar computer paper with the perforated edges and holes along the sides. It was the interim G/L!

I was livid and Langr knew it. He hung his head for a minute—in shame, I hoped. Then, he looked at me and fessed up. He explained that the entire department had lied to me all day. He was afraid that if the numbers changed between this report and the end of the month, he would be in trouble with the new owners. *What?!* The numbers were supposed to change. That's why it was interim. I didn't understand.

Yet in my gut, I was beginning to understand. So many of my experiences and my friends' stories were coming together to make some sense. Under the communist system, people were held personally responsible for any mistakes, errors, perceived errors, differences, anything. Oftentimes, the monetary difference would come out of their paychecks. I'd learned this about inventory, but apparently it applied to everything. Capitalism is about trial and error. What works gets rewarded. What doesn't work gets left behind. Under communism, there were no rewards, just punishment. Czechs still carried this with them—a culture of fear and blame that overrode logic and reason.

Back in the team's small, barren conference room, the enormous rotary dial phone rang. It was my manager, Stephen, back in Prague. He asked what we had accomplished that day. *Everything and nothing,* I thought to myself.

ME: "We got a copy of the interim G/L."

STEPHEN: "Ok, what else?"

ME: "That's it."

STEPHEN: "What? Did you review it? Did you start auditing cash? Accounts receivable?"

ME: "No. Incredibly, it took us all day to get the G/L."

There was silence on the other end. I knew this was not my fault, but I was worried he thought I was useless. How could I possibly explain why a five-minute task took eight hours? And somehow that wasn't the most ridiculous thing that happened that week. The notes we left for the manager were epic.

Notes for Stephen:

The construction department has nine employees. This seems excessive as there are no construction projects planned for the next year. (So what in the world will they do all year?)

The budget and analysis department has eight employees who prepare detailed monthly reports that nobody outside their group is aware of or uses.

The fixed asset listing is often inaccurate due to confusion regarding the status of ownership of some land. They don't know what they own or where it is, and they don't have a complete list of land they use.

The marketing department has a lack of resources, but this really shouldn't be an issue since there is no Czech word for marketing and they have no marketing activities.

THE CEMENTÁŘ

MAY 1993

IT HAD BEEN A LONG FIRST DAY AT HRANICE. I was looking forward to a hot shower and crashing out in my hotel room.

I retrieved my suitcase and went to the third floor. I unlocked my door, #305, and found myself in a hallway staring at three more identical doors. What in the world? I had no idea what was behind door number one, two, or three. Did I just get to choose?

But no, there had to be something . . .

I looked at my key again and saw that it said 305/2. I checked the doors in front of me and saw a "1," a "2," and a door with no markings at all. I chose door number two and hoped it wasn't the booby prize. Oh happy day, it was a bedroom.

The décor was what I would call "early dorm room." It was a small rectangle with two twin beds against either wall—almost exactly the same as my freshman dorm room at UCLA. I plopped down and turned on the little TV across the room. There were only a few channels: Czech TV, MTV, and the news—in German. Thank goodness I brought a book. There was a thin, very sad, small towel folded up at the end of the bed. But just like in college, there was no bathroom in my room. Ugh! I went exploring.

I went back into the hall and tried my key in the unmarked door. There it was! The bathroom I had to share with the strangers in the other room. Like we were roommates sharing a really weird suite.

The bathroom was a small, prefabricated plastic room plopped into the hotel with a toilet, a sink, and a showerhead on the wall. No shower door or curtain. I locked the door from the inside, feeling pretty relieved that that was possible. No shelf or hook for my towel, toiletries, or clothes. No toilet lid either, so that was out. I folded up my clothes and towel and set them on the back of the toilet and prayed they wouldn't fall in.

Finally ready, I turned on the shower. BRRRRrrrr. So. Cold. I stood naked in this plastic room for a while until the water warmed up. As I waited, I realized the water was going EVERYWHERE! This was not some well-thought-out plan for bathrooms in communist Europe—this was a mess! My clothes and towel were soon covered in a fine layer of mist. I took the fastest shower I had ever taken to stop the damage. Regardless, the entire bathroom was covered in water. The walls, the floor, the toilet. I dried myself off and then used my soggy towel to clean up what I could.

I put my dirty clothes back on and peeked out the door to the communal hallway. Nobody. I bolted back into my room and changed into my pajamas.

Later that week I would sometimes go into the bathroom only to find it covered in water. Clearly my neighbor had showered and the spray was still everywhere. I would need to come up with a better shower plan going forward to avoid this. It was uncomfortable and awkward in ways I couldn't articulate.

STEPHEN AND THE TWO
DESSERTS

MAY 1993

STEPHEN: "Can I get palačinky with strawberries and chocolate sauce?"

WAITRESS: "No. We have palačinky with strawberries or with chocolate sauce."

STEPHEN: "So you have strawberries, and you have chocolate sauce. Can we put those together on the same crepe?"

WAITRESS: "No."

We were in the center of town and Stephen, the manager who was usually back in Prague, had come out to see how things were going. (Probably because it took us eight hours to get a copy of the G/L.) Stephen was American. Serious. No nonsense. A good boss because you always knew what he wanted. On the first night, he decided to take the whole team out to dinner, Czechs and expats alike. There were only really a handful of restaurants in the center of Hranice. We always went to one of three: pizza, Chinese, or Czech. We chose the nicest Czech restaurant on the main square.

This restaurant served two desserts: palačinky s jahodami (crepes with strawberries) and palačinky s čokoládovou omáčkou (crepes with chocolate sauce). But Stephen had other ideas.

STEPHEN: "Can't I get a crepe with both strawberries and chocolate?"

WAITRESS: "No."

STEPHEN: "No, really, please just make one and put a little of each on it."

WAITRESS: "It's impossible. It's not on the menu."

STEPHEN: "But you have crepes, strawberries, and chocolate. Can you just put them all on one plate?"

WAITRESS: "It's impossible. Besides, I wouldn't know what to charge you."

Each dessert couldn't have cost more than 40 cents.

STEPHEN: "Ok, you got me. Charge me for both desserts and bring me one palačinky with strawberries and chocolate."

WAITRESS: "It's impossible. We only have crepes with strawberries *or* crepes with chocolate sauce."

STEPHEN: "What if I pay for both and then I go into the kitchen and put the strawberries and the chocolate sauce on one plate?"

WAITRESS: "It's impossible."

STEPHEN: "Ok, I'll order both."

WAITRESS: "You want two desserts?"

STEPHEN: "Yes. I'll have two desserts."

The waitress looked at him suspiciously, wrote it down, and shuffled off to place our dessert orders. She was flummoxed but left the table having won the battle.

When she returned, she placed the two plates in front of Stephen with the worried look of a mother feeding her child ice cream for dinner. The strawberry palačinky and the chocolate palačinky were identical except for three small strawberries on top of one and a few chocolate flakes on top of the other. The whole affair was just like the Jack Nicholson diner scene from *Five Easy Pieces* where the waitress won't let him order toast.

Stephen proceeded to reorganize the desserts. He put the strawberries on top of the chocolate sauce, discarding the extra crepes, and dove in. The Czechs watched him in silence like medical students watching their first operation. He put his fork into his concoction, took a bite, and smiled like a champion. Victory!

LETTER TO GRANDMA

Hi Grandma,

How are you? I'm doing really well here in Prague. I like my job, I adore my flat, and I LOVE Prague. The culture is VERY different and the shift from communism to capitalism is taking quite some time, but I'm really happy here. You do, however, have to have a lot of patience, and a very good sense of humour to live here! I've made a lot of friends with whom I work, spend my leisure time and travel! About half of them are American, and the rest are British, Irish, French, Czech, Australian, Canadian and Lithuanian. All of them speak English (more or less) but it is absolutely amazing how differently English is spoken even within the U.S.

When my friends and I go out there is complete chaos because we can't figure each other out! There are 7 of us that go out together on a regular basis and we are from: Los Angeles, Houston, Kansas City, Dublin/London, Lithuania, Czech Republic, and Sydney. Things that are insults to one person are harmless to another and we're learning loads of great slang from around the world.

The Lithuanian is one of our English/Czech translators (what a horrible job—to translate between two languages, neither of which is your first language!); her English is great but every now and then we have a real misunderstanding. I can usually translate Eva's comments to the rest of the group as she's got a very thick English accent and uses a lot of London/British slang! Nobody understands the guy from Sydney, so he's always playing charades and teaching us new words. Then, of course, there are the people who join us occasionally, like Laurent from Paris. Laurent's accent is so thick that he ALWAYS sounds like he's saying something lecherous and nobody can say his name with a straight face. (It's always said, "lau-RENT" with proper French pronunciation and a swing of the shoulders or hips in time with the "RENT.")

I've determined that in some areas of my life I am going to spend a lot more money than I normally would, but in other areas I'm going to save a bundle. When we all go out in the evening, we usually go to dinner, just split the bill evenly (it's cheap enough that you'd feel incredibly petty if you squabbled over the details), and then take turns buying rounds. I generally spend 200 to 300 crowns (Kčs) over the course of 5 to 10 hours) which is equivalent to approximately $7 to $11. (There are 28 Kčs to $1, thus 100Kčs = $3.50) I won't save any money this way, however, because we go out 3 to 4 times a week! (We don't know anybody else, and only on person has a flat in town so far!) I will save the bulk of my money because there is no shopping in this country.

Well—I'm sorry this letter is typed and may seem impersonal, but I'm at work and I need to at least *appear* busy.

Please write.

Love,
Melanie

FRIDAYS AT PIZZA TAXI: FLATS AND LANDLORDS

MAY 1993

"YOU WON'T BELIEVE what my landlord did!"

Another Friday, another episode of the Communist Mindf*ck. We experienced so many strange things with housing that it was hard to know where to start. We'd all been surprised by the décor. Wallpaper with psychedelic patterns. It felt like you were on some sort of acid trip. Blue velvet drapes that only clashed slightly with orange walls. And, of course, the framed nudes on Mike's wall. Jamie's flat was split in such a way he had to go outside to get from the living room to the rest of the flat.

BRENDA: "I came home for lunch and found my landlord and his girlfriend half naked. They had just finished having sex on my couch and were putting their clothes back on."

EVERYONE: "Ewwww . . . can you get a new couch?"

EVA: "Last week after work, I dropped by my place to pick up my wallet. I found my landlord taking a bath in my tub . . ."

Horrified looks from everyone at the table. The crazy news kept coming.

EVA: "Did I tell you I got my jewelry back? My landlord 'borrowed' it."

PETER: "My landlord keeps going through my clothes. I came home last week, and my underwear had been ironed. And they bought me new shirts! Was something wrong with the ones I have?"

ME: "Good Lord. What are you guys going to do?"

What could they do? What could any of us do? Nothing.

Under communism, the government was everyone's landlord. In 1948, they took ownership of all property and assigned houses and flats based on who was most favored by the Communist Party. They didn't have a housing lottery. Just pure state control. You lived where you were told to live.

In 1993, the concept of owning property and renting it for a profit was incredibly new to Czechs. So new that nobody had used a lease or rental agreement before. Some random lease agreement had become the standard in Prague. All the Czech landlords seemed to use it. Foreigners had money. And foreigners needed somewhere to live. Suddenly, Czechs could move to the country and rent out their city flats. It was a normal lease, but the interpretation was wildly different from what we were all used to.

PETER: "At least you still get to live there."

ME: "What do you mean?"

We all waited with bated breath . . .

PETER: "Remember how my friend came to visit last week?"

We did . . .

PETER: "Well, my landlord kicked me out."

What? Why?

PETER: "Because my lease said the flat was for personal use only, my landlord said I violated the agreement by letting someone else spend the night there."

JAMIE: "But that means you can't use it for business!"

PETER: "I tried to explain that to him, but he wasn't having it. I even had Roman call him since he arranged the lease. But the landlord wouldn't budge. I've been evicted and have to move out by next Friday."

Communist logic strikes again. There was no way to fight it. It was easier to find a new apartment than to argue with a Czech landlord. They believed that their place was their place, even if you were renting it. It was another thing we just had to accept. Because that was the way it was.

ME: "Did you hear what happened to Stephen and Sharise?"

MIKE: "Oh no. What?"

ME: "A few days before they were leaving on vacation, their landlord told them he would be moving back into their flat. At their earliest convenience, of course, but in no more than six weeks."

JAMIE: "Lease be damned?"

ME: "Pretty much. No warning at all."

MIKE: "Leases seem to be just for show."

We had all anticipated a normal rental situation. But our landlords saw it differently. They owned the flats. It was their property. Nothing was off-limits because it was, after all, their property. This was their concept of renting. Nothing any of us could say would change that fact. As hard as we tried to explain how renting worked—that once we were living there, they couldn't just come and go as they pleased, use our things, kick our friends out—we couldn't argue with their basic premise. That it was their property. It was like we were 20-something-year-old kids who had moved back home. We knew we had hit an impasse. It was so illogical that it was logical. Maybe logic was circular. We were never going to win.

BABY NAMES

MAY 1993

ME: "Why does everyone have the same names?"

MARKÉTA: "What do you mean, Mel?"

Jan, Jan, Jan, Jana, Jarda, Josef, Josefa.

Marcela, Markéta, Markéta, Martin, Martin, Martina, Martina, Miroslav, Michael, Michal, Michaela, Monika.

Peter, Petr, Petr, Pavel.

That's what it said in the office directory. Thank God for the occasional Běla, Ivan, and Václav of the world. Arthur Andersen in Prague wasn't big. We had about 25 Czech staff. But the names got even more repetitive when you included the tax team, the secretaries, and others: Iva, Irena, Eva, Ivana, Anna, Jana, and Ladislav.

Sitting around a pub table with pivos, I asked our Czech friends—Martin, Markéta, Markéta, Marcela, Pavel, and Josef—what was up with the names. I know in America we have our favorite baby names. This was more than repetitive. It was ridiculous.

I repeated the question: "Why does everyone have the same names?"

Blank stares from our Czech friends.

ME: "Come on. At the office, we have three Jans, two Janas, three Martins, a few Martinas, a few Markétas, Iva, Eva, Ivan, Ivana . . . why aren't there more names???"

MARKÉTA: "I see. Because of the calendar."

I sipped my beer silently, pretending that made sense. *Did I ask the wrong question? Had I had too many pivos? Let me try a different question.*

ME: "No, what I mean is . . . why are there so many men named Jan? And so many named Martin? And Petr? Do people just love these names?"

MARKÉTA: "Because they're on the calendar."

I looked around at the other expats hoping to see understanding in someone's eyes. Nothing. Not a flicker. Nobody said a word. Everyone was silently trying to make sense of the conversation. None of us had a clue.

I looked at the Czechs to see if anyone was laughing. The Czechs looked confused by our confusion. They clearly all thought this made sense, but the expats were mystified. We had reached a new level of misunderstanding.

We had to make a game-time decision. Did we say "thank you" and move on, cutting our losses? Or did we try a new question? I still didn't know what she was talking about but decided to wing it. She said they're on the calendar so I pretended I had some idea what we were talking about and hoped it would hit me soon.

ME: "What if your name isn't on the calendar?"

MARKÉTA: "It is on the calendar."

ME: "But what if it isn't?"

MARKÉTA: "All the names are on the calendar."

I tried to roll with it as if this made sense to me.

ME: "So . . . how many names are on the calendar?"

MARKÉTA: "About 365."

Ok, now we were getting somewhere. There were 365 names and 365 days in the year. Good.

ME: "Ah. So, a new name every day. So, there are 365 boy names and 365 girl names?"

MARKÉTA: "Neh. A total of 365."

ME: "Wait. Total? So half boys and half girls?"

MARKÉTA: "No, no, no." ("Yes, yes, yes.")

I was bothered that 365 wasn't an even number but didn't think we could handle that level of detail.

ME: "What if your name isn't one of those 365?"

MARKÉTA: "It is."

ME: "But what if it isn't? I mean, what if your name is Cynthia?"

I saw several puzzled Czech faces. Finally! I had stumped the Czechs. It was only fair; they stumped me all the time.

After some very animated conversations in Czech, they seemed to agree on an answer.

MARKÉTA: "It can't be Cynthia. Cynthia isn't on the calendar."

Ohmigod.

ME: "Wait, really? Are you saying you can't name your baby a name that isn't on the calendar?"

MARKÉTA: "Not unless you pay."

ME: "Pay for what?"

MARKÉTA: "To use a different name. Or a different spelling. But it has to be approved."

Wow. So, Czechs and Slovaks were only legally allowed to name their children one of the names on the official calendar. If they desperately wanted to use another name, they had to pay a fee and get it approved by the communist officials. Even a variation in spelling had to be approved.

ME: "Is this still true? Is this still the law?"

Shrugs. Nobody seemed to know and they didn't seem bothered.

ME: "So what determines whether a name is on the calendar or not?"

MARKÉTA: "On the Czech calendar, there is a saint's name associated with each day of the year, except national holidays. Also, some days have two names, and some names have two days."

Clear as mud. But she continued.

MARKÉTA: "If your name is, say, Bohuslava, July 7 is your 'svátek,' saint's day, or 'jmeniny,' name day. Your name day is more important than your actual birthday. People give each other cards or gifts and wish each other 'Všechno nejlepší k svátku,' 'All the best for your name day.'"

My head was spinning a little. *Should I keep asking questions?*

ME: "So everyone in the Czech republic and Slovakia does this?"

MARKÉTA: "Yo, yo. But the Slovaks have a different calendar."

WHOA. Despite having been one country for decades, the Czechs and Slovaks had different calendars with different names.

MARKÉTA: "Your name is on the Slovak calendar."

ME: "Wait, what? My name is?"

MARKÉTA: "Yes, you have a svátek."

I would have to figure out how to find said calendar and see which day was mine.

ME: "Ohhh. This is explains why nobody has any difficulty with my name and everyone pronounces it so beautifully: me-LAH-nee-ay."

I found it interesting that we had Czech friends named both Petr and Peter and Michal and Michael. The Americanized versions were not on the official calendar, so I wondered if they were Slovak spellings, if their parents had gotten approval, or if they had changed the spellings after the Wall fell. But my brain was full, so I let this detail go for now.

But now we knew why it felt like everyone had the same names. Making the situation worse was that some names were considered old-fashioned and weren't used much. On occasion, I'd meet a Svatopluk, or an Otakar, but not often. I'm just happy I didn't know anyone named Přemysl or Řehoř. If I ever did, I prayed they had an easier nickname.

NIGHTS WITH JAN HUS

MAY 1993

IT WAS MY FAVORITE PART of every night out. My walk to the tram through Staroměstské náměstí—Old Town Square.

Like most nights, it was deserted. The only sound was the clicking of my shoes on the centuries-old cobblestones. The Jan Hus statue stood proudly in Old Town Square as I walked towards his fierce gaze. Jan Hus means John Goose. He was a Czech theologian, church reformer, and dean of Charles University in Prague. He was burned at the stake for heresy because he challenged the Catholic Church. And we were hanging out together on the square.

I rested on the statue steps to savor the breathtaking view. The spires of the clock tower and the church were lit up in dashing gold and blue. The square was vast. Surrounded by tall, gothic buildings full of local cafés and restaurants. I hoped that when the weather was warmer, there would be tables and chairs outside. Endless rounds of pivo in the glorious sunshine.

But for now, I enjoyed the winter cold. The air was crisp; the silence, eerie. The streetlights put out a golden glow only for themselves. And then the snow began to fall. Just a small flurry at first. Tiny flakes melting when they hit the ground. Soon, it picked up. Huge snowflakes landed on my arms and legs and began to cover the ground in front of me. I could almost see that each one had a different design. I pulled my coat closer and watched the square fill with layer upon layer of snow . . . like a wedding cake being decorated by a master pastry chef. It was stunningly beautiful.

As I sat there, I realized that I was starting to get used to the sameness of some parts of life here. Especially the food. Sometimes I actually enjoyed it all. Even looked forward to it. God forbid. There was something comforting about always knowing who I was going to see, how bad the service would be, what I would eat (no matter how hard I tried to find something different), and that someone would bring me whatever beer they served. There was something strangely comforting in knowing you had no choice at all. No decisions to make. It was a lot easier.

I wanted to linger, but the snow was coming down hard, and walking across the cobblestones would be treacherous. I had to go catch my tram back to the place where they slit people's throats. But I would remember this night forever. And try to relive it every time I walked through the square.

MIKE AND THE SHOWER

MAY 1993

AS I WALKED INTO THE PRAGUE OFFICE juggling my audit bag, my purse, and my briefcase, I said hello to Gaby, our receptionist. She raised her hand in the air and stuck it inside her blouse. "Dobrý den!" she said in a sing-songy voice. She pulled her hand back out of her shirt and put it back into the other side. She was putting on deodorant . . . at her desk. I tried not to look horrified.

The managing partner had Arid Extra Dry shipped in by the case. Gaby kept a drawer packed full of it in case anyone needed a stick. I was happy she was using it, but maybe someone should have been clearer about the when and where. I wondered if this would be accounted for as office supplies.

We were back in Prague for a while after almost two months of going back and forth to our out-of-town clients. Every day, we went to the office at the bottom of Václavské náměstí (aka Wenceslas Square), the Times Square of the Czech republic. The office was in a five-story building located just above a subway entrance for Na Můstku. And it was an incredibly busy place most days. People swarming in and out of the metro. A Peruvian band, with their colorful chullo hats and dangling tassels, entertained the tourists with their flute music. Sometimes the Peruvians competed to be heard with the guy who played Muzak boomingly from his boombox. And then there was the sword swallower. He was my favorite. His sword wasn't straight; it zigged and zagged like pinking shears. But he swallowed it repeatedly all day, almost every day.

I arrived by tram at Vodičkova, a stop halfway up the square. I headed into the office and waited my turn to get into the tiny elevator up to our floor. The elevator was old and primitive. It held three people max, and some-one had to close two layers of doors to be sure we were safely inside. It took a freakishly long time to go three or four floors. It was so slow that I was never sure when we had arrived.

When I entered the staff room, I noticed that Mike had wet hair again, like he was just out of the shower. But then again, he was. There was a shower at the office (who knows why?) and he had been showering there for a few weeks. Today, he wasn't wearing any socks with his suit and dress shoes. We were starting to worry about what was going on. The no-sock look was the impetus Jamie, Peter, and I needed to finally sit him down and have an intervention. We decided to do it at lunch.

It took us a good 30 minutes to get from the office to the pizza place a few blocks away. The crowds were INSANE. Tourists, performers, dogs, and people standing in the street drinking beer. And the ever-present babičkas sweeping dust off the streets with their twig brooms. It was always a chal-lenge to navigate through the streets during tourist season.

When we arrived, we ordered a round of beer. We had beer almost every day at lunch. As one did in Prague in 1993. Cheaper than water. Cheaper than soda. It was as natural as breathing air.

After musing about why there was meat on the vegetarian menu—but knowing there would be no sensible answer—we ordered a couple of salami pizzas and dove right into our agenda.

JAMIE: "Mike, we noticed you've been showering at the office every morning."

MIKE: "Yeah, there's no hot water at my flat."

ME: "There's cold water? Just no hot?"

MIKE: "Yep. And the cold is arctic cold."

PETER: "Can't someone fix that for you?"

MIKE: "Well it not just me. It's the whole building. There's no hot water at all."

JAMIE: "Ok... and can't they fix that?"

MIKE: "They've chosen not to."

PETER: "What? Why not?"

MIKE: "Well... the guy who shovels coal into the furnace is on vacation."

ME: "What?! That's how they heat the building?"

We were in disbelief. The man shovels coal into the furnace all winter for a huge building?

ME: "Wait. Of course it is. Employment program?"

JAMIE: "So the guy is on vacation. What's the big deal? Don't they have someone to cover?"

MIKE: "No. 'It's impossible. He is on vacation.'"

We laughed at his imitation of the landlord telling him nothing would be done.

PETER: "Why don't they find a temporary replacement?"

MIKE: "They have one. But 'he is on vacation'!"

Peals of laughter. How was that acceptable? How was that the way they heated the entire building? How were the Czechs ok with only cold water for weeks? Why would they let both of them go on vacation at the same time? Again, we knew there would be no answer that was logical to us. And there was really nobody to ask. It just was.

We devoured our pizza and beer, marveling that an entire building of flats was heated by one guy shoveling coal day and night. We made our way back to the office, fighting against the tourists meandering around the streets. We were like salmon swimming upstream.

SUBJECT: LIGHTS

MAY 1993

"WHY ARE THE LIGHTS OFF AGAIN?" I thought as I entered the staff room at the office. I flipped the switch and the room was illuminated. Now I could see and get some work done. A few minutes later, a Czech got up and shut the blinds.

It was a beautiful sunny afternoon, and I wanted to see the sun and the snow on the ground! I whipped open the blinds to let in the natural light. Much better.

A few minutes later, a Czech turned off the lights. Another expat came in and turned the lights back on. A few minutes later, a Czech got up and closed the blinds.

Blinds opened. Lights off.

Lights on. Blinds closed.

Blinds opened. Lights off.

Lights on. Blinds closed.

Blinds opened.

It was like there was a strobe light in the staff room. What was going on? Finally, Jamie spoke up.

JAMIE: "What is happening? Why do you guys keep turning the lights off and closing the blinds?"

JARDA: "We can't have the lights on and the blinds open at the same time."

JAMIE: "Uhhh . . . why not? We want the light. We need to be able to see in order to work."

JARDA: "It's bad for you."

JAMIE: "Ummm . . . what's bad for you?"

JARDA: "The lights."

JAMIE: "Lights are bad for you?"

JARDA: "The combination of natural light and artificial light."

JAMIE: "Ummm . . . what's bad about that?"

JARDA: "The combination of natural light and artificial light will make you go blind."

JAMIE: "WHAT?!"

JARDA: "Yes. It will also turn your hair green."

JAMIE: "Wait. You know that's not true, right?"

JARDA: "Yes, it is."

JAMIE: "No. It isn't. I've been sitting in rooms with the blinds open and the lights ALL MY LIFE, and I am NOT blind and don't have green hair."

Jarda and the other Czechs shrugged. That same shrug that seemed to mean "I don't know," "I don't care," "I can't be bothered to have this conversation with you," and "I don't know why you're even asking this question" all at once. The conversation was over. There was nothing more to ask or say.

We later speculated that it had to have been a communist plot to save energy and money by keeping the lights off. It wasn't enough to tell people to save energy. The communists had to give it a spin. Perhaps this was why my cement client simply had no power in the afternoons. Energy savings.

We told them we'd been exposed to the combination for our entire lives with no negative effects. We told them natural light was actually good for them, even if it was combined with artificial light. But they had been told otherwise. Since birth. And there was no overcoming that anytime soon.

Soon after, we found a compromise. Détente. One room for the Czechs with the blinds open and lights off. One room for the expats with the blinds open and the lights on. Everyone was happy. But once again, it highlighted that our cultural differences were real. Tangible. Omnipresent on both sides.

I carried this lesson with me—just how hard it is to change someone's perspective when they have never known anything else. It was going to be a long road to recover from being lied to by their government all their lives.

A few weeks later, we each found a memo in our mail file:

TO: Prague Office
FROM: Managing Tax Partner
DATE: 21 May 1993
SUBJECT: Lights

In conjunction with the reorganization, we have decided to resolve the lighting position. Tax division policy will be to keep the ceiling lights on at all times.

I'm certain there was still a fight about the blinds.

X-GAMES:
SHOPPING BAGS

JUNE 1993

I WAS OPTIMISTIC. This time, I would go to the main Western-style grocery store in downtown Prague and avoid the canned goods. The store was underground, windowless, and connected to the Můstek metro station on Vodičkova Street.

I grabbed a basket and roamed the aisles of the store, looking for the things I needed. Eggs, fruit, jam, yogurt, cheese, and salami. I couldn't buy a lot since I would have to bring the food back to the office. The grocery store closed at five, just when everyone was getting off work. Convenient. We actually had not one but two office refrigerators so the expats could shop at lunch, store their groceries in the office, and take them home later by tram, metro, or bus.

There were no wrapped loaves of bread like there were at home. Only chleba. The word "chleba" literally means "bread." But here it was a specific type of bread. The traditional Czech, spongy, sort-of rye bread they served everywhere. There were also bins of rohlíky—the traditional Czech rolls. Like a day-old baby baguette. I settled for the rohlíky. They weren't bad with ham and cheese or butter and jam. I wondered how they would be with my peanut butter.

I went to the refrigerated section to get a few things. But I didn't find milk. Or eggs. *Weird.* They should have had both of those things, but for all I knew, those were sold at some other store. I was excited to find yogurt. I looked to see what flavors they had. Hmmm. No flavors. Just "yogurt." Alrighty then. I grabbed a few of those. Next, I grabbed a foil-wrapped slab of butter and tossed it into my cart. Wait! I needed to check it. Half the expats in Prague had gotten home from the store only to discover they had accidentally bought lard. They looked almost exactly alike. *Ok, whew.* It seemed to be butter.

I headed towards the sparse produce section. On my way, I passed the milk and eggs. They were both on regular shelves. Milk was sold in boxes. Unrefrigerated and stacked. I found that concerning. The shelf life of milk wasn't that long back home. But I decided to try it. Then, the eggs. They were rolling around loose in a box on the counter. I looked around for an egg carton to take some home in but finding none, I decided to skip the eggs. Anna carried them in a paper bag, but I was sure I didn't have that skill. I'd have to learn the secret to carrying eggs home some other time. I just envisioned coat pockets full of yolk.

On to the deli counter. I had no idea how to order salami. I was completely incapable of pronouncing the numbers three and four, tři and čtyři. They both have the dreaded letter "ř." My tongue was just not that acrobatic. So, I held up two fingers and pointed to the salami I wanted, having no idea whether I would get two slices or two kilos. One expat we knew always ordered five of everything. It was the only number she could pronounce. Pět. Pee-yet. The woman wrapped up three slices of salami for me. *What in the . . .* I looked at my hand with two fingers up and remembered. The Czechs used their thumb for one. *I have got to remember that.* With my two fingers, I'd actually asked for three slices. At least it was a minor misstep, and I wasn't going home with three kilos.

Upon arriving at the produce, I realized there really wasn't a produce section unless you counted the bin of cabbage in the corner. They had green and purple heads piled on top of one another. I would have killed for an apple.

Let's recount. No fresh veggies, no fruit, and no cans. I was left with bread, butter, plain yogurt, boxed milk, and beer. A good start, but the grocery scavenger hunt would continue.

I was thinking about how successful this shopping trip had been as I unloaded my basket at the checkout stand. The clerk was moody and seemingly unhappy to be dealing with a foreigner. No surprise there. She silently rang up my purchases, sending them down the conveyor belt. When finished, she coldly told me my total: "Tři sta dvacet pět"—I owed 325 Kč. I actually understood! A freaking miracle. I was getting better at numbers. I dug into my purse and gave her exactly 325 Kč. Success.

And then, I saw my pile of groceries. Nobody had bagged them. And there were no bags there for me to do it.

ME: "Excuse me, miss?"

She ignored me.

I tried my best Czech.

ME: "Excuse, me, miss? Slečna? Prosím vás, slečna."

I was clearly dead to her. She began ringing up the next customer.

Great. Any second, the purchases would be mingled.

I tried to get her attention again, but she pointed at my groceries and said something angrily as if she were scolding a child. Clearly, she expected me to pick up my stuff and go away. I didn't have a bag. She didn't have a bag. Or if she did, she had no plans to give it to me. Or even sell it to me.

I looked around to see if anyone was willing to help me. No. Clearly no. All I saw was the babičkas minding their own business and putting their groceries into the strange bags that they always seemed to carry around. These bags and old women were inseparable. They were woven plastic with rope handles. And they were indestructible. I eventually got two of those bags, and they never died. That was definitely something the Czechs got right. That and matches. The Czechs make the best boxes of matches bar none. They light immediately—you never have to strike twice. Like the bags, they're sturdy and do their one job brilliantly.

Resigned to not having a bag, I did what I had to do. I started putting food in my pockets and my purse. It didn't all fit. I stuffed the rohlíky into my shirt. Even still, I had to carry some things in my hands and pressed in my armpits. Riding up the escalator, I couldn't help but laugh at the ridiculousness of my plight. Incredibly, nobody was looking at me. The Czechs were minding their own business as always. But I felt certain some of them would be angry and yell at me if my food started bouncing down the escalator. I hung on tightly to my groceries and hoped not to fall down the escalator since I couldn't hold the rail.

Finally, I semi-waddled back to the office, and put my groceries into the fridge. I would need to find a bag for the trip home.

We could always identify the expats who were new in town. We would see them coming up the escalator onto Václavské náměstí with their arms and clothes full of cans and boxes, trying desperately not to drop anything. We'd all been there. Once they started ringing you up, you were on your own. No canceling the transaction. No stopping it midstream. No returns. No waiting for you to go get a bag. On occasion, someone would give up and abandon their groceries at the end of the conveyor. I always knew there was someone new in town when I saw a pile of groceries just sitting at the end of the conveyor. And it always made me smile a little. It happened to every expat once. And only once.

FRIDAYS AT PIZZA TAXI: SEXISM

JUNE 1993

ME: "Did you guys see the item in the *Fleet Sheet?*"

I pulled it out. I had been waiting all day to read it to them.

> (MFD/Sat/III) Carola Biedermannová, a devote feminist, says that she's been long convinced that men are immature creatures unfit for life in this world. Without women to take care of them, she says, they'd stand no chance. All the feminists she knows are married, overworked women who are fed up with waiting on their parasitic husbands hand and foot. Czech women who take this treatment lying down are making a big mistake, she says.

Everyone rolled laughing as the waitress set down a round of pivos.

We were gathering for our Friday session of "What in the world is going on here?" A bunch of our Czech friends had joined us.

MIKE: "Did you hear that Ed and Lenka are getting married?"

ME: "How many couples is that? That we know of between Czech women and expat men?"

JAMIE: "At least four men from work."

MIKE: "I know two more couples."

PETER: "And I know a third."

Wow. We counted at least a dozen such couples.

ME: "Does anyone know of an expat woman marrying a Czech man?"

Silence.

We looked at each other and wracked our brains.

BRENDA: "I don't see that happening for me. Most of the men in my office resemble the 'two wild and crazy guys' from SNL. And my family wonders why I'm single."

We all laughed as she assured us it was all the men. Americans, Brits, Aussies, and Czechs alike.

But then Markéta thought of one.

MARKÉTA: "Yo, yo, yo. My friend Petr is marrying an American woman."

ME: "Wow, ok! Any others?"

Nope. That was it.

ME: "So what is that about? So many expat men marrying Czech women but not the other way around? I mean, the expat men think Czech women are stunning, but there must be more to it."

EVA: "Well, you know, most of the Czech women that marry expats are staying home and cooking dinner every night."

ME: "Ohmigosh. So, all these men want old-school, traditional relationships? A wife that cooks, cleans, and stays home? Is this what Czech women want?"

MARKÉTA: "Neh. We only know one professional Czech woman who is marrying an expat, and the rest of us don't have the dream of being a housewife."

MARCELA: "And she'll keep working. She won't stay home to cook and clean."

We mulled this over and compared notes about the couples we knew. There were a few exceptions—some of the Czech women in our office were dating expat men. But they had no plans to quit work and stay home.

MARKÉTA: "I think this is not usual, Mel. I went to college and now I want to do interesting work and travel. Even if I do get married, I want these things."

MARCELA: "I agree. This is the same for most of us."

ME: "I saw a story in a magazine that said Americans were pouring into Prague for the 'cheap booze, pre-feminist women, and opportunities to get rich.' I'm glad to hear that's an exception, not the rule!"

MARKÉTA: "Definitely not the rule."

ME: "So I think my issue, then, is with all these American and other expat men that want to find the wives who DO want to stay home. It's like a throwback to the 1950s."

MARKÉTA: "For us too, Mel."

ME: "I can't believe it still happens, but I guess it's best if the people that want that find each other. Unlike poor Carola from the *Fleet Sheet* story, who is stuck."

We shook our heads and felt bad for Carola. We hoped she got out of her situation.

EVA: "Nothing personal, but what IS the fascination with Czech women?"

MICHAELA: "What do you mean?"

EVA: "Every man that has come to visit me from London CANNOT stop drooling over how beautiful Czech women are. Not that you ladies aren't beautiful, but are Czechs really more beautiful than other European women?"

ME: "Same here! Every American guy who visits is obsessed with Czech women. I have no other way to describe it. An obsession. Practically a fetish. They never stop telling me that Czech women are the most beautiful women in the world."

PETER: "They are!"

MIKE: "It's true. That's why I call them Hezky Českys!"

Another Mike-ism that somehow translated perfectly to "pretty Czechs" or "nice Czechs" but is not at all how one would actually say those things.

LAURENT: "Maybe not more beautiful than French women."

I laughed. The Czech women smiled and sipped their beer.

ME: "Don't get me wrong, I have no beef with Czech women. My issue is, yet again, with men."

I smiled, sipped my drink, and let it go.

EVA directed her next question at the Czechs: "And what is the story with all the orange hair? It seems like every fourth woman here has dyed her hair some shade from mandarin to cranberry."

The women all shrugged.

ME: "Good question. I recently got my hair cut here for the first time. The girl who cut my hair had orange hair and black fingernails. She cut my hair the way my friend's mom used to cut my friend's hair in their backyard. She pressed it all against my neck to try to flatten it out. Then she tried to cut it straight across. Of course, it wasn't straight, so she had to even it out. Then she asked me if I wanted her to dye it orange! I declined." My Czech friends nodded as if to say "That was to be expected" but still offered no explanation.

EVA: "Oh gawd. But it looks like it turned out ok."

ME: "Well, the evening-out process resulted in my hair being a good two inches shorter than I'd requested, but I've gotten used to it."

I was sure there was some sort of communist explanation for the orange dye. Maybe there was no other color hair dye available for 40 years. Or maybe it was one of the few luxuries they'd had. Who knew? Nobody here.

Mike chimed in now that we'd hit a dead end on the orange hair.

MIKE: "What's the '-ová' thing?"

ME: "Yeah . . . does it really mean 'property of'?"

Andrea and Markéta laughed.

IN UNISON: "Belonging to."

I failed to see a difference. It sounded an awful lot like "Offred" and "Ofglen" from *The Handmaid's Tale*, one of my favorite books.

Czech men and women have different last names. For as long as Czechs can remember, women have been given the suffix "-ová" to designate their sex. A daughter belongs to her father; a wife, to her husband. Andrea's last name was Horáková. Markéta's last name was Nechvátalová. Their fathers were Horák and Nechvátal.

In recent years, it has become controversial. Some people argue it's sexist. Other people argue it's an indispensable tradition or an important element of Czech grammar.

MIKE: "You know that Debbie and her American fiancé, Jim Woods, got married in Prague?"

ME: "A few months ago, right?"

MIKE: "Yep. Did you know that, when they got the official marriage license in the mail, she found out her new last name was Woodsová?"

PETER: "Noooo. Really?"

JAMIE: "Yeah. She had to legally change it to Woods when they moved back to the U.S."

ME: "That's crazy."

MIKE: "It's the law. If you get married here and are a woman, you are an 'ová' no matter where you're from."

We shook our heads in amazement. But I shouldn't have been surprised. I was Thomasová.

MOTHER'S MILK

JUNE 1993

VAŠEK: "Are you pregnant?"

ME: "Vašek?"

VAŠEK: "Are you pregnant?"

ME: "Do I look pregnant to you?! How can you ask me that?"

VAŠEK: "You're drinking dark beer."

I looked at my beer. It was dark. Dark Czech beer—tmavé pivo. So?

ME: "Yes . . . I am . . ."

VAŠEK: "It's mother's milk."

ME: "What in the world are we talking about????"

VAŠEK: "Dark beer. It's mother's milk."

Was he saying the Czechs considered dark beer to be wimpy or something? I mean . . . mothers aren't wimpy, but Vašek was pretty sexist, so I could only assume that's what he meant. Where was this conversation going? I tried the direct approach.

ME: "What does that mean?"

VAŠEK: "It's what nursing mothers drink."

ME: "Wait, what? Nursing mothers drink beer?"

VAŠEK: "Only dark beer."

Seriously, what was I missing? I briefly considered the possibility that I was losing it.

VAŠEK: "Dark beer is sweet and good for the bébé."

Well, this was new. Honey, I'm lactating. Bring me a cold one!

All their lives, Czechs had been taught that dark beer was good for babies and should be drunk by nursing mothers. Dark beer was considered feminine in the Czech republic. It was only drunk by women, especially pregnant women. Whereas in the rest of the world, dark beer is "manly." I never saw a Czech man drink a dark beer. And in my experience, doctors recommend against any kind of beer for babies.

PORPHYROPHOBIA

JUNE 1993

WE NEEDED MORE STAFF. Czechs who spoke English and knew something about accounting. Or numbers. Or who weren't afraid of numbers. Anything. But knowing the English language was the #1 skill requirement.

Arthur Andersen was having an all-day recruiting event at the Palace of Culture, a typical, drab convention center. I arrived in my usual attire in accordance with the very conservative Arthur Andersen dress code: skirt, blouse, jacket, pantyhose, and closed-toed shoes. No bare legs or even ankles. No bare shoulders. No cleavage. The expat men were easy to spot, dressed in their Android business uniforms: dark suits, white or light blue shirts, black dress shoes, and conservative ties. Shining knights of Western capitalism.

As I rounded the corner looking for the interview room, I saw a long line of people standing outside the room. It was a dizzying rainbow of attire. Some looked like they were going to a disco. Some looked like '70s shipping clerks. Some looked like performers in a Dadaist play. This couldn't be the right place.

ME: "Peter!"

He turned. I was relieved to see someone I knew.

ME: "Hey! What's going on? Where are we supposed to be?"

PETER: "Umm, yeah, this is the place."

I looked back at the crowd of people. This time, I spied our friends and colleagues mixed in with the Czechs. This was, indeed, the right place. Clearly, business dress was not the same here. It wasn't even consistent. It seemed there was no standard for business attire. The expats looked like they were going to a funeral compared to the recruits.

My first interview was with Zbyněk. He was easily 6′8″ and wore a pale pink blazer with dark pants. He was smart and spoke English. *Hired.*

Next was a man wearing a very short, waiter-style jacket with decorative gold buttons. Like a Czech matador. English not great. *Pass.*

Then came the purple man. A lot of purple was happening across the board, but this gentleman looked like royalty. Purple suit, purple shirt, purple tie, and purple socks. I could only wonder about the underwear. The other expats mercilessly mocked me about my purple London Fog coat, and I was starting to develop porphyrophobia—an aversion to the color purple. But his English was passable. *Hired.*

Some of the Czech men wore more Western-style dark suits. But always with a colorful shirt. Pink, mustard yellow, green plaid, checks, and every shade of purple. But never white. I'd never realized how boring American men's business attire was.

The ties were a mixed bag. Some wide; some narrow. The one thing the ties had in common was their length. Always a little short. Was it in fashion to wear them at rib-length? Or did they not know how to tie them properly by our standards? I had no idea.

The women were pretty consistently dressed in skirts and blouses. The skirts were of varying lengths, although most were tight and short. How could these women possibly be sitting comfortably in the chair? I think my ass would have been flush against the seat. But I'd never worn one THAT short, so what did I know?

A lot of the women had that ubiquitous dyed orange hair. Not a natural red or auburn color, although maybe that had been the goal. Closer to orange. But all shades of orange were coming through today. I wondered about this all over again. Why orange? Why so many of them? Was this a cutting-edge fashion choice? Did they all just love the color? It reminded me of Škoda orange. Was there an excess of orange hair dye in the country? Hence, the orange Škodas and the orange hair? The Czechs had had no answer when we'd asked them, and this day didn't provide any additional insights. I never found out what that was all about.

After the recruiting event, the hot topic of conversation was establishing a dress code for the office. We had strict dress codes back home in the States. Hopefully, it wouldn't be as strict here. I couldn't imagine that would fly, and I would have loved a little relaxation on the rules myself. I hated pantyhose with a passion. But our managing partner said we were a Western office, so we would have Western standards. We would turn our colorful Czech coworkers into boring industrialists yet. Skirts wouldn't be allowed to be shorter than six inches above the knee. And no house slippers permitted in the office.

Quarterly News

of the

WEIRD AND WONDERFUL

APRIL–JUNE 1993

THE NEWS BLURBS SHOWED THE PROGRESS the country was making as well as the many things it still needed to overcome. I loved the new focus on quality; I thought it might be slow going, but they had to start somewhere. I was absolutely blown away that compensating victims of Naziism was a current issue here, so many years later. The stories about companies not being worth what communist accounting indicated made me feel like my work was not in vain.

(MFD/14) Minister of Industry and Trade Dlouhý recommended yesterday as part of his campaign to promote domestic products that manufacturers here use "Czech Made" to denote goods made in the republic. Over time this should become known as a mark of quality, Dlouhý said.

This excited me.
A quality focus!

The good and the bad,
I guess.

(HN/3) Respondents to a recent poll rated the freedom to travel and to engage in business as the best fruits of the 1989 revolution. The deterioration of interpersonal ties was the most unwelcome post-revolutionary development, followed by the increase in corruption and vice.

(MFD/Sat/14) If Komerční banka had used international accounting rules for establishing reserves against risky loans, it would have shown a loss last year of 5.9 billion crowns instead of its reported profit of 3.2 billion crowns, according to Arthur Andersen. Komerční's reserves of 17 billion crowns were only about half what international standards would call for, the auditing firm said.

The change from communist accounting to international accounting standards created a swing from a $107M profit to a $196M loss. That's crazy!

(ČD/Wed/1) Charlie Kasal, the producer of Charlie Talk Show, says that the management of Česká televize is trying to put private producers of television programs out of business as a way to thwart future competition for their own shows. The weapon they are using, he says, is what they call hidden advertising. One of his programs, for example, was pulled because it allegedly contained advertising, Kasal says. It was weeks before he was able to get an official ruling. Though eventually cleared of the charge, the show never made it on the air.

What in the world was "hidden advertising" supposed to mean? Maybe nothing. Just suspicious about the concept?

(LN/Fri/X) Milan Jelínek wonders aloud in a column on language why foreign companies insist on using English, French or German in ads when few Czechs actually get the message. Of 20 people he asked to translate "You can't beat the feeling!" from a billboard, 17 shrugged their shoulders, two said something derogatory, and only one got it right. True, he says, a few did mutter something about it's probably having something to do with advertising Coca-Cola.

Oh dear . . .

How was this still at the forefront? It made sense; the communists never addressed it. But it was wild to realize that WWII was a recent memory for so many people here.

(MFD/1) Sources close to the Prague castle say that President Havel and German Chancellor Helmut Kohl agreed Mon. that as compensation for damage done to Czech citizens by the Nazis, Germany will invest about DM 120 million into constructing 40 modern facilities in the Czech Republic for persons who need permanent medical attention. Direct compensation for the more than 18,000 victims of the Nazis would come from the Czech government in the form of a cash payment.

(MFD/Sat/XII) One story goes that Vladimír Dlouhý dreamed up his "Buy Czech" campaign during a fit of spitefulness, writes Martin Komárek in a satirical Man-of-the-Week column. Dlouhý bought a Czech tennis racket and Czech tennis shorts, Komárek explains, and set out for a Czech hotel to play a match. The hotel was so hot, though, that the Czech shorts came unglued at the seams. While trying to hold them together, Dlouhý tripped and hurt his leg. Wanting everyone else to suffer a similar fate, Komárek writes, the minister began preaching the merits of Czech products.

Hahaha. I loved their ability to make fun of themselves.

Yeah, this was gonna take a while . . .

(MS/5) A Renčín cartoon pictures an unassuming Czech man making a clandestine radio call from a remote location in the woods. "Secret Agent Eagle here," he says. "Capitalism achieved. Send further instructions. Over and out."

(MFD/3) Fifty-one of the 105 nuclear operators at the Dukovany power plant gave termination notice May 31, citing poor management at the facility as reason. If workers do not withdraw their resignations, two of Dukovany's four reactors might have to be shut down, according to board member Ivan Cestr of ČEZ. Replacement personnel might be brought in from Temelín, Slovakia, Russia or Ukraine. Although workers denied that wage demands were a factor in the decision to quit, MF Dnes says that workers are asking for pay levels that approach those in Germany. Workers also denied that they are demanding the resignation of ČEZ's top management.

What?! They seemed to be really loosey-goosey with their nuclear power plants, especially given that the Chernobyl disaster was only seven years ago. *Note to self: Avoid the Dukovany area . . .*

Ohmigod. Hilarious. Advertising and marketing were totally new concepts. They would take a while to really catch on.

(RK(6) Jakub Horák, a 19,000-crown-a-month 20-year-old copywriter for Mark/BBDO, says he was shocked when he first learned that advertising is not fun and games but rather serious business. He says he really liked the way clients during meetings take out their electronic diaries and contort their faces over the figures. He, too, has learned to do this, he says boastfully.

I didn't understand this at first. But then I learned more about what communism was really supposed to be and that nobody ever achieved it.

(ČD/3) A cartoon pictures a pair of managers of a state enterprise raiding their company. "Everything's here for the taking," says one to the other gleefully. "Communism at last."

THUMPING

I HAD A HORRIBLE HEADACHE.

Now that we'd solved the lighting problem, we were all able to work late. Able to, had to, whatever. But I couldn't focus because my head was throbbing. *Throomp-da-da-wawa-throomp.*

It was busy season. We had a ton of work to do. Every Friday, our managers left us insanely long lists of things to follow up on and fix. This night was no different. We stayed past dinner time. We would meet up at a pub later.

Ugh, my head. *Throomp-da-da-wawa-throomp.* It was like when you have a headache that doesn't hurt but your head feels heavy and like you can feel your heart beating throughout your whole cranium. *Throomp-da-da-wawa-throomp.*

Wait. That wasn't my head. It was the building.

Throomp-da-da-wawa-throomp.

I looked out the window at Václavské náměstí. I could see the museum at the other end. The buildings were lit up. People were swarming around the square. And our office building was thumping. I stood still, closed my eyes, and finally heard it.

Music.

I looked above my head. It was coming from the ceiling. I asked the others if they could hear. Or could feel it. Everyone could.

What . . . the . . . hell . . . was . . . it?

We went to investigate.

The elevator in our building only held three people, and there were four of us. We tried to cram in, but once we did that, there was no way to close the door, which opened inward. We took the stairs up to the top of the building. As we exited the stairwell, we saw it. A line of people dressed mostly in black, a surly bouncer, and a hint of strobe lights from behind the door he was guarding.

It was a discothèque! On the top floor of our office building. There was a new dance club right above where we were trying to work.

Throomp-da-da-wawa-throomp.

Stunned, we went back downstairs and just stared at each other. It was a nightmare. This was sure to cause all sorts of problems. Not just the noise but all the people trying to use the elevator. How were we supposed to work like this? Well, we couldn't. We called it a night and headed to U Vejvodů.

We set a new informal policy then and there: If you're in the office so late that the disco music starts, it's time to go home.

CANDLE MAN

JULY 1993

WHEN PEOPLE ASKED ME IF I SPOKE CZECH, I told them I spoke "survival Czech." I could talk to a cab driver, buy a train ticket, and get what I intended to order at a restaurant. For a variety of reasons, this was a huge accomplishment in 1993. Especially at U Vejvodů, a classic Czech pub.

U Vejvodů was on a small, round corner in what felt like a dark alley that we walked through to get from New Town to Old Town. It wasn't actually an alley, but the stone façade was under rusty, scruffy scaffolding the entire time I lived in Prague, which gave it a dark, foreboding vibe. It always felt like we were sneaking into somewhere we weren't supposed to go. Inside we walked through a dark, dingy hallway to get to a large, dark, dingy space. It should have been beautiful—it was a large cellar with vaulted ceilings and beautiful archways—but it hadn't been maintained for decades. It was hazy from the cigarette smoke I'd need to wash out of my hair later. And there was no music like I was used to at home. In fact, I'd never heard music playing at any of the bars and restaurants. Weird. Still, it was cozy and served fresh Plzeň beer. Tourists had yet to find this place. This was a Czech pub full of Czechs. Everyone sat a long tables with whatever strangers were already sitting there or joined later. It made me feel more like a local when we went to U Vejvodů. Until we tried to get food.

We grabbed a big table and ordered a round of pivo. The waitress marked each pivo on that ever-present piece of white paper with a slash. By night's end, the paper would be blackened with dark slashes. All they needed to do was keep track of how many we ordered, not what we ordered, since there were no choices. And the bill would come to less than $20. Sooner or later, we would want to eat something, and we'd begin the long process of trying to get someone to wait on us.

We politely raised our hands.

EXPATS: "Prosím?"

We raised our voices.

EXPATS: "Prosím?"

We waved our arms.

EXPATS: "Prosím?"

We flailed our arms.

EXPATS: "Prosím?"

We cried out like banshees.

EXPATS: "Prosím?"

We often had to rise from the table and walk over to the waitstaff, as they huddled in the corner of the pub trying very hard to ignore us. It was like they were always on a coffee break.

Eventually, a waitress reluctantly came to our table.

WAITRESS: "Co?" *What?*

MIKE: "Dvakrát svíčková, prosím." *Twice sirloin steaks, please.*

WAITRESS: "Dvakrát?" *Twice?*

MIKE: "Ano. Dvakrát." *Yes. Twice.*

The portions here were much smaller than at home—not necessarily a bad thing considering the monstrous portions of American meals. Mike always ordered two sirloin steaks in cream sauce. The waitresses and our Czech friends were always confused by one person ordering two entrees just for himself. But at the equivalent of about $4 per steak, Mike didn't hesitate.

There were six of us altogether. I ordered vepřo knedlo zelo, the Czech national dish of pork, dumplings, and cabbage.

JAMIE: "Smažený sýr."

ME: "Fried cheese? Have you become a vegetarian?"

JAMIE: "I just like it. Mostly I like saying the nickname for it: smažák. I doubt it's vegetarian anyway . . . there's ham on the 'vegetarian' menu. And what do we think they fry the cheese in?"

We all laughed. He wasn't wrong. The vegetarian menu was called "bezmasa," which meant 'meatless.' But it seemed to just be a "no beef" menu. I don't know who needed to tell them that pork is not a vegetable.

BRENDA: "Pizza se sýrem." (Brenda WAS a vegetarian, so she ordered a cheese pizza. The best chance here of actually avoiding meat or animal fat.)

EVA: "Hovězí guláš." (Beef goulash.)

PETER: "Řízek." (A pork version of traditional Wiener schnitzel.)

JAMIE: "A pět piv, prosím." *And five beers, please.* Whatever kind they served.

When the food arrived, the waitress wordlessly set down four plates of food and walked away. We waited a bit, but the sixth meal never appeared. The waitress never returned. Where was Peter's řízek? Peter practically caused a scene trying to get the waitress' attention. I think he was the hungriest of all of us. She finally came back to see what we wanted.

PETER: "Excuse me, I ordered the řízek. Is it coming?"

WAITRESS: "We're out of that."

PETER: "What do you mean, you're out?"

WAITRESS: "We don't have that."

Peter looked at her like, *Why the hell didn't you tell me?*

PETER: "Well, can I order something else?"

WAITRESS: "Oh. You want something else?"

PETER: "Uhm, yes. I still want to eat."

WAITRESS: "Fine then."

Peter ordered the svíčková, and then Brenda spoke up.

BRENDA: "I didn't order this. I ordered a cheese pizza. I'm a vegetarian. This is pizza with ham."

The waitress turned quickly and just stared at her.

BRENDA: "I ordered the cheese pizza."

WAITRESS: "That is the vegetarian pizza."

Ah, now we got it. Cows weren't vegetarian. Pigs were vegetarian. But of course.

BRENDA: "But it has ham. That's why I ordered the cheese pizza."

Brenda handed the waitress the pizza and grabbed her pivo.

ME: "Pět piv mas, prosím." *Five more beers, please.* At least that what I thought I'd said.

The waitress look at me oddly. Jamie jumped in to help.

JAMIE: "Ještě pět piv, prosím."

ME: "What did I say?"

JAMIE: "I think it was five beers of meat, please."

I laughed. I'd tried. It wouldn't be the last time I said something crazy when I tried to speak Czech.

The rest of us had finished eating by the time the new meals arrived. Peter got his steak in cream sauce; Brenda got her cheese pizza. No ham. We drank our pivos while Peter and Brenda ate. Sitting in pubs chatting for hours was our standard evening activity, so no harm done.

Several rounds of pivos later, I noticed a man lurking in the restaurant. He was making his way around the tables studiously peering at the restaurant patrons. He was in a black, grayish trench coat. Extremely tall with long dark hair and a long beard and strangely hunched over. He couldn't have been creepier if he tried. He started walking directly to our table. I was wary.

He stopped at the edge and began to open his trench coat. I looked away. My God, a flasher? In a pub? Someone laughed out loud. I looked back. But what was I even looking at? Candles. He was selling candles. Not just any candles. Red, blue, and green candles of Lenin's and Stalin's heads.

Vlad's and Uncle Joe's heads in wax. The perfect addition to any home décor. They were cheap. About $1 each. How could I resist?

ME: "I'll take one of each. A Lenin and a Stalin."

Everyone bought a few. It was such a novelty. There was so little to buy in Prague; this was kind of a treat. From then on, whenever we went to U Vejvodů, we would hope for Candle Man to show up. I bought more every time. These would be the greatest stocking stuffers ever. One night Martina tried to speak with him. But I never heard him say a word.

Eventually, we used the universal sign for "check, please" by pretending to scribble in the air.

The waitress tallied the slashes on the beer slip, added that to our food charges, and gave us the bill.

Whoops. We'd been charged for six meals even though there were only five of us. Yet again, we had to flag down our waitress.

ME: "There's a mistake on our bill. We were charged for the ham pizza that we didn't order."

WAITRESS: "But we made it for you."

BRENDA: "But we didn't order it. I ordered a cheese pizza."

WAITRESS: "But we made it for you."

ME: "But why would we have to pay for it when we didn't order it?"

WAITRESS: "We made it for you."

We thought she was joking. We laughed, but she just stared at us stone-faced. She wasn't kidding. It was at this moment that a light bulb went on. She wasn't wrong. They had made it for us. Nobody else. And nobody else was going to pay for it, so we were the only option. There was no argument we could make. Customers were not always right here. They were most definitely wrong.

Everything was still rooted in the ways of a planned economy. They had produced a pizza, and someone had to pay for it. If we didn't pay for it, I'm certain the waitress would have been made to pay for it. She was not going to sacrifice a night's wages for a bunch of foreigners. We realized we were trapped in the vortex of communist logic. Illogical logic. So we all paid a little extra for another little lesson of life under the communist government and went on our merry way. From then on, we ate whatever they brought and celebrated when everyone got a meal they had actually ordered.

SLASHES

JULY 1993

IT HAD BEEN A LONG WEEK. Every week was a long week. We ordered a round of beer—five—pĕt piv—to be exact. The waiter put five pen slashes on a small slip of paper, dropped the paper on the table, and left. These stick figures were precious in the Czech republic. They were used by waiters and customers alike to track the table's beer consumption.

We weren't expecting stellar service, but the beers took a very long time. Others were being served around us. We flagged down the waiter and asked about our pivos. He slashed the paper five more times and left.

PETER: "Hell. He already slashed."

MIKE: "We'll tell him when he comes back."

The waiter returned with a round of beers.

PETER: "You slashed the paper for an extra round."

We tried pointing at the 10 slashes compared to our five beers, gesturing wildly with our hands. The waiter just walked away. Did he hear us? See us? Was he just ignoring us? Was he getting the manager to resolve this? Was he reporting us to the secret police? We had no idea.

When he appeared again, we ordered another round. He slashed five more times. Now, there were 15 slashes. Those beers never came.

Fourth try's the charm? We ordered for the fourth time, and he slashed for the fourth time. There were now 20 slashes on the paper. We finally got a second round and tried again to remind him that he had slashed the paper for two rounds we never received. Czech-English dictionaries out, we tried to find any words that would help us communicate the problem. He responded with the shrug. Like he was miming, "Not my problem."

When we got the check, we were not surprised to discover that we'd been billed for every time we ordered a beer, whether it was brought to us or not. We discussed our options and realized that, as usual, trying to fight it was futile. Beer was cheap. Literally, 50 cents a beer. And since this kind of thing didn't happen often, we paid and moved on with our lives.

COMMUNIST CUISINE

JULY 1993

ME: "Where should we go for dinner?"

MIKE: "How about the restaurace?!"

ME: "Very funny."

Virtually every restaurant in the country was simply called "restaurace," or "restaurant." A few were named after something they were near. "U" means "at" and is pronounced "ooh." There was U Medvídků (at The Little Bears because there was a metal plaque of three bears above the door), U Vejvodů (at Vejvodova Street), U tří pštrosů (at The Three Ostriches), and U Maltézských rytířů (at the Knights of Malta). Some new restaurants had popped up in Prague, largely owned by foreigners. Buffalo Bill's. Salty Dog. Red, Hot and Blues. But once we were outside Prague, all we ever saw were restaurants called "restaurace" or "čínská restaurace" (Chinese restaurant). And sometimes just "pizza."

The usual group of Czechs and expats from the office was wandering the streets of Prague looking for somewhere to eat.

ME: "Seriously, where should we go?"

As we approached a random Czech restaurant (maybe restaurace or maybe an U something—it didn't matter), we began discussing whether we should go to it.

MARKÉTA said eagerly: "Let's look at the menu."

ME: "Ummm. Why??? We know what's on it. They're all the same."

It was at that moment that I realized what I said was actually true. I was not trying to be snippy. Every restaurant—in the whole country—served the same things. There seemed to be maybe 25 Czech dishes, and each restaurant served 18 of them—their choice which ones. It was a sea of dumplings.

Every menu had vepřová s knedlíkem (pork and dumplings), svíčková (beef in heavy cream sauce), smažený sýr (fried cheese), and cabbage. They always had soup—hovězí vývar (beef broth) or dršťková polévka (tripe soup). Some had pork knuckle "cooked in its own lard" (*blech*). And if you were lucky, they might have a chicken breast with half of a canned peach on top or duck with red cabbage. I was always a little crushed to know that someone had found a peach or an orange and instead of eating it fresh, they cooked it and served it on top of a piece of chicken. Dessert was always palačinky (crepes) or zmrlinový pohár (ice cream with a little fruit).

We each came to have our favorites. I liked pork and dumplings. Mike always had two orders of svíčková na smetaně (beef in heavy cream sauce). The sauce was actually root vegetable cream sauce made with turnips, parsley root, carrots, onions, and celeriac. I never saw a carrot served, so I was skeptical. But it was a good dish. Martin loved his tripe soup. And pivo for everyone. Always beer.

MARKÉTA: "But this restaurant is a three!"

ME: "It's a what?"

MARKÉTA: "Look. It has a three."

She pointed to a Roman numeral three at the top of the menu.

Well, I'll be damned. There was.

ME: "Ok ... what does that mean?"

MARKÉTA: "It means it's good."

As usual, I had lost the thread of what we were talking about because my question and her answer didn't seem to go together. I stared at the menu, and they had—of course—pork, pork, beef, more pork, dumplings, and cabbage.

ME: "Ok ..."

It was the same menu as every other Czech restaurant, but Markéta seemed pretty excited about this place, so I took her word for it, and we went in for dinner. I don't know how her experience was, but as far as I could tell, there was nothing unusual or special about anyone's meal.

As I dug into my—*oh so the same as every meal*—pork and dumplings, I broached the Roman numeral situation.

ME: "What exactly does the three mean?"

MARTIN: "It means it's better than other restaurants."

ME: "Better in what way?"

Markéta looked back as if she didn't understand me.

MIKE: "Better ingredients?"

ME: "Better cooks?"

More blank stares.

MARTIN: "The number tells you which restaurants are better than others."

We were getting nowhere. I had never noticed it before, but at the top of every restaurant menu was a Roman numeral: I, II, III, or IV. A ranking system. Czech Michelin stars, I guessed. I never did get a clear answer as to what each number meant. Maybe it had to do with price. Maybe quality. Maybe both. For all I knew, it was a way for the government to imply excellence when everything was actually exactly the same. I truly couldn't tell the difference, and they couldn't explain it. But they had been told it meant the restaurant was better, and there was no talking them out of it.

I tried to dig into the bigger mystery.

ME: "So why do all the restaurants serve the same thing?"

MARKÉTA: "What do you mean?"

ME: "I mean, they all have pork and dumplings, svíčková, tripe soup, guláš, cabbage, and crepes or ice cream. Oh! And šopský salát."

MARTIN: "But some have pork knuckle."

MARKÉTA: "Some have bread dumplings instead of potato dumplings."

Bread dumplings? Potato dumplings? It was potato, potahto to me.

ME: "But nobody serves, say, sandwiches. Or other kinds of soup. Or tacos. Or a big salad!"

Blank stares. Silence. Another impasse. There was nothing left to do. I went back to enjoying my cabbage. They saw variety where we saw monotony.

Every week, the expats checked the *The Prague Post* and *Prognosis*—the English-language newspapers—for new restaurants. We were excited every time a new one opened—always hopeful that it would be good. But even if it wasn't good, at least it would be different.

FRIDAYS AT PIZZA TAXI: MIKE AND THE SHOWER REDUX

JULY 1993

ME: "Why are you still showering in the office? How long is this guy's vacation???"

We had realized Mike was still showering at the office because he had taken to putting a sign on the door while he was using it. At least he seemed to be remembering all his clothes these days. There was no way this was going unanswered. We asked him why.

MIKE: "I asked the same question! I called Roman and he called the landlord because I couldn't get a clear answer using my minimal Czech skills."

JAMIE: "What did Roman find out?"

MIKE: "It's a seriously spatny cislo."

Mike got us all using Czech words in absolutely incorrect ways, but we knew exactly what we meant. Špatné číslo was the only part of the recording we understood when we dialed a 'wrong number.' Mike's 'špatny číslo' meant something was a bad situation.

MIKE: "It seems the guy who shoveled the coal into the furnace died while he was on vacation."

ME: "Holy crap! How long has it been?"

MIKE: "It's been months. I asked Roman to call the landlord back to find out when someone new would start shoveling the coal."

PETER: "And? Soon we hope."

MIKE: "They said they have no plan to replace him."

JAMIE: "Wait, what? This is a big building. Aren't the other tenants unhappy and complaining about this?"

MIKE: "It seems nobody else cares and I'm the obnoxious American complaining about it. They won't fix it for me and nobody else has said a word."

PETER: "How is that possible?"

ME: "Dude . . . what are you going to do?"

MIKE: "I'm moving. I can't live like this, and they clearly don't plan to fix it. Let's have one last queso party at my flat before I move to Dejvická. It's closer to my favorite restaurant, U Cedru, anyway."

Insane that he had to move because of this. But we were all excited about U Cedru, or "At the Cedar Tree." It was a new Lebanese restaurant where we went for special occasions. They knew Mike by name. The food was great. We had plates and plates of Middle Eastern appetizers, bowls of hummus, kebabs, and more. It was exciting to have a new type of food available. Additionally, they had the best kung pao chicken in town. Go figure.

For Mike, that was that. There was no way to deal with the cold water issue except to move. The leasing company clearly didn't have any incentive to fix it. They would just rent the cold-water flats to people who wouldn't complain. This wasn't the first crazy reason an expat moved, and it wouldn't be the last.

JO'S BAR

JULY 1993

I FOUND A HAND-SCRAWLED NOTE on my desk.

> Melanie and Jamie
> Jo's Bar
> Tonight at 7 p.m.
> For Dunkin' Donuts
> From Brenda and Mike

We were in. We went straight from the office to the metro downstairs.

The metro voice rang out "Ukončete výstup a nástup, dveře se zavírají." We sang along with it, in Czech, as we always did. (Finish entering and exiting, the doors are closing.)

The ever-present metro announcement didn't include a please or a "prosím" at the time; I liked to think it was just silent. We jumped into the metro car and made our way to Malá Strana, across the river via the underground.

We walked to Jo's Bar and found our friends at a table with a big box of donuts they'd brought back from Budapest. Between us, we had about six dozen donuts. We took turns sharing. Today was Brenda's turn. We ordered American coffees—thank God for them—and sat down to catch up. Crowded House's "Weather With You" played over the sound system. We loved Jo's Bar. It was owned by some Australians who served American-style food. American coffee, nachos, and burgers. It was heavenly.

We'd finished our coffee and donut appetizers and asked for the menus so we could decide what Western delicacy we would have for lunch. The waiter looked chagrined as he handed us a simple sheet of paper—not the usual menu. I grabbed Jamie's arm as I saw what was on the menu:

Hovězí vývar

Šopský salát

Vepřo, knedlo, zelo

Svíčková

The list of Czech food went on.

ME: "What in the hell?"

BRENDA: "Noooooo!!!!"

PETER: "Hey mate! Mate?!"

He flagged the waiter back to the table.

PETER: "What is this menu? Where are the burgers?"

BRENDA: "And the nachos?"

WAITER: "Yeah . . . I'm really sorry. we've been busted by the Ministry of Health."

ME: "Oh, gnarly. Was there something wrong with the food?"

WAITER: "Oh! No. Not at all. But the dishes hadn't been properly approved by the authorities."

JAMIE: "What in the world does that mean?"

The waiter showed us a newspaper article. It explained so much.

In the late 1940s, the communists had established a state-approved cookbook *Receptury teplých pokrmů* (Recipes for Warm Dishes)[6] also known as "normovačka," or the "Book of Standards." The recipes were designed to use ingredients readily available in the planned economy and to provide well-balanced nutrition. The idea was that the more balanced people's meals were, the harder they would work.

Restaurants, which had all been owned by the government, used this cookbook for everything. What to cook, how to cook it, what ingredients to include, what dishes to serve together. The restaurants weren't "required" to follow the cookbook to the letter. If a cook or restaurant wanted to use different ingredients (assuming they could get them), combine the approved ingredients into a different dish, or otherwise deviate from the cookbook, they could totally do that. But they had to get approval from the Ministry of Health. And like all things under the communists, this process could take years. Virtually every cook gave up on creative cooking and stopped trying to make anything that wasn't in the cookbook. It was so much easier.

Now that foreigners were opening restaurants with different types of cuisine, there was massive confusion about what the rules were regarding food, kitchens, prices, and the like. Jo's Bar was in trouble because their Western recipes hadn't been properly approved by the health authorities, so they were relegated to using the state cookbook until further notice.

We were devastated. We were infuriated. We needed our nachos back. It would be weeks.

ARE WE THERE YET?

JULY 1993

HONZA INVITED A FEW OF THE EXPATS to his house. This was pretty exciting—it felt like acceptance somehow. We'd been outsiders for so long; we were something of a curiosity, really. Many, if not most, people in this country had gone their entire lives without meeting a foreigner from the West.

The four of us piled into the office Škoda we had borrowed for this excursion. The address was Svídnická 104/28 in Prague 8. Jamie was driving. Peter had shotgun. Mike and I were in the backseat with a huge map of Prague unfolded in our laps. By this point, we were all fairly confident in our navigation skills. We'd learned how to read a Czech map, even understanding Prague's districts and street names pretty well. After 20 minutes, we arrived at Svídnická Street and looked for number 104.

ME: "This is 345. We need to go further down."

Jamie sped up and drove a few blocks. We checked again.

PETER: "This is 74. We went too far."

Jamie turned around and went back a block.

ME: "Ummmm . . . this is 572."

MIKE: "What?!"

JAMIE: "What?"

ME: "I don't understand either. Let's go slowly and look at each building."

In order, down one side of the street, the building numbers were 345, 343, 58, 234, 74, 572, 712, 145, and 410.

Jamie pulled the car over. We looked again. Yep. 345, 343, 58, 234, 74, 572, 712, 145, and 410. Right in a row. We were in *The Twilight Zone*. That familiar surrealness began to descend upon us all.

JAMIE: "Why are these numbers out of order?"

PETER: "How can this be?"

ME: "Why are there odds and evens on the same side?"

JAMIE: "I think that's the least of our worries."

I laughed. Fair. And the other side was no better: 73, 541, 432, 278, and so on.

MIKE: "How are we supposed to find 104?"

JAMIE: "How does anyone find any particular address?"

ME: "Did Honza say anything about this?"

Everyone shook their heads.

PETER: "This is so communist."

We were totally stumped. This was way before the age of cell phones. And there were no pay phones. We had no way of calling anyone. This was on us to figure out.

ME: "Maybe we just drive the street from one end to the other, looking for 104."

JAMIE: "That seems like our only option."

So, we drove at a snail's pace down the long street shouting out the number we were seeing.

JAMIE: "272."

MIKE: "109."

ME: "312."

MIKE: "613."

PETER: "What number are we looking for again?"

JAMIE: "104."

PETER: "Right."

ME: "217."

MIKE: "218."

PETER: "219."

JAMIE: "Wait—they're in order? How did that happen?"

We all laughed. We were punchy now. And very late.

Eventually, someone saw it and pointed excitedly.

PETER: "104!"

Jamie pulled over immediately. We all stared at the building number—104. Right between 301 and 185.

Obviously.

PETER: "What the hell?"

We'd rung the bell that had Honza's name on it and gone to his apartment. Peter was fired up.

PETER: "Honza, how is 104 between 301 and 185?"

HONZA: "What do you mean?"

ME: "The building number. We've been driving up and down your street for at least an hour looking for 104. Why aren't they in order?"

HONZA: "They are in order."

Oh no . . . Back to the drawing board of questions. We tried again.

PETER: "Why isn't 104 between 102 and 106? Or 100 and 108?"

Honza looked at us quizzically.

MIKE: "Why aren't they in order?"

HONZA: "They are in order."

ME: "What order? It's NOT sequential . . . 15, 17, 19, 21."

HONZA: "It's the order they were built."

Was he kidding?

We all spoke at once.

JAMIE: "How does that make sense? How can you find anything?"

MIKE: "Do you have to know when the place was built?"

ME: "Even if we did know that, how would that help us find it?"

JAMIE: "Good point. It wouldn't."

We were incredulous.

HONZA: "You can look at the second number."

MIKE: "The SECOND number??? What second number?"

We all went outside to look at the building number. Lo and behold, we saw the second number. Honza explained.

HONZA: "My building was the 104th built in the district."

Not even just on this street? In the entire district.

HONZA: "That is on the red sign."

Every building had a standardized, red metal sign with three things: the building number, the district number, and the name of the neighborhood. Was he telling us that was just decorative? We weren't supposed to use it as the address?

HONZA: "About a hundred years ago, a blue sign was added below the red sign."

There was, indeed, a blue sign on the building with a totally different number.

HONZA: "The blue sign is the building's order on the street to help people find the building."

Ahhh. In order. The way we were used to. But there was a catch.

PETER: "But some buildings don't have a blue sign."

HONZA: "Well, it's not required."

Argh. Some buildings had them; some didn't. To confuse things further, some buildings had a sign indicating the profession of the person who once lived there, like a vegetable farmer or a goldsmith. Another clue. It was like a scavenger hunt.

JAMIE: "Honza, how were we supposed to know the blue number?"

HONZA: "It's right here."

On our piece of paper, it said 104/28. We had taken the 28 to be his apartment number. But it was the building's number, in order, on the street. THAT was the number we'd needed the whole time. Sigh.

Another communist riddle solved. Only one thing left to do. Pivo.

GOODBYE, PETER

PETER WAS LEAVING. Things just wouldn't be the same.

TO: Everyone
FROM: Peter
DATE: 6 July 1993
SUBJECT: Farewell

Well just as I started Czech lessons I have been forced to stop (I knew I should not have started them!!). There appears to be one too many expatriates (some might argue more than one!!) in the office and someone has to go. So it might as well be me!

So now it is time to continue what I originally set out to do, i.e., travel and enjoy the European summer (if it ever arrives!?!)

I have thoroughly enjoyed my 6 months in Praha and at Arthur Andersen and I would like to thank everybody, especially the Czech staff for making me feel welcome and at home (well, as much as possible). I will always remember my experiences here and the people I have met (and the food I have eaten!!; oh yes, and Radost!!)

Now to the more important announcement regarding the farewell. I do not plan to leave Praha until at least 1 August. Jamie and Mel are organizing a farewell and I'm sure they will keep you posted. It would be great to have a final pivo (or piv!) with you.

Finally, for all those (and I'm sure there are many of you!) who plan to come Down Under to Australia in the future, get in contact with me and I will show you some real "Aussie" culture. I will always be contactable via my parents. On Wongala Street ("Wongala" is an aboriginal term meaning "he who sings country music!") in Tamworth (i.e., the Country Music Capital of Australia!).

Na shledanou,

Peter

We left an invitation in everyone's mail files and faxed a copy to our friends at Price Waterhouse.

Peter's Pub Crawl and Roast

We'll be traveling en masse to as many of Peter's favourite local haunts as possible, reminiscing about the good things, the bad things and all those things we still don't understand, that have happened since Peter entered our lives! Below is a list of Peter's favourite hangouts, all of which we'll be attempting to hit, and you're all invited to join us at your convenience. Remember that the actual timing depends on a variety of factors such as weather (a sunny day will require that we spend more time outdoors than is currently scheduled), speed of service (probably the riskiest factor involved in Prague), and endurance (we will try to pace ourselves) but you can be sure to join up with the party at Red, Hot, and Blues; U pinkasu, U vejvodu, U radnice, or dancing at Lavka. And of course we'll end the evening dancing at our favorite late-night haunt, Radost. Hope to see you somewhere!

It was a celebration like no other.

I couldn't believe he left.

THE STINK TALK

ME: "You want me to do what?"

My stomach sank. Full of dread. I couldn't imagine having this conversation. I really, really, really did not want to do this.

I was told by one of my bosses that I had to speak to one of the Czech staff, Radka, and let her know that we were running an American-style office and that her body odor was too much. I was then to give her a stick of the Arid Extra Dry that Gaby kept in her desk drawer.

No, no, no. (And by that I truly meant NO.) This cannot be. How in the world was I gonna say this?

I'd heard about this. Other expats had done this before. It was so awkward and uncomfortable that we affectionally called it "the stink talk" to lighten the mood and help us push through.

Radka wasn't the only person in the office with strong body odor. Not by a long shot. This was a very common thing in the Czech republic, and much of Europe, at the time. It was a rare day when I didn't pass someone on the street who had an extremely strong scent. We encountered it in the office, on the tram, when our waiter or waitress came to the table, in the shops, and in the pubs. It was everywhere.

The staff rooms were divided into the Czech room and the foreigner room because of our different lighting expectations, but entering the Czech staff room on a hot day could be overwhelming for those of us not accustomed to the different expectations around body odor, particularly in the workplace. On the other hand, I suspected the Czechs were happy with the arrangement, too, since they weren't subjected to our lighting and they thought the expats smelled like soap. We were delighted when we heard this, but it wasn't meant as a compliment.

I felt terrible for Radka. She was so professional. We had recently spent a day organizing binders of audit documents. There were stacks of them. The room we were in had an entire wall of windows. Like we were working in a greenhouse. It started out fine. Then lunch came. And then the afternoon. The smell was undeniable. I tried to hide my discomfort. But I don't think it mattered. She knew, and she was probably more uncomfortable than I was. She gave me furtive glances; she occasionally smiled awkwardly. I felt so bad for her.

When I was told I needed to speak to her, I knew it wasn't optional. Our managing partner wanted a Western office, and that meant addressing this.

I invited Radka to dinner.

We had a great chat. I learned about her family, her boyfriend, and life in Czechoslovakia. We talked about work and being a foreigner in the country. Still, the impending conversation lingered in the back of my mind.

We ordered after-dinner espresso. I just couldn't pull the trigger. I ordered a second espresso.

As I saw the bottom of my cup, I knew my time was up. I had to do it now, and I still didn't have a plan. I awkwardly launched into it like my eyes were closed and I was trying to feel for the wall.

ME: "As you know, we work for an American company . . . and some things are different than they would be in a Czech-style office . . . I have American deodorant for you in my bag, in case you want to try it." At least, this is what I *think* I said. It was a blur.

She cut me off and said she would love to try the deodorant. I was slack-jawed. She continued.

RADKA: "Most of us shower or bathe every day. And most of us use deodorant. But the deodorant isn't always in stock and, even if it is, some of the options don't smell good."

I immediately thought of my own deodorant conundrums. When I'd been in Prague for about a month, I'd run out of deodorant. Most of my stuff still had yet to arrive. I'd panicked and bought a German deodorant, thinking that because it was Western, it would work better. I'd been right. It had worked. I'd had no body odor. But it had smelled like a urinal cake. Chemical-like and overpowering.

I leaned across the table, eager to learn more.

RADKA: "It was worse under the communists. We never knew if deodorant would be available. We had to get used to not using it."

ME: "Oh wow. I knew many things weren't available but never imagined it was something like that."

RADKA: "It was considered a luxury item, so it wasn't important."

ME: "Ohmigod. A luxury item? This explains so much. Thank you for telling me all of this!"

RADKA: "Also, some of the new staff don't have very many outfits for work. They're expensive, so we only have a few. And some of us don't have washing machines. We wash our clothes by hand. We don't want to wash them too often or the fabric could wear out. And we might not be able to afford more nice clothes."

ME: "And that's why some women wear so much perfume? To try to cover it up?"

RADKA: "Yes. Now we can get perfume so many people try to do that."

It was a misguided effort for sure. Nothing about it was working, and it actually made things worse. But I appreciated the effort.

I could have kicked myself under the table. Why hadn't I realized all this before? It was another impact of the communist government's planned economy! It was a perfect storm of issues directly related to that economy. Production was success. Things like bricks, cement, and other construction materials were high on the production priority list. Hygiene products, beauty products, certain crops and foods, and even cars, were not considered critical items. The state was always prioritized over the citizens. Cars and landline phones took years to get. The waitlist could last a decade in some cases. Demand was irrelevant in this model. It didn't matter that people needed and wanted deodorant, tampons, fruits, and vegetables. It only mattered what the government planned and wanted to produce. The state existed to take care of the state.

Even in 1993, we felt this. Products were not reliably or consistently available in the stores. We took what we could get. In our office, the staff were expected to wear suits or similarly formal clothes. Clearly, what we Westerners considered appropriate professional wear in line with our dress code was not readily available here. Or it was available but insanely expensive to the average Czech. The foreigners always shopped when they went home. I never bought a single item of clothing in this country. Except snow boots. They were great.

ME: "I had no idea. Thank you for making this conversation so much easier than I thought it would be. I've been dreading it."

RADKA: "Thank you for telling me! And thank you for the deodorant. I can't wait to try it."

And that was that. We never had to discuss it again. For the rest of my career, I was never afraid to give someone feedback of any kind—after giving the stink talk, everything else seemed easy.

X-GAMES: BASKETS

AUGUST 1993

BABIČKA: "BEZ KOŠÍKU NEMŮŽETE JÍT DO OBCHODU!!!"

I froze.

We were heading into a grocery store to pick up a few things. The woman was following us, yelling in our faces, and pointing outside.

ME: "What do we think she's yelling at about?"

JAMIE: "I have no idea."

There is nothing more terrifying than being yelled at by an angry Czech woman and not knowing why. And she seemed angry—*very* angry. Did we drop something? Did we leave the car running? Was there someone chasing us? No. Did she think we'd stolen something? That didn't make sense since we were on our way in. We were stumped.

We hurried outside so she would stop yelling. She pointed to the back of a long line of babičkas waiting to go into the store. In the bracing cold. Nobody else seemed bothered.

JAMIE: "I wonder what we're in line for."

ME: "Same here."

JAMIE: "Do you think they know why we're in line?"

ME: "Honestly, I don't know. Queuing for hours on end is a way of life here. Maybe they just like it."

Jamie laughed. Clearly, the Czechs seem to have long ago given up on trying to do any kind of shopping quickly. They were used to this. We weren't. And we didn't get it.

JAMIE: "How did this happen? Is this how communism worked?"

ME: "They yelled at people until they just complied?"

JAMIE: "Or forced them to stand in line for no reason as a means of control?"

ME: "At this point, I'd believe anything."

JAMIE: "I'm going up front to see how people ever get to go inside."

He was gone for a solid five minutes but the line never moved. He returned no smarter. We tried asking, but our Czech was abysmal, and nobody spoke English (or would admit they spoke English; this happened from time to time when people couldn't be bothered to help us). We took turns running up front to try to figure it out but kept returning to our spot because people gave us dirty looks.

Eventually, my timing was right, and I witnessed it. I could *not* believe it. And I couldn't wait to tell Jamie.

ME: "We're waiting for shopping baskets!"

JAMIE: "What?! But we only need a few things. We don't need baskets. Let's try again."

We went back to the doors and tried explaining that we didn't need a basket because we were just getting a few things. We got out our trusty dictionaries and tried out some Czech. Total failure.

BABIČKA: "Bez košíku nemůžete jít do obchodu." ("You can't go into the store without a basket.")

At least she wasn't yelling now. We tried just walking in quietly. We tried just one of us going in. No and no. There was a security guard there to make sure we didn't do that.

All of us were queueing outside a store in the freezing cold waiting for a basket to be available. Everyone was required to have a basket to go shopping. This turned out to be true even at the tiny corner stores. I had never tried to just run in to grab something small before. I'd always had a basket, but I hadn't realized it was *required*!

We got back in line and waited a very long time to get a basket. And we each had to take one. No sharing allowed.

It took us a while to come up with a possible explanation. Crowd control. By only having a handful of baskets, they could control how many people were in the store. Did they think people would shoplift? Honestly, what would they steal? There wasn't much of interest or value in the stores. I suppose compared to what it was like pre-1990, the stores were well-stocked with exciting new goods. Or was it crowd control just for the sake of control? I didn't know why this was a rule; I just knew I didn't want to get yelled at—or worse—so we learned to get in line. In more ways than one.

After that, we always planned a much bigger part of our day to buy our groceries.

ABSURDISM

AUGUST 1993

> **Absurdism** *(n.):* a philosophy based on the belief that the universe is irrational and meaningless and that the search for order brings the individual into conflict with the universe
>
> *—Merriam-Webster Dictionary*

I HAD A NEW PROJECT. Markéta and I were going to a small town a few hours outside of Prague to find out how many employees the company had. Easy, right? I was told the project was scheduled for two weeks. *Two weeks?* I found this confusing, but I was often confused here. I knew better than to ask too many questions, so I packed my bags and headed out on Monday morning.

The town was small and the roads were dusty. I saw two restauraces and one čínská restaurace. That was pretty much it. Nothing else to see. The next morning, after the hotel breakfast of rohlíky, cheese, and salami, we went to the client's main office to introduce ourselves and get started.

Week one.

MARKÉTA: "Dobrý den. We are here from Arthur Andersen."

Mercifully, pani Liškařová was expecting us and knew why we'd come. This was a nice change.

We set up in a sparsely furnished office with a handful of desks. Several employees were working here, but there was one free desk for us. It faced a large window that overlooked the dusty street. At least it was bright in here.

MARKÉTA: "Can we get a list of all your employees, please?"

We both assumed we would get the list and just head back to Prague. But we waited.

And waited.

And waited.

Eventually, someone returned and handed us a handwritten list. The list had 97 people on it. Ninety-seven random names. No departments, no employee numbers, no positions. Just 97 handwritten names. The company was supposed to have hundreds of employees. Where were the other names? Why was it handwritten? Why was there no breakdown of employees? Didn't they have a computer printout from an HR system?

ME: "I don't think this list is complete. There should be a lot more employees. Can we please get the list from your HR system?"

Markéta translated, but the client knew I'd posed the question. And she stared at me. Right into my eyes. Steely but somehow blankly resigned. As if to say, "I can't believe you're going to make me do more work." She left the room—hopefully to get a new list. For all we knew, she was done for the day and wouldn't come back. But we waited. It was still mid-morning, so she would definitely come back. *Right?*

We waited.

And waited.

After a few hours, she returned with another list. Also handwritten. This time with 302 people on it. Ok! We were getting closer. We assumed the shorter list was just a partial list and the new list was correct. But we wanted to confirm.

MARKÉTA: "Can someone tell us the difference between these two lists?"

Liškařová shrugged. Crap. The shrug. She didn't know. Or she didn't care. Or she was just the messenger. Or all of the above. It wasn't good news for us. We would get no assistance.

Markéta and I sat at the desk with the lists and did a side-by-side comparison. We were wrong. The short list was totally different from the long list. The names on one did not appear on the other. What in the world?

We looked closely and realized the lists were in different handwriting. Maybe this was a clue. Maybe one came from, say, human resources? And the other came from—maybe—payroll? But then they should be the same list, no? Who knew? We were grasping at straws.

I looked up and saw that Markéta and I were alone in the office.

ME: "Where is everyone?"

MARKÉTA: "It's lunch break."

ME: "Already? How long have we been here?"

I checked my watch. It was 10:45 a.m. Work always started early at the factories, so it was, indeed, lunchtime. Realizing there was nothing more we could do at that moment, we headed to the kantýna. I was relieved they had yogurt so I didn't have to resort to the standard factory lunch of tripe soup.

After lunch, we tried again.

ME: "These lists are different. Where did they come from?"

Shrug.

MARKÉTA: "Is it possible to get a list from your human resources department?"

ME: "And maybe with identifying information like what department each person works in, their job title, or their employee identification number?"

I hoped for any tidbit that would help us reconcile these lists.

The woman left.

So, we waited.

And waited.

And waited.

The woman finally returned with a new—you guessed it—handwritten list. This one had 289 employees. Again, there was no additional information. Just more names.

Arrggghhhh. What. Was. Happening?

We compared all three lists. None of the three aligned with the others. There were missing people and new people. There were people who appeared on two lists or all three, but there were also people on each list who appeared on no other list. Absolutely no clarity at all.

I was ready to bang my head against the desk, but it began to get dark and the workday was coming to an end. There would be no more lists today, thank goodness. We decided we each deserved a velký pivo (huge beer) tonight with our chicken kung pao.

Day after day, we went to this office to try to figure out how many employees they had. We confirmed we had lists from the heads of human resources and payroll. Who else could we ask?

We tried the head of accounting. A new and different list.

We tried asking each department head and got a new and different list every single time. Nothing was adding up. There were names on the department lists that didn't appear on the longest list. And there were names on the longest list that did not appear in the department lists.

We poured over the lists. We sorted the lists. We cross-referenced the lists. There was always a disparity. Didn't these people actually know who worked for them? The numbers weren't adding up at all. Looking at the longest list, I could see there were groups of people that didn't appear on any of the department lists. I decided they probably had some crazy communist departments I couldn't even conceive of. And that actually didn't do anything I'd ever considered to be a job. *Sigh.* I had absolutely no idea how to ask a question about them.

Every time we asked for a new list, it took hours. The person being asked would handwrite a list of the employees they knew about. Were they doing it from memory? No one would review someone else's list. It was like they wouldn't dare.

We asked about the new names, the missing names, the different groups of names.

Shrugs. Shrugs. Always shrugs.

It was nobody's problem but ours. Even Markéta was horrified. She couldn't explain the craziness of it all. At the cement factories, she usually had an explanation for the convoluted nature of things. But not this time. We decided to just do it ourselves.

We went to human resources and asked to look at the personnel files. Those had to exist, right? We were shown the back offices. Filing cabinets to the ceiling. All crammed full of paper files. We glanced at each other. We were going to be in this town a lot longer than I'd anticipated. The two-week estimate suddenly made sense. We needed a plan.

Week two.

I assumed the foreign investor who bought the factory had promised to keep all the employees for some amount of time. We were supposed to figure out who those people were. And we were failing spectacularly. It would take us weeks to dig through the paper files to compile our own list. We had no way of knowing if the files were accurate or complete.

We tried a new approach.

We decided to stop asking for more lists. We would make one master list and go from there. We compiled all the lists and discovered we now had 712 employees. *Argh.* Could this possibly be right? How could there be so many people when we kept getting shorter lists? There was only one thing to do. Go person by person.

ME: "What does Sylvia do?"

LIŠKAŘOVÁ: "She works in the kantýna."

ME: "Why isn't she on all the lists?"

Shrug.

I guessed it didn't matter why—she should be on the master list.

ME: "What does Bohuslav do?"

LIŠKAŘOVÁ: "He's in the military."

Ok . . . he was off the list.

ME: "What does František do?"

LIŠKAŘOVÁ: "He works in the warehouse."

Great. He'd go on the list.

ME: "What does Evička do?"

LIŠKAŘOVÁ: "She had a baby."

I didn't know what to say to that. That wasn't an answer to my question.

ME: "Ok . . . so does she work here?"

LIŠKAŘOVÁ: "Yes."

ME: "Great. What does she do?"

LIŠKAŘOVÁ: "She's at home with the baby."

Hmmmm . . . we put her on a separate list—a "no idea what to do with these people" list.

ME: "What does Ivan do?"

Shrug.

Shrug. Shrug. A tidal wave of shrugs. But we soldiered on. Because there was one thing we couldn't do when we returned to Prague. Shrug.

Week three.

We needed to not be here anymore. Our manager would never understand why we were still here. We continued going through the 700+ names one by one. Name by name, we asked who the person was, what department they worked in, and what they did. We took copious notes, especially when we got nonsensical answers like "She had a baby," "He's in the army," or "He's retired." At long last, we had gotten through everyone on the list. We began grouping the employees based on our notes, and it started to become clear what we were dealing with.

Every list we had been given was a different category or set of categories of "employees." Some included only laborers. Some also included office workers. Some included management. Some included women on maternity leave (which lasted for three years!). Some included men completing their mandatory military service. Some included retired workers who were still permitted to eat in the kantýna. Each list included one or some combination of groups.

We came to learn that there were numerous categories of "employees." And there was no blanket word in Czech for "employee." There were company employees (zaměstnanec), civil servants (státní úředník), workers or laborers (pracovník, dělník, pomocný dělník), skilled workers (kvalifikovaný pracovník), and more. Women on government-supported maternity leave were still considered employees of the company, as were people on military duty. I guessed that the retired guys eating in the kantýna were on some sort of government pension.

I had no idea how the word "employee" had been translated every time I spoke it. But I suspect it was like a nightmarish game of telephone. It must have driven the Czechs as crazy as it had driven me.

But after *THREE WEEKS* of shrugs, new lists, and the runaround, I could say with absolute certainty we had our number.

563. (I think.)

MY KITCHEN TRIED TO KILL ME

MAYBE I WAS OVERREACTING, but I really didn't think so.

Jamie and I rented a Škoda to go to the big grocery store in the paneláks—the ubiquitous apartment buildings of the Communist East. To be fair, they were actually introduced in the Netherlands after World War I, but they flourished later and became heavily associated with the Soviet era. Prefabricated, they were built from panels which were obvious to the eye. Hence, paneláks. This hulking housing had been built, row-after-row, on the outskirts of Prague. They were faceless. Unadorned. Repetitive. Soviet relics of soulless living. Millions of Czechs lived in them. Shortly after he became president of the country, Václav Havel called the paneláks "undignified rabbit pens."[7]

But the good news was that they needed large grocery stores to feed all those people.

We routinely rented a Škoda to trek out to a larger store and stock up on EVERYTHING. We filled the car. The trunk, the back seat, the window ledge. No space was spared. My kitchen was fully stocked, so I decided to cook dinner for Jamie.

It was a tried-and-true family-favorite recipe: chicken and rice made with three kinds of Campbell's soup that I had brought from the U.S. Super easy. Not gourmet. I had that strange instinct to impress him with my "cooking."

I was hoping to have dinner ready as soon as Jamie arrived, so I started early. I found a baking dish that would work well. I filled it with chicken breasts (I didn't even have to pluck the feathers myself), rice, and the Campbell's soup. A delicacy. I hadn't used my oven before but assumed it should be simple. But of course, it wasn't.

I put the chicken in and turned the heat to my best guess at 350 degrees and went to set the table. I returned 15 minutes later to check on the chicken and discovered the oven was still cold.

Oh man. I hadn't noticed that my oven was connected to a propane tank. Like an outdoor grill at home, but this was inside my flat. *Is that even safe?* I opened the gas line and crossed my fingers. I felt it start to heat up—whew—and returned to my preparations.

Jamie was on his way. The table was set. The pivo was cold. The chicken was about done, so I went to pull it out of the oven. The door didn't move. I pulled harder. It didn't budge an inch. Or a centimeter.

Are you kidding me?

I took a deep breath and tried to focus on the problem at hand. *Is there some trick to this? A latch?* I probably shouldn't have waited until now to actually use the oven, but here I was. *What the hell?* I put my foot on the wall next to the oven to get some leverage and pulled as hard as I could. Ugh. Nothing.

I wanted to bang on the door and try to unstick it, but the oven was connected to that gas tank, and I was afraid of jostling it too much. Common sense got the better of me. I turned the gas off and *then* yanked violently. I looked for a secret switch or dial or anything to free the door. None in sight.

I heard Jamie knock on the door. Holy hell. Maybe he could figure it out and get it open before the chicken was overcooked.

I let him in and had to tell him the problem. He went into my kitchen and was dazzled—not in a good way—by the bright red plastic cupboards. He assessed the oven door and gave it his best shot. He gave it that manly second chance. Nothing. That door was determined not to let us reach the chicken.

All we could do was peer into the small oven window and watch the chicken fade away. We gave up and headed into town. I was just grateful I hadn't somehow blown us both up.

The next morning, I went downstairs and found Rudolf, my landlord. I mimed to him that I needed help upstairs, and he followed me. We entered the kitchen, and I turned to look at the oven, that vile thing. Rudolf stood next to me and looked at it with me. I again mimicked trying to open it but the door staying shut. I feigned the strain of trying to open an unopenable door. His face lit up. He understood!

He walked up to the oven and grabbed the door handle. I was dying to know what the secret was. But the door opened right up! No trick. No pulling. No strain. No problem. Easy peasy.

He looked at me and shrugged. Typical. Just like the car that doesn't rattle when you finally take it to the mechanic.

Sigh.

For weeks, every time I went into my kitchen, I heard a strange noise. Constant but not very loud. I just closed the kitchen door so I couldn't hear it. In hindsight, that was probably the wrong choice.

A month later, I went into the kitchen expecting the same noise, but this time was different. The noise was loud. And I mean LOUD! I walked around the kitchen (not a long walk). I didn't see anything. But the noise seemed louder closer to the kitchen window. I peered outside. I didn't see anything suspicious, so I left the kitchen and closed the door. I couldn't ignore it much longer.

I struggled to sleep that night. *Is it mice? Snakes? Very loud snakes? Ok, not that, but some sort of animals camping out in the wall? Electrical lines? Something getting ready to explode?* I was determined to figure it out the next day or I might never sleep again. I needed to know.

After work, I cautiously opened the kitchen door. I looked around, a little afraid something would appear and attack me. Nothing. Just that infernal noise. It now sounded like a buzzsaw. I was once again drawn to the kitchen window. This time, I looked up.

Bees.

Flying back and forth. Only a handful of them, but it made me curious. I went outside and looked up at my kitchen window. There were bees flying in and out of a small hole just under the overhang.

Ok, I thought, *bees are manageable.* But then I thought about how loud they were and realized there must have been thousands. Thousands. In my walls and ceiling. Nothing else could have made that INSANELY LOUD BUZZING!

I went back into my flat, shut the kitchen door, and went to inform the landlords. I never learned whether they addressed it because I never opened the kitchen door again.

MARKÉTA
(OR NO MEANS YES)

SEPTEMBER 1993

MARKÉTA: "Yo, yo, yo, yo, yo. Špagetko!"

Markéta had taken to calling me Small Spaghetti. She was quite tall. I was not.

ME: "Hey, Markéta. Sorry. Markéto."

I could never wrap my brain around this language. So complex. So confusing. Czech declensions were going to be the death of me.

Markéta just laughed.

MARKÉTA: "Don't you want a cup of coffee?"

I was taken aback. I did want one, but that seemed presumptuous of her. But it was coffee, so I just carried on.

ME: "Sure. Where should we go?"

MARKÉTA: "Let's go to Velryba. It's the best, Mel."

On the walk from the office to Velryba, Markéta told me things that had happened here before the Velvet Revolution.

ME: "I keep hearing about Prague Spring, but it seems to be something different every time I hear it."

MARKÉTA: "Yo, yo, Mel. It is two things."

ME: "Oh good. I feel better. What are they?"

MARKÉTA: "Well now it is the name of a music festival, but the first

Prague Spring was in 1968. After 20 years of communist rule, President Dubček implemented 'socialism with a human face' and loosened the rules. People had more freedom to talk, do art, and travel. But the Soviets were not happy. They sent troops into the country. Their tanks rolled through Wenceslas Square. The people protested the occupation, but more than 100 people were shot and killed."

ME: "Oh! And Jan Palach set himself on fire?"

MARKÉTA: "Yes. And another man. And everything went back to the way it was. Nothing had changed. It might even have gotten worse."

ME: "How awful."

MARKÉTA: "They even gave it a name. They called it 'normalization.' Going back to the way things had been before the Dubček's changes."

ME: "Oh man. As if that was the 'norm.' That's brutal."

We walked silently except for the clacking of our shoes on the cobblestones. As we walked by a new shop filled with alcohol and candy, I laughed at the combination.

ME: "They really sell alcohol and candy? Nothing else? Is this for adults or children?"

She shrugged.

MARKÉTA: "That store used to sell brown suits."

I stopped walking. *What?*

ME: "They sold suits?"

MARKÉTA: "They sold brown suits."

ME: "No gray suits? No black suits? No blue?"

MARKÉTA: "No, only brown suits."

Good Lord. I couldn't contain my laughter. The absurdity struck a chord.

ME: "Were they all the same size?"

Markéta joined in the laughter. They weren't all the same size, but it wasn't a ridiculous question. They could have been.

Still chuckling, we arrived at Velryba, just off Národní třída. Velryba was a basement-level coffee house with graffitied walls. Or at least someone's childlike artwork on the walls in pretty patterns and pastels. You could just see into the basement through ground-level windows covered with soot.

There was no rhyme or reason to the décor. The tables were old and mismatched; the chairs seemed like each person simply brought their own. It was eclectic. Like a bunch of squatters decided to open a café. It felt subversive. I loved it. It became my favorite café too.

Markéta ordered kávu s mlékem (coffee with milk); I debated which specialty coffee to order. I loved Vídeňská káva (Viennese coffee—with whipped cream on top) and Alžírská káva (Algerian coffee—with egg liqueur whipped cream). The second was actually a Czech invention, but they loved to name things after exotic places. I opted for Algerian—it was delicious. We ordered two pastries (they had my very favorite—makový koláč—poppy seed) and grabbed an empty table. I was pretty sure it was also covered with some sort of grime, so I tried not to touch it much.

ME: "I have a question. We just walked through the center of Prague and passed tons of restaurants and pubs. But not a single one of them has outdoor seating. What is that about?"

MARKÉTA: "What do you mean, Mel?"

ME: "The weather is beautiful, and there's plenty of space on the squares. Don't people ever sit outside to grab a drink or eat a meal?"

She actually looked pensive. Like she'd never thought about it. Maybe I'd asked a good question.

ME: "Is it not permitted? Is it just not something Czechs like to do?"

MARKÉTA: "It is something non-standard. Too much work for the waiters, or the furniture would be stolen."

ME: "Hire more waiters? Take the furniture inside at night? Maybe that's too much work too."

MARKÉTA: "There are some garden pubs but not many. And actually, I think they don't serve food outside. Only beer."

ME: "Wait. There's a garden pub, but you can only drink outside? You have to go inside to eat? Is this like the cows living in houses?"

MARKÉTA: "I guess maybe it is not allowed."

ME: "I guess not. Well, I put in my vote for patio seating when someone finally changes the rules."

We talked about her family—they lived in the paneláks on the outskirts of town, in Prosek, not far from my flat. We talked about work. I wasn't sure auditing was her passion, but she was really good at it. One of my best staff, in fact. And she happily welcomed my every question, no matter how big, small, or absurd it was to her.

ME: "Why are there no green doors?"

MARKÉTA: "What do you mean, Mel?"

ME: "The doors on the houses are very colorful. Red, blue, brown. But never green. None of us have ever seen a green door. We keep looking but no luck."

MARKÉTA: "I never noticed this, Mel."

Admittedly, it was a strange thing to notice. But it became something of a game amongst the expats. Pick out all the things that just seemed a little off or struck a chord with us.

ME: "Ok, let's try another one. Why are most of the Škodas orange?"

MARKÉTA: "Because that's what they had."

My brain hurt. What did that even mean?

ME: "What?"

MARKÉTA: "What?"

We were both confused.

ME: "What do you mean that's what they had? What if you wanted, say, a white car?"

MARKÉTA: "My parents were on the waiting list for seven years. The year it was their turn, the cars were orange."

Ahhhhh ... in one small detail, Markéta had summed up the entire socialist economy that had existed here for 40 years. The planned economy. The government sold whatever it had decided to produce; demand be damned. Production for production's sake with zero regard for what people needed. Or, God forbid, what they wanted. Everyone was at their mercy. It took years on the waitlist to get a home phone. Years to get a car.

And no matter what you got, you were happy about it. Because at least you got one. I didn't dare ask why the only colors ever used for Škodas were orange, white, gray, '70s yellow, and pale blue. Did they never have black paint? Or red? I knew I would get the "asking questions was futile" shrug. But I was starting to understand.

ME: "Oh duh!"

I slapped my forehead.

ME: "That's why all the suits were brown and there are no green doors!"

MARKÉTA: "No, no, no."

ME: "No?"

MARKÉTA: "Yes."

I belly laughed.

ME: "Right! No means yes. Up is down. Cars are orange. Suits are brown."

I've made a rhyme.

MARKÉTA: "No, Mel. I mean yes, Mel. You've got it now."

We sipped our coffees and people watched while we talked. The people watching was always good here.

ME: "You know what I need to learn?"

MARKÉTA: "What, Mel?"

ME: "How to swear in Czech."

She laughed at me but then thought about what the best thing would be to teach me.

MARKÉTA: "Ok. I have one for you."

ME: "Rad. What is it?"

MARKÉTA: "Do prdele."

ME: "Do purr-de-lay."

MARKÉTA: "Yes! Perfect, Mel."

ME: "Wow cool. What does it mean?"

MARKÉTA: "Well, technically it means 'to the ass' or 'to the anus.'"

I almost spit out my coffee.

ME: "Umm . . . kind of like the way we say 'up yours'?"

MARKÉTA: "No, it's more like a simple swear word. The way Americans say 'damn' or 'shit.'"

ME: "Ha! Do prdele!"

I realized I should probably keep my voice down. So I started whispering it repeatedly, to practice.

ME: "Shit. Do prdele. Damn. Do prdele. Just trying to get the hang of using it the right way."

MARKÉTA: "Oh, I like that, Mel. Shit prdele. Shit prd. Shit prd!"

ME: "Ooh. I like that 'shit prd.'"

And that's how Markéta starting using 'shit prd' as her new English-Czech swear word.

It had been quite the educational day. We finished our coffee and pastries.

MARKÉTA: "Tak. We are finished with our coffee. Don't you want to get pizza?"

Tak meant "so."

ME: "Yes, but what is that about? How do you ask that question in Czech?"

MARKÉTA: "Nechceš si dát pizzu?"

ME: "Interesting. Ok. It's an exact translation."

MARKÉTA: "Why?"

ME: "In English, we would ask, 'Do you want to get a pizza?' In Czech, you ask, 'Don't you want to get a pizza?' In English that would be sort of presumptuous, I guess. Like you have an expectation of their answer. If I didn't want pizza, I would feel like that would disappoint you."

MARKÉTA: "Oh! That is very good to know, Mel. Do you want to get pizza?"

She said it with a smile.

ME: "Yes! Where shall we go?"

MARKÉTA: "We must go to Pizzeria Kmotra. It's the best, Mel."

FRIDAYS AT PIZZA TAXI: A GOOD LAUGH AND A TERRIBLE COUGH

SEPTEMBER 1993

ME: "Have you guys seen today's *Prognosis*?"

Prognosis was one of the two English-language newspapers in Prague; the other was *The Prague Post*. Both were our lifelines.

MIKE: "Not yet, why?"

ME: "Someone named Steve included the 'Top 10 Possible Ad Slogans for the New Czech Republic.'"

JAMIE: "Oh boy. Let's see them!"

I pulled out the paper and we looked at the list. We each had our favorites.

The same old Czechoslovakia you've always loved—now in a new, easy-to-visit size!

The Czech Republic. Easier to spell than ever before.

The beauty of Paris. The mystery of Venice. And a lot more pork!

Don't worry. There's a McDonald's.

Take the German autobahn to Exit 5, turn right, and WE'RE RIGHT THERE! YOU CAN'T MISS US![8]

We couldn't stop laughing.

JAMIE: "These are great. We need to meet this guy, Steve Fisher. Anyone know him?"

We shook our heads. We never ended up meeting him. But we appreciated his sense of humor.

JAMIE: "Did you see what a McDonald's employee told a reporter about working there?"

ME: "Oh no . . ."

JAMIE: "He said he can earn more working for a foreign company, which helps make up for the psychological pressure of having to smile for customers."

Funny—not funny. At least it was honest.

ME: "Did you read the article[9] about how McDonald's wants to buy all local products, but they can't?"

MIKE: "Why not?"

ME: "There's not enough quality control over the products. They aren't checked regularly. We don't have Egg McMuffins here because they're afraid the eggs may have salmonella."

JAMIE: "That's not at all concerning . . ."

ME: "But there's some good news! A few beef producers have agreed to stop raising the cattle indoors in exchange for a contract with Mickey D's."

We all enjoyed that. There really were cows somewhere! Now we needed to find the pigs.

Oh man. What was happening? Call us dumb Americans. But after a year, we were starting to "get it."

MIKE: "There was a hilarious article in the paper last week where they interviewed people about paying to use restrooms, including at least one babička working the door."

JAMIE: "Oh lord . . ."

MIKE: "The things they said were unreal. For example . . ."

BABIČKA: "Some of the men say, 'I really didn't piss that much so I should get a discount.' But we aren't going to measure it. We aren't going to fall for that."

BABIČKA: "Sometimes he goes in the toilet side, sometimes the urinal side. It all depends."

TOILET VISITOR: "When you notice the stalls and the urinal are both two Kč, it's a rip-off. It's a crime. It's more valuable to the customer to take a crap. Consider the value to the customer."[10]

We were crying laughing. Of course it "depends." But the value to the customer stuff had us rolling! So close, but no cigar.

LAURENT: "Have any of you seen the memo called 'You know you've been in Eastern Europe too long . . .'?"

ME: "Oooh. Tell us!"

Laurent pulled the memo out of his bag and read aloud.

You've started to think that not only is drinking at lunch perfectly acceptable, but you feel it's perfectly normal to be expected to do shots during the day.

Purple and teal sport coats and suits seem relatively fashionable, along with gym socks.

A "light" meal consists of fried pork and potatoes. The heavy version would include cheese, sauerkraut, & dumplings as well.

You no longer expect the "vegetarian" part of a menu to mean "food without meat."

Knee-length skirts seem long.

You think the air back home in L.A. or New York is pretty clean!

The list went on, and we could relate to all of it.

ME: "Speaking of the air . . ."

JAMIE: "Don't get me started. I could feel the coal dust every time I breathed in the other day."

MIKE: "It was worse up north. Did you see the *Fleet Sheet?*"

He pulled it out and showed us.

ME: "Ugh. And I think it gets worse in the winter."

JAMIE: "I read that air pollution is the cause of 3 percent of all deaths in the Czech republic."

MIKE: "Well, they say breathing the air here is like smoking 10 cigarettes a day, so that makes sense."

ME: "Wow. And the children here have 'smog holidays'[11] where they close school for the day. Or a few days."

> (MFD/1) After five days of danger-
> ously high levels of air pollution, resi-
> dents of Northern Bohemia were fi-
> nally able to open their windows yes-
> terday. Health Minister Petr Lom said
> yesterday that he would join with the
> environmental ministry to release
> funds to be used to treat individuals
> affected by the inversion.

JAMIE: "Like snow days back home."

MIKE: "Yes, because all the paneláks and apartment buildings have coal-burning fires to heat the buildings."

JAMIE: "They say the pollution causes ear infections, hearing loss, head-aches, and nausea. Of course, they also say the combo of artificial and natural light turns your hair green, so who knows."

ME: "Not long ago, the news said that seven of 13 air monitoring stations registered such high levels of sulfur dioxide that it was deemed a 'natural disaster.'"

We all sighed. Nothing had been shut down in our world during the air quality "disaster." Who knows how many cigarettes our lungs thought they'd smoked. Winter would be even worse. We braced ourselves.

THE SHOEBOX

I OPENED THE LID OF THE SHOEBOX and saw receipts and numbers scribbled on scraps of paper. Alrighty then.

I had a new client: The Civic Forum Foundation (Občanské Forum Foundation) run by Dáša Havlová, the sister-in-law of President Havel. (Not to be confused with Dáša Havlová, the president's wife. Again, there were not enough names to go around.) This was going to be cool. The foundation was born from the famous Občanské Forum (OF), a movement that led the peaceful transition to democracy and provided the first non-communist president of the country.

My main contact was an American woman named Claire. I was excited we'd be able to communicate clearly.

CLAIRE: "Welcome to The Civic Forum Foundation. We're excited to have an audit done and see how we're doing. Here you go."

ME: "I'm happy to be here, but what is this?"

CLAIRE: "Our accounting records."

I looked down at the shoebox now in my hands.

ME: "Is this the backup documentation to your system records?"

CLAIRE: "We don't have a system."

ME: "Do you have a general ledger?"

CLAIRE: "No. We have this."

Sh*t.

I figured I'd better get started.

Martin and I created a set of books and financial statements from the paper scraps in the shoebox. The organization was tiny—and I mean *tiny*—so it didn't take us long. Their annual budget was less than $1,000. It was the first and last time I audited a shoebox.

WE HAVE A KMART!

THE CIVIC FORUM FOUNDATION was holding a dinner dance at the Barrandov Terraces. The terraces were a beautiful, historic building complex overlooking Prague, built by the Czech president's family, the Havels, in the 1930s. It had been confiscated by the Communist Party and had only recently been returned to the Havels, its rightful owners.

The client had invited me plus a guest. Jamie said he would join me. But it was black tie. And the only such event either of us ever went to in Prague. My choice was easy. I would wear a beautiful little black dress that I'd purchased for $5 at a Salvation Army years before and had thrown into my shipment at the last minute. Just in case.

Jamie's, not so much. He needed a tux. And nothing less would do.

We decided to start at the newly renovated department store. Gone was the old communist Máj department store. In its place was Kmart. Five floors of Kmart. I never imagined, in my wildest nightmares, that I would be so thrilled to be able to shop at a Kmart. But here we were. They clearly had A LOT of stuff. Floors and floors of it. But was a logistical hell. We had to make our purchases on one floor before moving to the next. Fortunately, we only had one purchase to make that day. Did we expect to find a tuxedo? No. But you gotta start somewhere. And Kmart had a new Little Caesar's. We were thrilled. Crazy chleba. (Crazy Bread.) So exciting!

The building had been built by the Communist Party and was said to be modeled after both a factory and the Pompidou Centre in Paris. I wasn't initially sure how those went together AT ALL, but once I read that explanation, the craziness made a little more sense. At first glance, it looked like almost every other squat, boring, cement and glass building in town. But the escalators were on the outer edge of each floor and visible from the street through glass walls, giving it a Pompidou-esque look.

We made our way up to the men's clothing section and looked around. Not surprisingly, there were a lot of low-to-moderate quality clothes. And a plethora of mustard yellow, pale pink, and purple choices. We browsed, not bothering to ask anyone—we knew how that would go.

ME: "Oh psych! Over here!"

JAMIE: "You found a tux?"

ME: "I think so . . ."

We stared at it as if we were interpreting a Rorschach blot. It was a black suit with satin lapels and satin stripes down the legs of the pants. Honestly, if we'd simply found a black suit, that would have sufficed. But this was legitimately intended to be a tuxedo. At Kmart.

We found a white tux shirt nearby and Jamie headed for the changing room.

JAMIE: "I can't believe it."

I heard him through the door.

"Oh no. What? What's wrong with it?"

I was nervous. He stepped out of the dressing room and much to my surprise, he looked fantastic. Very debonair. My jaw dropped open, but then I furrowed my brow. Something had to be wrong. We just hadn't found it yet.

We checked the entire tux. No weird pockets. No strange seams. Nothing out of the ordinary. We looked at each other in astonishment. We'd found a black tux with no bizarre features that fit him perfectly. It was a miracle. We checked the clothing tags for washing instructions.

And there it was.

"100% pes."

We stared at it in silence for a long time. Our Czech wasn't great, but this one we knew.

JAMIE: "That says '100 percent dog,' doesn't it?"

ME: "It does . . ."

JAMIE: "Maybe it means something else too."

ME: "God, I hope so."

We looked it up in our dictionaries. Yep. Dog. A dog-hair tuxedo? We knew it had to be wrong, but we couldn't get our minds around it. Desperate times call for desperate measures. Jamie bought the tux. He'd only have to wear it once. Hopefully.

Afterwards, we asked around—a lot. Nobody knew. They didn't have a clue. Not the expats. Not the Czechs. Nobody.

So, I wore my $5 cocktail dress. And Jamie wore his Kmart dog tux.

The food was Czech, the wine was Czech, the views were amazing. We had a wonderful time on what we took to calling The Night of the Dog Tux.

The mystery of the material would haunt me for decades. I finally learned many, many years later that pes is a term for polyester. Whew.

Quarterly News

of the

WEIRD AND WONDERFUL

I LOVED CZECH HUMOR. The self-deprecating realism of their past. The bemused positivity about the future. The skepticism. The satire. I loved it all. It was infused in almost everything.

(EK/XXI) In a 32-page section on U.S. business activity here sponsored by the American Chamber of Commerce, Prognosis Editor-in-chief John Allison writes that the secret to successful Czech-American business relations lies in finding the happy medium between the can-do attitude of Americans and the can't-be-done attitude of Czechs. Each side has a bit to learn, Allison suggests.

Ahhh. This was exactly right. Americans thought we could make anything happen. Czechs had grown accustomed to assuming it couldn't. "It's impossible" did seem to be a favorite phrase.

Ohmigod, the lines! To get my ID, get a basket for the grocery store, exchange currency, pay utility bills at the post office. Always the lines.

(MFD/6) Tomáš Marek suggests in an editorial that the Czech government might intentionally be trying to discourage people from participating in the second wave of coupon privatization. How else can you explain the requirement that people stand all day in one line to prove their Czech citizenship and then stand all day in another line to actually register, he asks? The government has done nothing to make participating in this wave easy, he says, and many people will get weary and give up.

(MFD/Sat/XII) Václav Havel says that the same anti-German Czechs who vote for the communists or for the right-wing Republican Party often have "Zimmer frei" signs up in front of their homes and gladly make a few marks from any German who comes along. This inconsistency in behavior is typically Czech, he says.

I wasn't sure . . . I'd seen a lot of consistency. But then again, political viewpoints and economic needs were two entirely different things.

So . . . $1.30.

(HN/4) Elektrárna Opatovice will pay a 40-crown dividend for 1992.

(MS/5) A cartoon by Renčín pictures a farmer out inspecting his beehives. "They've stopped making honey," he laments to a passerby. "Like everyone else, they've turned into middlemen. Now they buy tobacco for 16 crowns and sell it for 20."

When they put it this way, it doesn't sound great.

(MFD/3) Czech health officials issued thousands of crowns in fines this month when an inspection of 365 beer glasses from various bars revealed that more than 80% of mugs were unsanitary. Inspectors were surprised to find how many bars still clean beer glasses only by rinsing them in cold water.

Ohmigawwwwwd. Gross.

(RP/Sat/2) President Havel said Fri. that he has one staff member whose job it is to check out Prague's new taverns. Whenever possible, Havel said, he likes to hold low-level official meetings in some bar or restaurant instead of at the Castle.

I loved this so much. So Czech. So cool.

So many questions ... but I started with why is Semtex "in"??? What does that mean? Terrifying.

(MFD/Sat/M4) What's in and what's out, according to Prague grade-school students? In is sex, contraception, promiscuity, drugs, McDonald's, Harlequin romances, Czech films and Semtex and other plastic explosives. Out are phosphorescent colors, discotheques, the Smurfs, American films and stretch miniskirts.

(LN/Fri/2) Prague now boasts a new American-made fire engine with a 46m extension ladder, which outstretches the old models by 9m. Unfortunately, the mayor's office forgot to take the truck's height into account. The vehicle (with its ladder down) is too high for many underpasses or tram wires, which renders the 20-million-crown technological wonder virtually useless in the city.

I have no words.

Hahahaha. The world was going to take a while to get used to the new name and it not being Czechoslovakia anymore.

(RP/1) The Russian film "Chekhov" by Nikita Mikhalkov will be - by mistake - the sole Czech entry in this year's Venetian film festival. It seems that the event's organizers confused "Chekhov" with "Czech" and slotted the film into the wrong country.

(MS/6) Jan Kašpar wonders aloud why the "Czech Made" slogan is in English if the goal of the campaign is to promote the sale of Czech goods on the domestic market. The choice of "Czech Made" is all the more curious, he says, when you consider the Czech people's inherent disrespect for things sacred. You can almost certainly bet, he says, that they will humorously rework "Czech Made" into "Ček šmejd" (Czech Schlock).

LOVE their sense of humor!

(MS/3) Vladimír Renčín, the cartoonist, says that although he was on the commission set up to pick the winning design for the Czech Made logo, he refuses to accept responsibility for the final selection. Inexplicably, he says, the logo the ministry of industry finally chose was not even among the top three picked by the commission. If nothing else, he says bitterly, Czech goods now at least have a realistic chance of being of a higher quality than the quality logo itself.

Hahahaha. How is this true?
Amazing.

(Strategie/3/4) Commercials for feminine hygiene products are banned on Czech television before 8 p.m. It seems lawmakers think that the moral development of children is at stake, the magazine says. The same lawmakers probably teach their children that storks bring babies, the author writes.

Wow.

Who let this happen? I felt like there was supposed to be a rule against this . . .

(RP/1) "Who's in charge here, anyway?" asks writer Robert Dengler. All top Czech officials are on holiday, including President Havel, Premier Klaus and Parliamentary President Uhde. The nation is being run by telephone, Dengler concludes, with the premier's office manager, Mrs. Mrázová, at the control panel.

JOSEF AND THE TRABANT

OCTOBER 1993

IT WAS POURING RAIN when it was time to leave the pub. Josef offered me a ride home. I was grateful. Otherwise I faced waiting in the rain for a tram and then a bus and then walking for 20 minutes. He ran to get his car and picked me up at the pub door.

Josef had a Trabant.

The Trabant was known as "a spark plug with a roof." Communism's most famous car. East Germany's finest. Even by the most ardent Marxist, it was considered small, uncomfortable, loud, slow, and poorly made. A quintuple threat.

If it hadn't been pouring rain, I would have heard the *putt putt* sound as he came around the corner. I folded myself into the tiny passenger seat as quickly as I could. I'm 5´3˝. Nothing is ever too small. But my knees knocked against the dashboard, and my briefcase was pressed against my chest. I slammed the door shut, and it shook the car. Josef pulled onto the road, and the car rumbled over the cobblestones. It was bouncy as hell. The rain was pelting the car loudly, like we were inside a tin can. I couldn't see a thing out the window through the torrential rain.

ME: "Josef, I can't see out the window . . . how are you driving like this?"

JOSEF: "I can see."

ME: "Ummm really? How?"

JOSEF: "I'm used to it."

The Czechs must have really good eyesight, I thought. No lights required. Rain be damned.

I really couldn't see a thing. As we continued the very bumpy journey, I was beginning to get nervous.

ME: "Do you think maybe you should turn on the windshield wipers?"

JOSEF: "Yo. Yo. Sure."

He rolled down his window. In the hard rain, with sheets of water blowing in, Joseph reached his hand out and around to the windshield . . . and moved his hand to and fro on the glass. What in the world? His hand was his windshield wiper? The car was so small, his hand could reach the outside of the front window with little effort. I was dumbstruck. And a little terrified. I burst out laughing. Josef thought nothing of it.

ME: "Josef, don't the windshield wipers work?"

JOSEF: "It doesn't have any."

My brain slowed for a minute while I processed what he'd said. The car had NO WINDSHIELD WIPERS.

ME: "What? Why not? They seem kind of necessary, don't they?"

JOSEF: "It didn't come with any."

ME: "Uhhhh can you get them if you want them?"

JOSEF: "I don't know. I bought this from someone else, and it never had any."

I have never laughed so hard while fearing for my own life. We flew through the cobblestone streets of Prague in essentially a golf cart with Josef driving and wiping the windshield simultaneously. I was jolted and bounced for the entire ride. I'm not sure the car had shock absorbers. We were soaking wet. Visibility was zero. I held on and just prayed we'd make it in one piece.

When I finally arrived home, I was certain I was now wetter than if I had walked. Still, this would be one trip I would never forget.

MY ŠKODA

I BOUGHT A ŠKODA. (I sure as hell wasn't going to buy a Trabant.) It was a 1988 Škoda 105 L in light gray. I was pretty excited it wasn't planned economy orange.

I was tired of borrowing the office car or renting one every time I wanted to go to the big grocery store. My friend Iva from the office and her father had taken me to a small town a few hours from Prague to buy it from a man named Vladimir. For $1,600. After handing over the cash, he started to remove the license plates.

ME: "Wait. Why is he taking the license plates? I need those."

IVA: "Because you are not Czech."

Ummm.

ME: "What does that mean? I still need license plates."

IVA: "You need the blue plates. These are white."

Ummm.

ME: "Why do I need the blue plates?"

IVA: "Because you are a foreigner."

I didn't understand, but I couldn't disagree.

ME: "Yes, I am a foreigner."

I immediately thought of another trip to some bureaucratic hellhole.

ME: "Ok, wait. What will happen if I have blue plates?"

IVA: "People will know you're a foreigner."

ME: "And is that a good thing?"

Iva shrugged.

ME: "So the police will know I'm a foreigner?"

IVA: "Well, yes."

Hmmmm.

ME: "That seems bad. Like I'll be a target."

IVA: "Yes, probably."

Argggghhhh.

ME: "Is there any way I can buy this car but have white plates?"

IVA: "It will need to be in someone else's name."

ME: "Ok . . . is that possible?"

Iva spoke Czech with her father and the seller for a few minutes and then smiled at me brightly.

IVA: "Sure! I will put the car in my name so you can keep the white plates."

ME: "Wow! Are you sure? That would rock."

IVA: "Yes, sure."

I hugged her and said, "Diky. Diky. Diky." (Thanks. Thanks. Thanks.) And so, I got to keep the white plates. I was a local. And I had wheels.

FRIDAYS AT PIZZA TAXI: ŠKODAS

OCTOBER 1993

ME: "You guys won't believe what I did last week..."

EVERYONE: "Oh no... should we be afraid to ask?"

ME: "I bought a Škoda!"

They all spoke at once.

EVERYONE: "No way. You didn't."

ME: "I did! I got a Škoda 105. The engine is the size of a lawnmower engine and it's in the trunk. Seriously. It feels like I'm driving a golf cart."

Škoda jokes immediately followed.

Q: "How do you double the price of a Škoda?"

A: "Fill the gas tank."

Q: "Why do Škodas have heated rear windscreens?"

A: "To keep your hands warm when you're pushing it."

Q: "Do you guys know why most of the Škodas are orange?"

A: "Because that's what they had!"

The last one was mine. All the jokes were easy laughs.

MIKE: "Do you guys know what Škoda means?"

ME: "Oh God . . . what?"

MIKE: "Damaged!"

We rolled with laughter.

MIKE: "That cannot be true. Why in the world would they name their car Škoda?"

JAMIE: "Of course they did . . ." and shook his head in disbelief.

BRENDA: "It really does mean that. They say 'to je Škoda,' and it means 'It's damaged' or 'It's a pity.'"

ME: "Dude. That would have been a marketing nightmare. Oh wait . . ."

MIKE: "The inventor of the car was named Emil Škoda."

ME: "And there's not even a word for marketing in Czech, so I'm pretty sure the irony was lost on everyone."

JAMIE: "Have you seen the new Volkswagen ads for Škodas?"

Volkswagen had begun partnering with Škoda after the Velvet Revolution. In 1993, they launched a new advertising campaign for the "pitiful" Škoda. We couldn't stop chuckling as we shared the various advertisements we'd seen.

"It isn't just the car that's been turned around."

"You're looking at a car that's been changed almost beyond recognition—the 1993 Škoda Favorit."

Eva: "How is this a selling point? This car was so bad we decided to buy the company?"

We thought that was hilarious.

ME: "Did you see the *Fleet Sheet* entry about the latest Škoda improvements?"

JAMIE: "Which one?"

He laughed. There were many. Many entries and many improvements. I pulled a *Fleet Sheet* out of my bag and shared.

> (MFD/Sat/XII) In a satirical column, Martin Komárek honors Škoda Auto Spokesman Jiří Hrabovský as the Man of the Week. Hrabovský is the most honest guy on earth, says Komárek, but he nevertheless carries out his job admirably. To his credit, notes Komárek, not a single hint of mental anguish is evident when he tells the public that the "994 significant improvements" to the Favorit actually almost make up for the increase in price.

JAMIE: "994 significant improvements? I wonder how many minor improvements they made."

We all laughed and carried on sharing ads we'd seen.

> "With no complicated 'deals' or long lists of optional extras. Just the features you want at extraordinary value for money."

Ok . . . no options. So, it was still a communist car, after all.

> "Call in at your local Škoda dealer and see for yourself the car that prompted *Car* magazine to say: 'Now you can drive a Škoda and look the world straight in the eye.'"

That one killed me. A Škoda used to be so bad that it was embarrassing to drive one.

ME: "Hey, I almost died in Josef's Trabant the other day. A Škoda has to be better than that."

MIKE: "I rode with Josef the other day. We were dropping the partner from London off at the fancy new Hilton Hotel. And here we came in putt-putting up in his Trabant. The doormen seemed shocked to see us amongst all the German cars."

We laughed and drank Frankovka and laughed some more. At least Volkswagen was honest.

CAFÉ SLAVIA

JAMIE AND I WERE HAVING SOME PIVOS at U Medvidků when some-one ran in and said, "Hurry! Café Slavia is open!" Everyone in the place jumped up and left their beer on the table. We walked briskly and en masse down Národní (National street) towards the river.

Café Slavia sits at the corner of Národní and Divadelní (Theater street) and overlooks the Vltava River that runs through Prague. For decades, it was known as the place where dissidents, artists, and intellectuals gath-ered to discuss their plans and ideas. It was an iconic landmark. Yet it had closed in 1991 due to a contract dispute. We were crushed. The Czechs were angry. We all wondered when they would resolve things and re-open. Everyone wanted the opportunity to sit where all the famous rebels had convened. Just to imagine Franz Kafka or Rainer Maria Rilke or Václav Havel sitting in the Café Slavia, talking about how to fight the communist government or what to put in their next poem or play and how to obscure the meaning from party officials.

But we couldn't. Because the doors had been shut indefinitely. We used to peer through the windows just to get a glance at the interior.

ME: "What do we think is happening?"

JAMIE: "I have no idea, but let's get there before it ends."

We walked faster. The street was full of people rushing to see what was going on. We arrived at the double doors of the café and saw that it was true. The doors were open and there was a crowd of people at the entrance.

JAMIE: "Is it actually open?"

ME: "Well, the doors are open . . ."

JAMIE: "Some lights are on, but it's still pretty dark in there."

We pushed a little closer. The heavy chains that had been holding the doors shut for years had been cut off. The doors were wide open now. There was a table in the entrance behind which someone was pouring beer into small, flimsy plastic cups. Another person was passing the cups out to the crowd. We each took one and entered the café. It was like a pop-up speakeasy.

The room was packed with people smiling, laughing, and enthusiastically talking about how cool it was to finally be inside this hallowed place. The room was filled with cigarette smoke, many of the lights were burnt out, the tables were worn, and there was trash piled up in the corners. A group that called themselves the Society of Friends of Café Slavia had gained access but had no legal rights to the place and no permits to sell drinks. There was a container on the bar where we dropped donations in exchange for a beverage. But we were inside, where so many incredible things had been plotted, conceived, and written.

In the 1970s, Havel and other dissidents had met there regularly to discuss their plans. I wondered if the Czech heroine, Milada Horáková, had spent time there with other members of the underground resistance. (She'd fought against the Nazis and then the Communist Party. She'd been interrogated by the Gestapo and ultimately executed on false charges of treason and conspiracy.) Government spies had also met there to try to hear what the dissidents were planning. The waiters were rumored to have been working with the secret police. My favorite Czech author—Milan Kundera—had spent time here. Maybe he'd conceived of *The Unbearable Lightness of Being* here. The cathedral of Bohemian life. We were in awe.

We huddled in the dim light and reveled in the rebelliousness of the moment. We had all broken into this mythical, subversive mecca. Like the next wave of dissidents. It was silly, but we felt part of something bigger than any of us.

By the end of the month, the interlopers had been locked back out, and Café Slavia was closed once more. The break-in was a one-time event. A once-in-a-lifetime opportunity for many. I don't know who made that happen. I don't usually support trespassing, but I'd thank them if I could. It was an incredibly special moment for everyone there.

CHEERS

I WAS ROBBED!

I came home from work and discovered that my nightstand had been opened and a gold necklace taken. It was a gift from a friend, and I was crushed. Weirdly, my camera wasn't taken. But more upsetting was that my door had been locked. It had to be someone with a key—from the landlord's family. I assumed it was the teenage kids, but I didn't feel safe anymore. I needed a new flat and dreaded the process. More weird layouts and retro décor to work through. Maybe I'd just decide to live in a '70s home for the next year. Finding a new place was at the forefront of my mind when the group got together the next night.

Jamie had just received a package from his friends back in Nebraska. Labeled as important work documents so it could be sent through interoffice mail, it was actually a care package of food and fun goodies. Unfortunately, one of the three bottles of syrup had leaked, so everything smelled like maple. Fortunately, the VHS tape wasn't ruined. A friend had sent him the series finale of *Cheers*! It had aired in May 1993, but we were excited to have it by November, six months later.

We reserved a large room at U Medvídků. Who knew that was a thing?!

U Medvídků was one of the oldest breweries and pubs in Europe, and somehow, it had a party room? We were amazed. We pulled together every American we knew because what expat here hadn't been glued to "America's Best Night of Television on Television" (re-branded to "Must See TV" in 1993) in the 1980s? *Fame, Taxi, Hill Street Blues, Diff'rent Strokes, Family Ties, The Cosby Show,* and *Cheers.* We'd dedicated more than 10 years to *Cheers,* and we wanted—no, we NEEDED—to see how it ended.

We invited all our American friends, not just from our own office but from other firms, people we'd met around town, and new clients. (Some of our Czech clients had recently hired Americans!)

I had a new client—a video distributor. They bought movie rights, dubbed the movies into Czech, and distributed them throughout the Czech republic and Slovakia. The audit was a mess. Their IT system didn't work, their records were incomplete and inconsistent, their branch chief could easily steal all their money, and their entire product line was at risk of being easily counterfeited. Super. But they'd just hired a guy named Mitch who shared my frustrations with their records. I invited him to come watch *Cheers.*

Brian had a new client—TV Nova, the first and only private TV channel in the country. TV Nova was a huge hit in the country—the only programming not run by the government. But it was beginning to feel like every company's books were a black hole. They compiled financial information based on interviews and judgment. (That is very dicey.) There may have been missing transactions. And maybe a bunch of debt. Who knew? Not them and not us. The company had two cars, a fax machine, a copy machine, and 200 steel display cases. The display cases had wandered off. Nobody knew where they were. They wanted to depreciate the other assets in accordance with Czech tax regulations. But no one actually understood the details of those regulations. So every single calculation was wrong. At least they knew where the fax machine was.

Tereza worked there selling advertising time. That sounded like a thankless job in a place where there had been no such thing as advertising until recently. No marketing. No TV commercials. But if anyone could do it, she could. She was friendly, outgoing, funny. And she spoke Czech! She grew up in New York state, but her parents were from Eastern Europe. What a huge plus that would be—to actually speak the language. Brian invited her to come watch *Cheers* too.

Turned out that Mitch and Tereza were already friends, so it was an easy evening. Tereza and I hit it off immediately and spent much of the evening hanging out and chatting. She hadn't been in town long but had just found a flat she loved and NEEDED A FLATMATE! For several reasons (let's see . . . I was robbed, the oven was a death trap, and there was an ever-growing beehive in my ceiling . . .), I jumped at the opportunity and said I would love to move in with her. (I don't think she asked, but I was bold about it, and she said yes immediately!) She told me the flat was quirky, but honestly, unless it had snakes in the walls and a deathtrap of a kitchen, it had to be better than what I was used to. Flat unseen. Neighborhood irrelevant. I'd escape my now-sort-of-hellish flat and have a fun roommate to boot.

The *Cheers* finale party was a huge hit and a great time.

But most importantly, I would be moving before I left town for the holidays.

CHRISTMAS SHOPPING
(OR NOTHING TO BUY HERE)

I NEEDED CHRISTMAS PRESENTS for my visit home. But what the hell was there to buy? Shopping was pretty dismal. The Czech republic had a handful of specialties, and they were cheap to us. Every expat in town was the proud owner of at least one full set of crystal glasses, a colorful crystal globe paperweight, a wrought iron picture frame, and some garnet jewelry. There was also a weird obsession with marionettes in Prague. I found them creepy, and they were literally hanging around at every tourist store in town. I never understood the draw. Prague was largely a shopping desert, but there were some fun new things available.

Before WWII, Czechoslovakia had been a country full of intellectuals. Painters, authors, poets, sculptors, playwrights, and artists of every kind. After the Soviet takeover in 1948 and until the Velvet Revolution, the country experienced a "brain drain." More than 500,000 skilled workers, professionals, and artists fled the country. After the Velvet Revolution, some of those people returned. Others had stayed but hadn't practiced their skills. During the summer of 1993, a number of new galleries and shops opened. I went through the tourist district, looking for unusual Christmas gifts for my family. Maybe not things they needed or knew they wanted, but they definitely couldn't get them anywhere else. I returned to my flat from my shopping excursion and set my plastic tote bags down. I'd finally caved and bought some of the shopping bags all the babičkas used. They were fantastic. They held a lot, didn't get dirty, and were indestructible.

I took off my coat and enjoyed the warmth of my flat. I washed my hands and face and watched the black water swirl down the drain. Then I sat down to unpack my loot. Everyone at home was getting one of everything. Except the hat. That was for my dad.

- Stalin and Lenin head candles from the Candle Man.
- Russian Matryoshka dolls (the doll within the doll) of the old Soviet leaders—Gorbachev, Brezhnev, Khrushchev, Lenin, and even Czar Nicholas.
- Bath salts from Karlovy Vary.
- Traditional Czech wooden toys.
- Crystal paperweights.
- Ceramic mugs—some made by burgeoning artists, others that said Kmart Praha.
- Authentic Soviet military and sports pins.
- A fur hat with the Red Star on the forehead that I bought from a Russian standing on a street corner.
- And for myself, an antique glass bowl with a metal stand from the shop on Bethlehem Square.

THE MOVE

OH. COME. ON.

It was moving day, and we were having a snowstorm. I had to delay a day.

Oh! Come! On!

I had loaded the car, filled with excitement to take my first load of belongings, but the freaking car wouldn't start. This had happened once before, but then it miraculously began starting again a few days later. I refused to let this delay my escape from Hrdlořezy much longer, so I had someone help me find a repairman that would come to my flat to repair it then and there. The repairs cost almost as much as the car had, but finally, I was able to move my things and my person out of the beehive.

My new flat was in Vršovice on a street called U Vršovického nádraží. "At the Vrsovice train station." It was a mouthful, but at least it didn't make me think someone was coming to slaughter me. As soon as I moved, I was headed home to California for Christmas for three weeks. I could not wait!

I was mentally drained from how hard it was to get our work done here, and I had been cold for months. I was craving Tomboy's chili burgers and warmer weather. I loved Prague and living in the Czech republic, but every few months, I craved a good dose of friendly service, great food, efficiency, and logical logic.

I wished my coworkers and friends "Veselé vánoce!" (Merry Christmas!) And just like that, I was off.

Manhattan Beach or bust!

Quarterly News

of the

WEIRD AND WONDERFUL

OCTOBER-DECEMBER 1993

CHANGE WAS HAPPENING. We could feel it, and the *Fleet Sheet* reflected it. Motivations were changing. Advertising was taking off slowly and awkwardly. Entrepreneurs were navigating the new world. Air pollution was still terrible due to the heavy use of brown coal. But the nuclear power plants continued to struggle. And worst of all, Café Slavia was closed again. Indefinitely. People were furious. The Czechs. The expats. The tourists. And it did not go unnoticed.

(RK/2) Karel Kánský, a professor at CERGE in Prague, says that public toilets have started to stink again as Czechs have lapsed back into their bad habits of the past. Poorly maintained toilets, he says, are a symbol of the apathy overcoming Czechs. For a brief period after the revolution, toilet attendants, sales clerks and waiters found pride in their work. But only through proper economic reward can people now be motivated, he argues.

Public bathrooms were my nemeses. The babičkas kept them clean and sat outside the door, charging a few Kč for a few squares of scratchy toilet paper. But even if I had my own tissue, I was often turned away because I didn't have the right coins. I almost never did. But at least they used to be clean!

(MFD/2) More than half of Czechs (52.9%) say they would prefer a government that ruled with a firm hand, according to a recent poll. Vice Chairman Daniel Kroupa of ODA says that this does not mean that they are yearning for a dictatorship, but rather that they want an end put to the chaos that overwhelmed postcommunist countries when the former totalitarian regimes were pushed out.

Oh wow. Just wow. I supposed it was a little chaotic, but hopefully they would push through!

(LN/2) Director Vladimír Velenský of the Konstruktiva underground parking garage on Prague's Jan Palach Square says that he might have to rent out part of the underused 450-car facility as a storage site for potatoes to increase revenues. Laxity on the part of the police in enforcing parking rules on the street is the major cause of the garage's misfortunes, he claims.

I loved it. Someone took initiative! A true entrepreneur.

(MFD/2) A cartoon pictures Czech Defense Minister Josef Zieleniec talking with NATO head Manfred Worner. "We know that the Czech Republic represents an island of peace in the postcommunist world," Worner says. "But what's this we've been hearing about a cruel battle in Prague over some café?"

Café Slavia was international news!

I went to see *Jurassic Park* when it came to the theater. It was subtitled in Czech, so I was excited to simply watch a movie in English. Sadly, the sound system was so bad that I couldn't understand a word. But the dinosaurs were great.

(LN/2) Because Czech theaters need the money, they reportedly gladly welcome all children to such films as "Jurassic Park", even though this particular one is considered too scary for those under age 13.

Christmastime carp sellers were on street corners all around Prague. Huge vats of carp. Wooden blocks for the killing, scaling, and gutting. And rivers of blood flowing down the streets.

(MFD/PR1) Street sales of (live) carp, a traditional Czech Christmas food, began yesterday at several Prague sites. Prices average about Kč 60 per kilo. Scaling and gutting are often extra, but killing is included in the price.

Almost every day during the winter, when I blew my nose, it was black. Schools were shut, and people were told to keep their windows closed. I came from L.A. with its well-known air pollution. We had nothing on Prague.

(HN/1) Pollution levels reached record highs in Northern Bohemia yesterday. In Prague, the police are considering restricting car travel.

(MFD/Thur/3) Czech men, it seems, don't have the well-publicized problem faced by their British counterparts in finding a condom that is big enough. Vulkán, the major Czech producer, has never heard any complaints from customers about size. But then Vulkán's are up to 40mm longer and 10mm wider that the British versions.

I was amused that this was considered a news highlight.

For real. Thank goodness we weren't trying to drive. The metro and trams were much smoother. You would have thought snow was new here.

(HN/2) As usual, the paper says, the year's first snow caused calamity on the streets of Prague yesterday.

(MFD/Sat/X) Czech Television will air the finals Sat. of a wet t-shirt contest that attracted nearly 300 entries. Producer Čestmír Kopecký says he hasn't been satisfied with the Miss Czech pageants, where language knowledge and public speaking are more important than beauty. Make no mistake about it, the paper says, Sat.'s contest will be about breasts.

Charming.

(MFD/Sat/3) The Dukovany nuclear-power plant, which supplies one-fourth of the Czech Republic's electricity, will likely remain in use for 35-40 years instead of the 20 years originally planned because experts agree that the facility's useful life is longer than previously assumed. Dukovany's first reactor was put into use in 1985.

This seemed to be going from bad to worse! How was this a good idea?

Ummm . . . nothing to see here . . .

(MFD/1) More than 100 kilograms of Semtex plastic explosive - enough to blow up 300 medium-sized airplanes - were reported stolen near Carlsbad over the weekend.

PRAGUE
1994

NEW FLAT

JANUARY 1994
PRAGUE

I COULDN'T SLEEP.

Thwink. Thack. Spach. Sprrrrrrrrrrr.

It was my first night back in Prague after going home for Christmas. I was in my new flat. I opened one of my suitcases right away to unpack the cheddar cheese I'd brought back with me. The microwave popcorn, Reese's peanut butter cups, and instant oatmeal could wait. I was surrounded by duty free bags from a wild shopping spree at Heathrow Airport. New clothes for me!

Tomorrow, I would be heading to Arthur Andersen's new office. We had moved from the disco building on Wenceslas Square to a beautiful, modern building on Husova. It was like I was getting a fresh start this year. Or was it?

Thwink. Thack. Spach. Sprrrrrrrrrrr.

I couldn't sleep . . .

The new flat was modern, freshly painted, and in good condition. The floor plan was a huge square dissected into four equal-sized squares. One of these squares was a massive entryway with a small bathroom. There were doors to the two adjoining rooms. One of these rooms had a door to the fourth room—Tereza's bedroom. I was left to choose one of the rooms off the entryway to be my bedroom. One was clearly the family room. It had large windows and a fireplace. It was lovely. But Tereza would have to traverse through it to get in and out of her bedroom every time she wanted to come and go or even use the bathroom. That just seemed awkward for everyone. So I checked out the other room that would *have* to be my bedroom . . . and there was the kitchen.

IN. THE. BEDROOM.

I had flashbacks to the Dušní flat where the bedroom was in the kitchen. Was this normal? Although the flat had been advertised as a two-bedroom, it was unclear what the intent was. Neither of these rooms was suitable to be a bedroom, and I certainly wasn't going to sleep in the entryway. Out of sheer curiosity—and because we were gluttons for punishment—we decided to ask our landlord, the elderly pan Vobruba. The next time he dropped by—which he often did at random—we were standing in the kitchen as we chatted.

ME: "So which room was supposed to be the second bedroom?"

VOBRUBA: "This one."

He waved to the room we were in. The kitchen with a bedroom (or the bedroom with a kitchen). A straight answer. I was pleasantly surprised.

I ventured further . . .

ME: "So, why is the kitchen in here?"

VOBRUBA: "I knocked the wall out."

Oh geez . . . this was intentional. I had to know more.

ME: "But why?"

VOBRUBA: "I heard that Americans like open floor plans, so I knocked it out."

I chuckled. That may be more open than anyone wanted. Somehow it made total sense even though it made no sense at all. I was getting really used to that. More importantly, I'd gotten an answer to a "why" question, which was, in and of itself, a huge accomplishment.

Thwink. Thack. Spach. Sprrrrrrrrrrrr.

But I couldn't sleep in my chosen bedroom. There were no big windows, it was plenty dark, it was nice and cool. The way I like it. I'd had no issue sleeping in the kitchen at Dušní. I hadn't, however, accounted for the fact that the refrigerator at Dušní didn't work.

Thwink. Thack. Spach. Sprrrrrrrrrrrr.

The NOISE! The freaking noise! The refrigerator made a shocking amount of noise cycling on and off. It kept me up at night for weeks.

Thwink. Thack. Spach. Sprrrrrrrrrrrr.

Tereza got up and headed into work earlier than I did, so I never needed to set an alarm. She just woke me from my groggy sleep while she made herself coffee. I am sure I looked like a red-eyed, crazy mess, but she never said a word. And that was the beginning of my day. Every day.

Thwink. Thack. Spach. Sprrrrrrrrrrrr.

NEW FRUSTRATION

I WAS IN HRANICE, in my usual room at the Cementář, after a long day at the cement factory trying desperately to get something done. We still didn't have CNN here, so I was flipping between music videos on MTV, strange game shows on Czech TV, and the German news. I stopped and looked with horror at what I saw on the news. It took me a while to grasp what I was seeing, but there had been a huge earthquake back home in L.A. The telephone in the hotel room only called other rooms, so I had no way to call home to make sure everyone was ok. I watched the German news all evening, trying to figure out where it had happened and how bad the damage was. I finally figured out it was big one—6.7 on the Richter scale—but that it was centered in Northridge, 30 miles from home. Whew. My family was nowhere near there, so they were fine. But so many other people weren't. It was hard to watch, but I couldn't look away.

NEW OFFICE

WHAT WAS I LOOKING AT? There were three coffee machines brewing coffee in the breakroom. Was there a difference? The three pots sat there like some game of three-card monte. Should I risk it and just pick one? Or was that just a disaster in the making?

We had moved into our new office space. It was much nicer. More modern and clean. It lacked some of the amenities we'd valued, like multiple fridges and a shower. But it also didn't have a disco, Peruvian flute players, or Muzak. It was on Karlova Street, right in the heart of Old Town and smack on the tourist walking route. We were excited.

As I pondered my coffee choices, paní Křížová walked up from behind and pointed at my blazer. I looked down and back up at her, confused. Paní Křížová was a lovely addition to the new office. She worked in the breakroom, making sure it was clean and that there was always coffee. She spoke no English and my Czech was still terrible, so we communicated through facial expressions and our hands. She pointed again, but this time, I could see she was pointing at the button on my blazer. She motioned for me to open my jacket. When I did, she scowled. My button was held on by a safety pin. She signaled for me to give her my jacket. She seemed to know my type. She had correctly guessed that I was a "hold it together with a safety pin or duct tape" kind of girl. As I removed my blazer, she went to get me a cup of coffee.

She touched the top of the first coffee pot and said: "Americký." She moved to the left, touched that pot, and said: "Evropský." Then she touched the furthest pot to the left and said: "Český."

Ahhh.

ME: "What's the difference?"

Ok, time for the dictionary. I looked up "difference."

ME: "Rozdíl?"

She nodded her understanding and walked me over to the coffee machines to show me. She opened one at a time and showed me how much coffee was in the filter and then motioned on the pot how much water she'd included. The American filter had 10 cups of coffee for 10 cups of water. What I would consider the appropriate amounts. The European one was stronger; the filter was full of coffee, but she only used about eight cups of water. And the Czech pot was absolutely atomic. She packed the grounds into the filter like brown sugar in a measuring cup before making a pot. Three coffee pots to appeal to three different groups in our office. I was kind of impressed at this level of customer service. And at least it was filtered coffee, so nobody would have grounds in their mouth anymore. She gave me a taste of each before finally handing me an Americký coffee. Good call.

I thanked her for the coffee and handed her my blazer. Fifteen minutes later, she found me at my desk and gave the blazer back—with the button sewn on properly. She shook her head and tsk-tsked me. I knew she thought I was a sad excuse for a woman.

But paní Křížová and I developed a great relationship. I brought her clothes I didn't need anymore. She gave them to her daughter. She checked my clothes every day. As I walked into the kitchen, she put out a flat hand to stop me. I would stand there like a four-year-old as she looked my clothes over, always making me open my blazer just to make sure. When she spotted something, she sewed on buttons or fixed tears as needed.

One day, she excitedly hustled me to the refrigerator because she'd brought me a gift. Homemade slivovice. Of course, she poured me a shot at 9 a.m. because she wanted me to try it. It was even more shocking as a breakfast drink than it would be any other time of day, and somehow, I was always served before 10 a.m. It would have been rude to refuse it, and she was so proud of it. Her husband made it at home. She gifted me a bottle full of liquid that I'm sure could clean a carburetor. I thanked her profusely and knew I had to take it home or she'd notice that I'd abandoned it at work. At some point, pan Kříž (paní Křížová's husband) began working in the office too. I'm not quite sure what he did, but it always felt like I was visiting someone's grandparents when I went to the kitchen for coffee. Or slivovice.

I got up from my desk to get more coffee. I was tired and seriously considering drinking from the evropský pot that day. But as I walked towards the kitchen, I smelled something unpleasant. Had I forgotten to put on deodorant that morning? I ran to the bathroom and locked myself in a stall to check. *Sniff. Sniff.* Whew! It wasn't me. Maybe I'd imagined it.

I headed to the breakroom and the scent returned. It seemed to be following me. I realized it must have been one of our new staff. I didn't know her name, but I'd heard her story. She had been taught that it was bad for your hair to wash it too often. So she only washed it once a month. We could tell where she had been because the scent lingered. The Czechs called her "šmudla." There was no clear translation of this word, but they said it was like the famous photo of the little kid with a bowl of spaghetti poured over his head. I wondered if I should try to tell her, but I'd been here before. I thought twice. The Czechs didn't believe us about the lights. I assumed she wouldn't believe me about washing her hair. I knew she'd been taught this all her life, maybe as a ploy to save water or because her family couldn't afford shampoo, or maybe her local store never stocked it. The Czechs didn't try to tell her either. We couldn't fight every battle. Šmudla would continue to be šmudla, and we would carry on.

FRIDAYS AT PIZZA TAXI:
FLATS AND LANDLORDS REDUX

JANUARY 1994

ME: "How was everyone's Christmas break?"

Lots of murmurs. "Good," "fun," "nice." And then we launched into our reverse culture shock experiences.

ME: "I had forgotten how little there is to buy here. As soon as I hit Heathrow, I bought a TON of new clothes. And shoes! My high heels are totally impractical here and my flats are worn to hell. Cobblestones are no joke. Heathrow was like a carnival of stores. And I had a credit card. Suddenly, I knew how Jana had felt the first time she went to Harrods. It was almost overwhelming, but I fought my way through it and channeled my inner American."

Everyone nodded in agreement. I think we'd all done some shopping.

JAMIE: "I had forgotten how small the beer bottles are at home. Nobody else thought anything of it, but I felt like a giant every time I grabbed one!"

He was right—the difference between a Czech bottle, which holds about 17 ounces, and an American bottle, which holds 12 ounces, was substantial. When we first came here, the beer bottles seemed huge. But, like everything else, we got used to them. After a year, they seemed normal, and we drank every drop.

Jamie showed us a photo of him holding an American beer. We burst out laughing. He did, indeed, look like a giant holding the tiny "American" bottle.

MIKE: "I brought back a suitcase full of Velveeta, RO*TEL, and tortilla chips. Ready for our next late night queso party after we go dancing."

There were a lot of places to go dancing, but we routinely hit Fx, which was attached to a new vegetarian restaurant, Radost. Eva loved Bunkr. It was in an old Cold War bomb shelter that had been painted black inside and served drinks in flimsy paper cups. I was always afraid to touch anything. It seemed sticky. My favorite was Lavka. It was on the river, and there was an outdoor bar area where you could sit and look at Charles Bridge and the Prague Castle all lit up. It was one of the best views in Prague.

ME: "I brought Oreos and cheddar cheese."

JAMIE: "I brought tortillas and flavored coffee."

We were excited for our next get-together with the expats to enjoy all the treats.

We ordered our usual. Frankovka, wine, beer, and pizza. The pizza here wasn't the best in town anymore—we actually had a lot of great Italian restaurants and pizza places now—but it was tradition to air our grievances here.

Ordering done, I launched into my latest grievance. I was dying to talk to everyone about what I'd encountered upon my return.

ME: "You won't believe what I found when I got back to my flat after the break."

MIKE: "I can only imagine . . ."

ME: "The taxi dropped me off at home. I lugged my luggage up four flights of stairs. And when I walked into my flat, pan Vobruba was there. Alone. He just let himself in."

EVA: "Oh, I HATE when they do that. I know they own the flat, but once they rent it out, they really need to understand that it's not ok to just come in unannounced!"

ME: "Oh, and worse than that . . . he was standing in my kitchen eating
sausage and raw onions."

JAMIE: "What?!"

ME: "Not a care in the world. Just frying sausages and onions. "

MIKE: "But . . ."

ME: "That's not even the most disturbing part."

They stared at me expectantly, waiting for the other shoe to drop.

ME: "It was the fact that he was in his tighty-whities."

EVA: "Holy sh*t, dahling. His tighty-whities?"

Laughter broke out immediately at the image of this 80-year-old man,
with his skinny legs and his tighty-whitey underwear, standing in my
kitchen having a sausage and onion snack.

JAMIE: "At least he was in the kitchen." He snickered.

ME: "Well yes, but since the kitchen is IN MY BEDROOM . . ."

We gasped for air through the laughter.

ME: "I asked him what he was doing. He just looked at me like I was a
moron and said, 'I am having a snack.'"

They lost it. There was no good response to that.

The rest of the night was full of questions. Why was he there? Where were
his clothes? Why had he taken them off? Couldn't he have eaten his snack
somewhere else? With his clothes on? Had he bathed? Had he napped in
my bed? The questions went on and on. We entertained all sorts of possi-
bilities. Not a single scenario seemed reasonable or acceptable to us.

ME: "Stephen and Sharise got a new flat after being abruptly kicked out of
their last one. The new flat has all sorts of showering problems."

MIKE: "But do they have hot water?"

We all laughed. Mike's coal shoveler incident would never not be funny
to us.

ME: "The hot and cold water come out of separate spouts, and turning one
on turns the other off. That alone sounds horrible. But they also don't

have a showerhead on the wall, just the handheld kind, so they decided to get one installed."

JAMIE: "This is not going to end well."

ME: "Actually, they got their showerhead! But when Sharise showed him how high up she wanted it, the man asked her—in all seriousness—'Your husband stands when he showers?'"

Jamie shook his head and Mike laughed.

ME: "Sharise tried to keep a straight face as she shrugged her shoulders and answered 'yes,' as if there was nothing she could do about his crazy behavior."

We rolled with laughter.

ME: "They're having a hell of a time. There was a tenant meeting in the building, after which their landlord told them nobody likes them."

MIKE: "I'm afraid to ask why."

ME: "Well, they had a clogged kitchen sink and made the mistake of calling a plumber."

Jamie chuckled.

ME: "Their drain was fixed, but the plumber moved the clog down and stopped up the flats below. A big group de-clog was scheduled for a few weeks out. Until that happened, they weren't able to use their kitchen. And then the sink gurgled. Black, greasy water filled the sink and overflowed onto the floor. Then the washing machine joined in. Their house stayed that way until the big de-clog."

So many things were maddening. But we learned to roll with it.

We clinked our glasses. Na zdraví!

MATRÓNA AND THE MACHO PIG

FEBRUARY 1994
HRANICE

WE WERE HEADED BACK to the cement factories for the new year's audit. Vašek and I had learned a lot about each other over the past year. Vašek was clearly raised in a very chauvinistic way. He didn't treat women badly. In fact, he coddled them. He did so because he self-assuredly felt he was much smarter and stronger than they were. He thought women were weak: mentally, emotionally, and physically. I made it my mission to show him he was wrong.

One day, we were chatting away as we worked.

VAŠEK: "I know you like yogurt. Do you like village cheese?"

ME: "Well. I've never heard of village cheese."

VAŠEK: "Yes you have. You know, it's the cheese with all the curds. I can never remember the right name."

ME: "You mean cottage cheese?"

VAŠEK: "Yes! That's the one. Cottage cheese."

ME: "That's hilarious. Any other terms you're not sure of?"

VAŠEK: "Yes. What is the right name for shark arms?"

I giggled. Just the image of a shark with arms.

ME: "Fins?"

VAŠEK: "Yes! That's it. Fins. Need to remember that. I'm always trying to get better at English."

ME: "Your English is very good, Vašek."

VAŠEK: "Díky."

He used one of the short, informal version of "děkuji," or thank you. I felt happy he was being informal with me.

ME: "I've heard that you're 'really good in the Czech language.' All the Czechs say so. But I really don't know what that means. Isn't everyone here good at Czech?"

VAŠEK: "Not everyone." He shrugged.

Great.

ME: "Still no idea what that means."

He smiled. As if he had a secret that I hadn't figured out yet.

A few minutes later, he threw out something new.

VAŠEK: "When I heard that my new boss was a woman arriving from America, I thought you would be different."

ME: "Oh? What did you think I'd be like?"

VAŠEK: "I thought you'd be an overweight, nerdy accountant with thick glasses, a pocket protector, and . . . what do you call these?" He motioned up his lower arms.

ME: "Sleeves?"

VAŠEK: "The plastic ones that go over your clothes."

I couldn't help but smirk. I was pretty sure accountants hadn't worn plastic sleeves to prevent ink from staining their shirts since the 1950s when they still used pocket protectors and green eyeshades.

ME: "Well, that's not a pretty picture. Were you surprised when I showed up?"

VAŠEK: "Oh yes. But I still call you the same name."

ME: "The same name? What name?"

VAŠEK: "I call you matróna."

I snorted and would have spit out my coffee if I'd had any.

ME: "Matróna?! Like matronly?"

Now Vašek was grinning. It had been a running joke with others in the office awaiting my arrival. Until then, it had been almost entirely men. I was the only female expat in the audit practice.

VAŠEK: "In Czech, a matróna is a big, burly woman who is a prison warden or hospital administrator."

I can only imagine their surprise when I showed up. I was a short, outspoken, feisty 25-year-old from California with a perm from hell. An emotionless bureaucrat, I was not. I struggled constantly to keep my thoughts and emotions off my face and from coming out of my mouth. I was, in no way, this "matróna" they had been expecting.

It wasn't a compliment. But I didn't take offense. I figured it was only fair for him to call me matróna since I affectionately called him "Vašek, the Macho Pig" to my friends back home.

Back at Cement Hranice, they put us into a new conference room. No more socialist library. This room was a little more cozy. Largely because of the enormous orange and brown shag rug hanging on the wall as if it were some sort of art.

It was midmorning and I needed more coffee. I poured water over the grounds so it would be drinkable in 10 minutes or so.

ME: "Markéta, can you go talk to paní Polášková? I don't understand the documents she gave us."

MARKÉTA: "Yo, yo."

Markéta grabbed the files and left our conference room. While she was away, I chatted with Ladislav. He was a Czech statutory auditor; we had one every job. He was a little older, with flyaway eyebrows and a mischievous smile. He also let us call him by his first name; the other statutory auditor did not. He would review the same records we did, but his report would align with the Czech accounting standards, while our report was done in accordance with international standards. The results were wildly different, and I was delighted I wasn't responsible for the Czech report.

I had barely started chatting with Ladislav, and was still waiting for my coffee to settle, when Markéta returned. Way too soon. And she was empty-handed.

ME: "What happened?"

MARKÉTA: "She said she's too drunk to help me right now."

It took me a minute to process what Markéta had just said to me. Not only was the client drunk at work, but she told Markéta that as if it was a totally rational explanation for not helping us. Not to mention, it was 10:30 a.m. on a Monday. Paní Polášková was one of those Czechs who was probably 40 but looked like she was 60. The smoking, the fried food, the cold, and the day drinking in this case. You unmistakably saw it in some of their faces.

I looked at Ladislav to see if he thought this was a problem. He gave me the shrug, and I realized this was out of my hands. I mean, what were we going to do? Another situation I'd never encountered at home.

ME: "Ok then. We'll try again tomorrow."

My Czech lessons were finally paying off! My brain had somehow absorbed something.

The team was discussing how long they should depreciate an item and debating—in Czech—whether or not to ask me a question. They were worried about looking bad if they should have already known the answer. After listening to them discuss it for some time, I simply provided the answer in English.

ME: "10 years."

Their heads all whipped towards me in disbelief. Vašek whispered, "She's dangerous . . ."

Mission accomplished.

We turned our attention to their land. We had a list of properties with a lot of crazy notations on it. The three of us went to see Langr, the economic director, to get a better understanding of what it said.

ME: "Can you tell me what this notation says?" I pointed to a note that seemed to point to several line items. Markéta and Ladislav took turns translating.

LANGR: "These parcels of land belong to us, but not everyone agrees."

ME: "Ummm . . . what does that mean?"

LANGR: "We know we own them but can't find proof. A few other companies think they own them, so we're in a dispute."

Perfect.

ME: "Ok . . . so what's the item written in different handwriting at the bottom of the page?"

LANGR: "That's a piece of land we own that hasn't been properly recorded in the accounting system."

ME: "How so? Can you fix it?"

LANGR: "We need to find documentation showing how much we paid for it."

Oh great. Property they own isn't on the books. Property they can't prove they own IS on the books.

ME: "Ok . . . anything else we should know?"

LANGR: "Yes. We have some plots of land in other parts of Moravia. They were not properly marked or blocked off from the public and people have been using them as rubbish heaps."

ME: "Oh dear. Is there a plan for dealing with this?"

LANGR: "We might be liable for environmental penalties due to the dumping."

That must be some horrific rubbish.

ME: "What kind of plots are these? What would Cement Hranice have used them for?"

LANGR: "They're old quarries."

Oh, fantastic. Quarries full of toxic rubbish. I made a note to myself that we may need to consider whether someone could get sick or injured, and then there could be insurance claims. If those were a thing here.

That was four accounting issues to contend with that I'd never imagined or come across before. Never mind the bigger business problems. I had a lot of research to do.

Sigh.

On top of everything else, the computer network at Cement Hranice was a sh*tshow.

Ladislav and I interviewed the head of technology, pan Nechvátal. We had no idea what we were dealing with here.

LADISLAV: "Tell us about your computer system."

NECHVÁTAL: "We have a network with three main programs: accounting, sales, and fixed assets."

ME: "They have a sales program? I'm surprised. Can you ask him more about that?"

NECHVÁTAL: "We use it to track our inventory."

Ummmm. Ok . . . that isn't right. Where do they track sales?

ME: "Can you ask him about the other systems then?"

Ladislav asked a bunch more questions. The answers weren't any more sensible to me than the first one had been. Accounting was used for accounting but not payroll. And fixed assets weren't used to track fixed assets at all. They kept track of those on paper.

ME: "My brain hurts, but let's find out how they pay people."

NECHVÁTAL: "We have a wages software program, but it's not on the network."

ME: "Why not? Where is it?"

NECHVÁTAL: "We run it on a separate computer to ensure confidentiality."

ME: "What? Don't people have passwords?"

NECHVÁTAL: "It's impossible to have this program password protected on the larger company network."

ME: "Wait. There are no passwords used here?"

NECHVÁTAL: "Each network user has his or her own name and password assigned. But then everyone can see all the programs."

I had so many questions. Where to start?

ME: "Ok. How often do you change passwords?"

NECHVÁTAL: "We don't."

ME: "Never?"

NECHVÁTAL: "They haven't ever been changed since we started the network."

Oh, dear God. When that was, nobody seemed to know. It could have been decades. And clearly, there was never, ever any intention to change the passwords on a regular basis. I felt certain the passwords were written on paper and taped to the desks.

ME: "Ok. New question. How often do you back up the system? And where is it backed up to?"

NECHVÁTAL: "All backup tapes are stored in a cupboard in the room where the server is located."

I hung my head a little. That defeats the purpose of a backup.

ME: "How do you keep that room safe? Is there a security system or fire alarm system?"

NECHVÁTAL: "We don't have either of those in the tech department."

So the server and all the backup tapes could go up in flames together. Fantastic.

Simply put, the entire computer system was as trustworthy as a blowhard politician. We couldn't rely on these controls at all.

Notes for Stephen:

They might own the land on the books, but they might not. They might own land that isn't on the books, but they might not. They own land they don't use, and now it's hazardous and could present legal liabilities.

All the records could go up in smoke at once.

They have unsatisfactory safeguarding of the computer. I guess they would let everybody in.

LETTER HOME

FEBRUARY 1994

Dear Mom and Dad,

Hi! How are you? I'm in Hranice na Moravě right now. My "favorite" town in the Czech republic. (UGH!) I'm staying at the Cementář hotel and going to work at 7 a.m. every day in -15°C (4°F) cold. It's really the life, isn't it? Actually, it gives me a lot of free time to read, write letters, and watch the Olympics with no distractions whatsoever. Shockingly, the Cementář now has not only MTV but Eurosport as well! Still no CNN but at least I get to watch the Olympics with English commentary! Tonight was fairly thrilling. The U.S. played Slovakia in ice hockey. Tomorrow night, the Czech republic plays Germany so we may have a beer and hockey "party" in my hotel room. (Oooh!) And right now I'm actually watching the pairs figure skating. (I was getting so sick of ice hockey!)

Love,

Melanie

CHAIRS AND STOOLS

FEBRUARY 1994

THE RESTAURANT WAS EMPTY but for our group and the waitstaff. *Empty.* Stephen was in town again and took the whole team out to dinner at our favorite Czech restaurant in the center of Hranice. We always chose this restaurant when Stephen was in town because it was more expensive, and he always picked up the tab. Stephen and I were the only foreigners on the team, and the Czechs were appreciative when he bought dinner. But for whatever reason, we always seemed to cause a stir when we were there. Last time, you would have thought he asked them to put a man on Mars when Stephen tried to order a dessert that wasn't on the menu. But on this inglorious night, I was the cause of the drama.

Reservations weren't a thing in the Czech republic at the time. Not that it mattered. The restaurant was completely empty. Serving us was the only thing the waitstaff had to do that night. The hostess seated us at a table in the corner.

The restaurant had low tables and seating. Some of the seats were low chairs with backs, but others were backless stools. Our table only had stools. I was tired and wanted to be able to lean back in my chair. The table next to us had all chairs. As everyone was looking at the menu (I didn't need to; I knew what I would order), I swapped my stool for a chair from the next table. I sat down and looked at the menu just for fun.

WAITRESS: "Teď musíte odejít! Tady nesmíte jíst! Nesmíte sem znovu přijít!"

I whipped my head. The waitress was yelling directly at me and was clearly pissed off about something. I looked at the team as if to say, "What is she yelling about?" The Czechs calmly put down their menus, stood up, and grabbed their briefcases. Stephen and I swiveled our heads in confusion. What was going on? What the hell had happened? Was there a fire? Why was she yelling at me directly?

WAITRESS: "Vstávej! Musíš okamžitě vypadnout!"

She wouldn't stop. How could we make it end?

The entire team was standing except for Stephen and me.

MARKÉTA spoke up: "We have to leave."

ME: "What? Why?"

MARKÉTA: "We need to leave right now. *Right. Now.*"

She seemed anxious but calmly hustled all of us out of the restaurant as quickly as possible.

The waitress stopped yelling as the front door was closing. I stopped outside and caught my breath.

ME: "What happened?"

MARKÉTA: "We can never come back here."

ME: "What do you mean?"

MARKÉTA: "We can never come back to this restaurant."

ME: "Ever?"

MARKÉTA: "Ever."

ME: "Why?"

MARKÉTA: "Because you moved the chairs."

ME: "Wait, what? Seriously?"

MARKÉTA: "Yes."

ME: "All I did was swap my stool for a chair."

MARKÉTA: "Yes. You moved the chairs."

ME: "I don't understand."

MARKÉTA: "We can never come back."

I couldn't get any real explanation as to why this was such a big faux pas. *Is the waitress just angry she'll have to move the chair back? But why would she have to move it back? Is there a government-mandated chair and table configuration? Does the waitress just want an excuse to kick us out so she won't have to serve us? Is she just having a bad day?*

Whatever it was, it was a serious bummer since there were only two other restaurants in town. The Czechs took it in stride. This was just the way things were. I was totally frustrated. How could I avoid making such a big mistake in the future if I had no idea what the rules were or what I'd done wrong?

Years later, I would ask Markéta about this incident. There was still no explanation. She just laughed, gave me the shrug, and with a glint in her eye said, "I would have known not to move the chairs."

CAPITALISM?

LANGR: "We've made some investments."

ME: "Oh?"

This was a huge surprise, and I had no idea what to make of it.

Investing was a completely foreign concept. There had been no shareholders and no stock exchange. Investing didn't exist. Only now, Czech citizens had vouchers they could use to invest in Czech companies, thereby transferring some ownership to the people. They would be the first shareholders. Additionally, foreign companies were making significant investments in Czech companies. Somehow, Cement Hranice had invested in several smaller Czech companies in the building/construction industry as part of their effort to appeal to foreign investors and emerge as a leader in the new market. This was cutting edge in 1994. We needed to know more.

The chief accountant, Langr, gave us an overview of their investments. There were a shocking number of them. They had 100 percent ownership of two companies and direct investments in seven others. Everything from machinery maintenance to paint to design services. We also learned that they owned the Hotel Cementář! It explained so much. Why in the world was a cement factory running a hotel? Now I knew why we had to stay there even though there was a much nicer place nearby.

As part of the audit, we needed to confirm the value of these investments. We planned road trips to visit five of these companies to make sure they were being valued properly. First up was Tiles Olomouc.

JASON, THERESE, THE TRAM, AND THE COFFEE MUGS

JAMIE AND I WERE TAKING THE TRAM from my flat into the center. Very few expats lived out that way so we were always the only foreigners on the tram. Until this day.

THERESE: "Hey! Are you guys American?"

We were surprised someone was speaking English to us.

ME: "We are! Are you guys?"

JASON: "Yes. We just moved into a flat on U Vršovického nádraží."

ME: "No way. I live there too."

We did, in fact, turn out to live in the same building. We had to be the only expats.

JAMIE: "Was it super obvious we're American? How did you know?"

Therese pointed at our travel coffee mugs.

I laughed so hard. It was a dead giveaway but we'd never realized it. Czechs absolutely never carried beverages around with them. There was no coffee "to go" here. No innovation. No new ways of doing things. The customer was always last. Jamie bought coffee beans in Austria, brewed coffee at home, and carried it in to work so he could avoid the office coffee.

JAMIE: "Ha. Totally makes sense but I mean, I can't drink that office sludge every day."

THERESE: "Have you tried the new Seattle place?"

JAMIE: "What Seattle place?"

THERESE: "There's a new coffee shop that sells coffee TO GO! It's called Seattle Takeout or something like that."

ME: "Ohmigod. Where is it? We have to go try it."

JASON: "It's on the main tourist drag, Karlova. You can't miss it. They also sell T-shirts with different Prague logos and sayings on them."

JAMIE: "No way. Real souvenirs?"

We were floored and couldn't wait to check it out. Or Czech it out, as one of the T-shirts said.

ME: "So what are you guys doing in Prague?"

THERESE: "I teach English."

JASON: "And I'm about to start working at a not-for-profit focused on education."

There were four types of expats in Prague: professionals, entrepreneurs, English teachers, and backpackers. The backpackers were easy to spot—drinking on Charles Bridge, writing in their journals, pretending they were Kafka. The entrepreneurs were brave souls, trying to open Western restaurants in a completely foreign business and customer environment. The English teachers were welcomed by people who'd been taught Russian for decades and now pretended they didn't speak it. And the professionals worked at generally large Western companies supporting the transition.

ME: "Oh cool. But how's your Czech?"

Therese launched into two sentences in Czech that were complete gibberish to Jamie and me.

ME: "Was that Czech?"

THERESE: "Yes. I said 'Please take your seats. Let's begin today's lesson.'"

Whoa. I had never heard any of those words except "prosím."

ME: "Ok let me try one. Jsem auditor. Mohu prosím dostat kopii hlavní knihy?"

JASON: "What was that?!"

JAMIE: "She said 'I'm the auditor. Can I please have a copy of the general ledger?'"

We all laughed. It hit us that not only were we in different factions of expats, but that those factions probably all knew wildly different Czech words and phrases. But we all knew the words for please, thank you, beer, and pork.

We became fast friends.

U ŠATLAVY

FEBRUARY 1993
ČESKÝ KRUMLOV

A FEW MONTHS BACK Anna had told all of us about a restaurant she'd found in the medieval town of *Český Krumlov*. She'd been wandering around the town and kept seeing people go in and out of an unmarked door. Not a lot of people but a steady stream. After watching this for a while she'd decided to see what it was. And what she'd found was amazing to me. After hearing about it, I knew I had to go. She told me how to find it if I ever made it to *Český Krumlov*.

Jamie and I had heard great things about *Český Krumlov* so decided to go for a weekend.

The town has been there since around 1250, when the castle was built. The old town is surrounded by part of the river running through town and most of the buildings were built from the 13th through 17th centuries in Gothic, Baroque, and Renaissance styles. And since around 1700, the castle moat has been occupied by bears—and still is today. A trip to *Český Krumlov* is like going back in time.

After visiting the castle and roaming through the medieval streets, we decided to try to find this mysterious restaurant. We navigated the streets using a map Anna had drawn on the back of a beer coaster. We came to the spot she'd marked and saw a door with a goblet hanging above it. After seeing a few people go in and out, we decided this must be it. We cautiously pushed the door open.

It was dark, lit only by a fire and candles. There were a handful of wooden benches and tables; only a few already occupied. We sat at one of the tables and a waitress, dressed in medieval peasant clothing, came with a piece of wood for each of us on which the menu was engraved. There were only three items: pork something, pork something, and beef something. We ordered beef and beer.

We enjoyed our beer served in ceramic steins, while the waitress cooked the meat over the fire in the center of the room. The meat arrived on a wooden plank with a knife that was curved at the end so it could also be used as a fork. Beautiful celtic music played from the only item giving away that we were in the 21st century—a boombox. Other than that, it felt like we'd stepped through a magical doorway to medieval times. If only I'd worn my Renaissance Faire costume, and I would have fit right in.

My favorite restaurant in the world. U Šatlavy. At the goblet.

Ok that turned out to be wrong. It was U Šatlavy because it was at Šatlavksá street, not because there was a goblet hanging above the door.

Sigh.

To me it would still always be "at the goblet."

ANDREA AND THE BAILEYS

FEBRUARY 1994

IT WAS 9:30 A.M. AND I NEEDED COFFEE. I went to the office kitchen to see paní Křížová and choose from the various coffee pots. I was wearing a long, black wrap skirt that I loved. It had three buttons down each hip and was made of a heavy fabric that hung nicely and made me feel slim.

Before I could even think of grabbing a coffee cup, paní Křížová pointed at the buttons on my skirt. She pointed insistently. She wanted to know if they were properly sewn on or if, perhaps, I had safety pinned any of them. *Dammit.*

I flipped the waist down a bit, and she saw a safety pin. She motioned for me to hand her my skirt.

I was paralyzed. Could she possibly mean that? I held up my hands in an exasperated gesture. I couldn't take off my skirt in the breakroom! She signaled for me to follow her. Where were we going?

I followed her into the restroom. She nudged me into a stall and put her hand under the door. Waiting impatiently for me to hand her my skirt. *Sigh.* I had no real choice in the matter. She would not relent. I removed my skirt and sat on the edge of the toilet seat, wondering exactly how long I would be trapped in the stall wearing nylons and a blouse. Three of the six buttons were going to need to be sewn on. I wished I had gotten a coffee first.

A few women came in and out of the restroom. I stayed quiet so as not to draw attention to the fact that I was just hanging out in there. Mercifully, paní Křížová was a quick seamstress. She returned in a few minutes and gave me my skirt back. When I emerged, now properly dressed, she handed me a cup of americký coffee. She knew me.

I went to office entrance to say hi to the new receptionist, Andrea. Most of the staff walked right past her as she answered the phones and greeted visitors to the office. She was a bit of a scowler, but that just made me want to try to connect and get to know her better. I loved a challenge, and I was curious what was up with her. So every day I made a point of saying hello. On this day, I finally broke through the proverbial wall.

ME: "Dobrý den!"

ANDREA: "Dobrý den. Jak se máš?"

ME: "Good! How was your weekend?"

ANDREA: "Dobrý. Dobrý. Chceš Baileys?"

Did I want Baileys? Maybe this meant something else. I mean, it wasn't even 10 a.m.

ME: "Baileys?"

ANDREA: "Yes."

She signaled for me to look behind her desk. She did, indeed, have a bottle of Baileys Irish Cream in her desk drawer. Well, ok then! Definitely better than slivovice. I said sure and waited to see how this was going to go down.

She stood and signaled for me to follow her. We went into the massive, cold, stone stairwell of the building and sat on the steps. She poured a generous splash of Baileys into each of our coffee cups. Wow. That definitely made this coffee more palatable.

And this is how Andrea and I became friends. Once a week, we would hang out on the stairs and drink our coffee with Baileys. We talked about our countries, men, the expats, and the future. But mostly about men.

TILES OLOMOUC

MARCH 1994
OLOMOUC

IT WAS OUR FIRST SITE VISIT. As was typical under the communist government, the company was named after the product and the city it was in. No creativity here. We entered a completely empty and silent production facility. No workers on the floor. Machines eerily still. The director was proudly telling us about the tiles they made there. We had a lot of things we wanted to know about the company. About the customers, the facility, the suppliers, and the tiles but were stopped in our tracks after the first question.

ME: "What are the tiles made from?"

VAJDIČKA: "Wood and asbestos."

ME: "Ummmm . . . what?"

I hoped I'd misheard Vajdička or that his English was terrible. I looked at Martin and was delighted to see that he looked equally stunned.

ME: "Asbestos?"

VAJDIČKA: "Yes. Our customers love them. We also make tiles without asbestos, but they cost more, so nobody is interested. They want the cheaper asbestos tiles."

That seemed like a high price to pay for cheaper tiles. Like with your life.

ME: "What's the price difference?"

VAJDIČKA: "Asbestos-free products sell for almost 50 percent higher than asbestos products. But it's a challenge because the workers can only work in this environment for 36 hours a week compared to 42 for the asbestos-free tiles."

My eyes bulged a little. How did that one little fact not make it clear what a bad idea this was?

ME: "So . . . how many customers do you have?" I held my breath hoping there weren't a lot of people buying these tiles of death.

VAJDIČKA: "It's very sad. We used to have a lot of customers but not now. New environmental regulations require that we stop producing these."

Sad indeed. No more homes covered in asbestos. At least this explained why the facility was a ghost town. And thank goodness! Otherwise, we'd be standing in a swirl of asbestos.

ME: "Oh! Is that why this place is so quiet today?"

VAJDIČKA: "Yes. We've slowed down production because nobody wants the regular tiles, and we aren't buying any more asbestos. We'll use up what we have, but then we plan to shut down and scrap the machines."

Our work was done here. We thanked the director for his time and got out as quickly as possible, eternally grateful to get away from asbestos ground zero.

Company value = zero.

FRIDAYS AT PIZZA TAXI: SOCIALIZED MEDICINE

MARCH 1994
PRAGUE

BRENDA: "You won't believe what happened when I went to the doctor."

She opened the first bottle of Frankovka and began pouring. I popped some pre-hangover preventative Advil, washing it down with the red Czech wine.

ME: "Oh God—you had to see a doctor here?"

BRENDA: "Yes—remember I broke my leg while I was home for a visit and came back with a cast? Well, this week, I had to have the cast removed."

ME: "Yes . . ."

That sounded easy enough. Our interest was piqued.

BRENDA: "After waiting hours for my turn to go in, I limped into the doctor's office. I expected him to pull out a cast saw like they use at home."

ME: "He didn't?"

BRENDA: "No . . . he pulled out an enormous pair of scissors!"

JAMIE: "Scissors?"

We all gasped in horror.

BRENDA: "Like hedge trimmers! He put one blade under the cast and started trying to cut it. He tried again and again. The cast wouldn't cut. The blades simply weren't sharp enough."

ME: "But of course not."

BRENDA: "So he kept trying and pressing harder and harder. Next thing I know, he shoved the tip of the scissors into my leg, and I started gushing blood!"

ME: "No way!"

BRENDA: "Yes way!"

We shook our heads in horror, waiting for the rest of the story.

BRENDA: "Now the blood was dripping down my leg and out of the cast. He still didn't stop. Blood was everywhere. My leg was covered. Finally, he managed to get the cast off. And then I needed seven stitches. Unreal."

My eyes widened as I realized how bad this was. Everyone started talking at once, asking if she was ok now. We were glad she had lived to tell the tale.

MIKE: "I had to go to the doctor a few weeks ago. I think it was supposed to be free, but he wanted payment."

JAMIE: "Like a service fee?"

MIKE: "More like a bribe . . ."

JAMIE: "Well, you're a foreigner after all. How much did you have to pay him?"

MIKE: "I gave him a bottle of whisky. He seemed happy with that."

So many things were wrong with that, but somehow it was believable. As always, we closed our eyes and shook our heads. And had to laugh. The standard response to life's absurdities. We were always paying more because we were foreigners. But paying a doctor with alcohol? Maybe he should switch doctors.

ME: "I heard that Stephen's wife has a good doctor."

JAMIE: "But isn't she going back to the U.S. to give birth to their baby?"

ME: "I guess the doctor wasn't THAT good. And they had that vaccine incident, so maybe they're wary."

JAMIE: "What vaccine incident?"

ME: "It seems there was an encephalitis-carrying tick scare—not sure why nobody told us this—and elementary schools were recommending that children and parents get vaccinated."

MIKE: "I never heard about this."

JAMIE: "Great. Me neither."

ME: "Same. But anyway, Sharise and Stephen went to the hospital for shots, expecting a long line."

MIKE: "Did it take all day?"

ME: "No . . . there was no line at all, and it took them twenty minutes to convince the doctor that such a vaccination existed."

BRENDA: "For the love of . . ."

ME: "The doctor told them they had to go the pharmacy, buy all the shots for a three-dose series, and come back."

MIKE: "But of course. Nothing is efficient."

BRENDA: "Please tell me they actually got their vaccines after all that."

ME: "Oh, they did. The first dose was administered and then they were told to take the remaining doses home, refrigerate them, and come back for the second dose."

Everyone looked at me, waiting for the punchline to the story.

ME: "IN A YEAR!"

Everyone rolled laughing. I mean . . . how is this the way it works?

LAURENT: "I had to go to the doctor a few months ago."

MIKE: "Uh, oh. Why?"

LAURENT: "Well, I had a fever and chills."

MIKE: "Oh no! What was it?"

LAURENT: "Remember how I went to Nicaragua?"

ME: "Uhhh, no. You went to Nicaragua???"

LAURENT: "Yes, on vacation. I've always wanted to go."

We were all pretty surprised that a Frenchman living in Prague wanted to vacation in Nicaragua. But that was beside the point.

LAURENT: "He kept telling me it was different things. I asked him to please test for malaria, but he said I couldn't possibly have malaria. Even after I told him I'd been to Nicaragua, he wouldn't test for malaria. I don't think they've ever seen it before. For all I know, he might not even have the test for it."

ME: "So what did you do?"

LAURENT: "This went on for a few weeks. I told each different doctor I saw that I thought it might be malaria. I got the same reaction every time. It couldn't possibly be malaria and must be something else. So finally, I flew home to Paris. They tested for malaria and—no surprise—it came back positive. They gave me medication, and I was better almost overnight. So now, I am back in Prague. Easy."

We knew we were lucky. We had terrific options back home when it came to healthcare. Czechs didn't.

JAMIE: "So, how was your actual vacation?"

LAURENT: "It was great . . . except for the malaria."

We ate pizza, drank Frankovka, and chatted for hours, grateful for every day we didn't have to see a doctor.

Healthcare News

MARCH 1994

I WAS PRETTY STUNNED by all the stories we'd shared about seeing doctors here. I wanted to do a little more research the only way I could—by reviewing the past *Fleet Sheets* for any stories about healthcare. What I found alarmed me greatly!

That's maybe $1.25 an hour to do heart transplants!!!

(MS/50) Heart surgeons at Prague's Institute of Clinical and Experimental Medicine calculate that they earn 36 crowns per hour for performing transplants.

(MFD/Sat/12) In a satirical column, Martin Komárek honors Health Minister Petr Lom as the Man of the Week. Lom, says Komárek, is fond of praising the nation's health system. Václav Klaus himself was quite pleased with Lom's work until a muscle injury sent him to the hospital not long ago. After facing the lines and the surly nurses, Komárek says, the otherwise physically fit Klaus now figures it's better to give up tennis than risk experiencing the republic's health system again first hand.

Even the leaders of the country don't want to go see a doctor.

(MFD/2) Premier Klaus said yesterday that a new system for rewarding doctors will be introduced at the first of the year. The current point system, whereby doctors are paid according to the number of procedures they perform, should be altered so that doctors are not motivated to increase the number of procedures, Klaus said. One proposal calls for physicians to receive a fixed fee for certain routine visits, regardless of the number of procedures required.

Ohmigod. Paid by number of procedures? That cannot be good.

(MFD/Sat/XII) In a satirical column, Martin Komárek honors Education Minister Petr Pit'ha as the Man of the Week for having such confidence in the school system as the new year begins. If some children are able to survive treatment in Czech hospitals, Pit'ha says (according to Komárek), then there's reason to hope that more than half of students will survive the school system as well.

Ha. This just makes me wonder what the hell is wrong with the school system.

(HN/2) The Czech Dental Association charges that Universal Health Insurance's refusal to pay for local anesthesia during treatment of caries "grossly limits the patient's right to painless dental care." The Association said it is prepared to go to court to have anesthesia covered.

Note to self: Definitely never go to a dentist here. Fly home.

(MFD/3) A Brno dentist who fell into a patient's lap in a drunken stupor while drilling away at the patient's tooth will perhaps be forced to withdraw from the profession, MFD says.

Ditto.

Ummm . . . how was this not easily clarified? Either it was the right one or the wrong one. Right?

(MFD/2) An Ostrava patient says he will sue a private clinic for Kč 1m for operating on the wrong shoulder. He said that after he awoke, he wondered how his right shoulder could feel so good. No wonder, he soon learned. Doctors deny that an error was made.

(MFD/3) A judge yesterday ordered a tuberculosis patient from Carlsbad to be jailed after he escaped several times from a hospital and wandered aimlessly about the country, endangering others. He will likely be charged with spreading an infectious disease.

Oh great. Now we need to worry even if we go nowhere near a hospital or doctor's office.

And now I was committed to never, ever, *ever* needing to see a doctor or dentist here. Under any circumstance. *Sigh.*

HARDWARE ZLÍN

THE NEXT INVESTMENT WE NEEDED to value for Cement Hranice was a chain of hardware stores. We hit the road and made our way to one of the stores. We browsed a bit and then spoke to one of the store managers, pan Netopil, directly.

ME: "I'm not understanding the pricing I see. Can you tell us how the prices are set?"

NETOPIL: "The price of each product is based on the cost of that product."

ME: "Ok, but I see identical items with different prices."

NETOPIL: "That's right. The price of each product is based on the cost of that product."

I could see I was going to have to ask this differently.

ME: "How can two identical products have different prices?"

NETOPIL: "If we bought one of them for 100 Kč and another for 120 Kč, they will have different prices. The first one will be 150 Kč, and the second one will be 170 Kč."

I felt a little light-headed. This was so illogical that it was logical. There was a 50 Kč profit on each item and that was that.

ME: "So if I'm the customer, I can go find the cheaper one?"

NETOPIL: "The prices are separately indicated on a price list available at the store, but if a customer doesn't look at the list, staff are instructed to sell the higher priced product."

But why? The profit to the store would be the same no matter which one was bought. So it didn't matter if they bought the more expensive one. Did it? Was I losing my mind? My brain was going in circles. And I was going to have to start shopping differently ...

We suggested that management consider adopting a radical new pricing approach that took into consideration what the market was prepared to pay for products. While the initial cost of a product was clearly part of pricing decisions, so were competitor prices, sales volume, and market demand. It fell on deaf ears. At least for now.

But in the end, it wasn't going to matter. The inventory would be counted on November 30th and the stores closed on December 1st. Most leases were expiring, and the stores were being returned to their original owners. It would be part of the restitution process—returning property taken by the Communist Party decades earlier and still owned by the government now. The goods in these stores would also be transferred to the owners of the buildings, gratis.

Company value = zero.

Maybe.

Or zero + 50 Kč profit.

ČÍNSKÁ RESTAURACE

CHINESE FOOD WAS ONE OF the very few types of foreign cuisine available in the Czech republic under communism. It was still widely available throughout the country. We were always on the lookout for a uniquely good čínská restaurace in the center of Prague. There was a new one on Vinohradská, so we decided to check it out.

Upon walking in, you could see a modest effort to decorate a "Chinese" restaurant. Like all good Czech čínská restauraces, there were as many red and yellow signs, chair cushions, and red and gold lamé curtains as they could stuff into a bland, kantýna-style room. There were plastic tablecloths and a few outdated Chinese calendars on the walls. Still not really warm and welcoming, but they'd tried, and we appreciated the effort.

The menu was extensive, all things considered. Lots of options. Each item was translated from Mandarin into Czech and English. We read through the dozen or so dishes, but I paused when I came to the seventh item on the menu. I raised my eyebrows and looked at Jamie to see if he'd read it yet. He looked back at me with a bemused smile.

JAMIE: "Chicken in a strange way?"

ME: "What can that possibly mean?"

We studiously analyzed the Czech wording. No help whatsoever. It actually said something similar to "strange chicken." We needed someone who could tell us what the Mandarin said. We called over the waiter.

We asked about the dish in English.

Shrugs.

We asked about the dish in Czech.

Shrugs.

Speaking no Mandarin, we resorted to pointing. We held up the menu and pointed to item #7 and gave him the universal face and arm motions for "what is this?"

Shrugs.

In the end, we weren't brave enough to actually order it and try it, but it struck me how perfectly it encapsulated this entire experience. Each word was clear, but they didn't mean anything when put together. Everything was a little off. It was the perfect metaphor for how it felt to be an expat in this no-man's land between communism and capitalism.

Quarterly News

of the

WEIRD AND WONDERFUL

I'D BEEN IN PRAGUE FOR A YEAR. I had already witnessed incredible change. Companies converting to Western accounting. Customer service making its first appearance. Not successfully, but at least it was a topic of discussion. More food choices. More new businesses. A few more things to buy as gifts. My new favorite shop was Patio, a home décor store where almost everything was made from wrought iron: picture frames, candle holders, and furniture. I furnished my new flat and bought gifts there. And the Czechs maintained their self-deprecating sense of humor about it all.

(RP/Sat/2) Miloš Zeman of the Social Democrats says he wishes that, like Bill Clinton, Czech leaders played the sax or some other musical instrument. This would have a much more beneficial effect on society than what these politicians are doing in office, he says.

The chaos continued.

We all bought the CD.

(MFD/1) At the Reduta club yesterday, Clinton played a few jazz numbers on a new sax given to him by President Havel. Singer Bára Basiková said that Clinton's playing was clean and without any errors.

(LN/1) Václav Klaus writes [in what appears to be the first of a regular column] that few Czechs are actually justified in expressing discontent with their standard of living under the new political and economic order. The others, he says, have simply not learned to live with the new era of freedom, which brings with it the responsibility to fend for oneself.

Before I got to Prague, I couldn't have conceived of how things worked. This freedom was a huge change. I was finally starting to understand just how huge.

Hilarious.

(MS/27) The main cause of divorce, says Mladý svět in an article on failed marriages, is marriage itself.

(LN/Sat/1) A cartoon pictures a couple out gazing at the stars. "If you see the Iron Curtain fall," says the husband, "quick, make a wish."

Hahaha.

WHOA. The Russian leader was something else.

(LN/1) Zhirinovsky says in an interview that he will gladly visit the CR. He criticizes Havel, asking why a playwright should be president, and says that in 10 years Czechs will damn Havel just the way Russians damn Gorbachev today. Czechs in 10 years will be forced to speak German and will forget their native language. They will attend German churches and will clean the boots of German officers, he says. For this reason, he continues, all Slavic nations should join together in a single society. And not serve the West.

(RK/14) In response to Václav Bělo-hradský's salute to McDonaldization [see FS 491], Zvonimír Šorm, a cleric, compares McDonaldization to communism in the way they cast aside tradition. Communism contributed to today's problems of aggression, xenophobia and racism by breaking down culture, he says. McDonaldization promotes an illusory way of life, one that can lead to anarchy and caprice. Given the similarities, he argues, McDonaldization in the CR might be in the wrong place at the wrong time. Czechs need to rebuild their culture and values, he says, not tear them down.

I found it hard to believe McDonald's had this power, but perhaps this was how many of the old guard viewed capitalism.

Hahaha. They were marketing a car by giving away a bike with each purchase. At least they were trying.

(MFD/14) Beginning in early May, Škoda Auto will give a free mountain bike made by Favorit Rokycany with the purchase of each vehicle in a promotional campaign called Bike Line. This is expected to provide a significant boost to Favorit, which is having financial problems.

(HN/2) A fire broke out at the Dukovany nuclear plant yesterday. No injuries were reported and no radioactivity was released.

!!!!!

Ohhhh boy. I knew they didn't understand commercials, but this seemed a bit melodramatic. Maybe?

(HN/19) Head Physician Jan Cimický of the rehabilitation ward at the Bohnice mental hospital in Prague says, referring to Nova, that interrupting films with commercials disturbs the viewer's concentration so much that he won't be able to listen in normal life. A person bombarded with commercials will see his partner just as a TV screen that doesn't require attention, Cimický argues.

(HN/2) Average monthly wages in Czech industry reached Kč 6,283 for Jan., according to the Statistical Office. Construction wages averaged Kč 6,339 monthly.

This was about $200/month. I was shocked how low it was.

Ahhh, the McBůček. A burger with a big round piece of mostly fatty bacon. I passed.

(MFD/XV) In celebration of gaining use of the Czech Made logo, McDonald's will offer a McBůček menu March 18-27 for the reduced price of Kč 29.

Note: We regret any inconvenience caused by our decision to use more abbreviations beginning today.

I really wondered who complained.

Arghghgh.

(RP/3) Nova, which begins broadcasting Fri., plans to interrupt long programs with commercials after 45 minutes, according to Director Vladimír Železný. The Radio and Television Council says that it will take Nova to court if it does.

(LN/1) A legal-support group, Klub právní podpory, has pointed out to justice officials and investigators that some companies - such as Harvard Capital and Komerční banka - were registered in Prague 1 court in a matter of days although many companies must wait months. Those who accompany their request with a gift for the judge are accommodated immediately, the group said.

Well, of course.

PANELS TELČ

MARTIN AND I WENT TO VISIT the panel manufacturer, where we spoke with the chief accountant, paní Milačková, and the production manager, pan Poslušny.

ME: "Please tell us about the panels you make."

POSLUŠNY: "We produce panels made from 80 percent wood and 20 percent cement. They're used in the construction of family houses as molds for the walls. Cement is poured between the panels to form the wall and the panels are left as part of the wall."

I was no construction expert, but this sounded weird to me. At least it wasn't something I'd ever encountered auditing manufacturing companies in Los Angeles.

ME: "And how is business?"

POSLUŠNY: "Production did not start out well initially. A Slovak company was contracted to build the machinery, but they went bankrupt. We paid their bills so they could finish. Finally, in November 1993, production began. Due to a number of mistakes in the production line, the first panels produced were inferior. But we can make 600,000 panels a year now."

Nothing about that sounded like good decision-making to me.

ME: "And do you have customers lined up for these panels when these problems are resolved?"

MILAČKOVÁ: "Rektor at Cement Hranice is responsible for marketing the panels. In November 1993, advertising began, and we received phone calls from many interested parties. Unfortunately, the products were inferior and most of the potential customers did not buy them. We only sold 800, but then we were able to sell the inferior panels to a Hungarian company at a reduced price. We do believe the product will be quite popular once quality control is fixed."

This was all over the place. I couldn't track the thought process at all. Yay—customer inquiries. Boo—few sales. Yay—capacity. Boo—bad quality. Yay—someone buying the crappy panels. Boo—Hungarian houses falling down? I was so confused.

ME: "So, where do you think this business is headed?"

POSLUŠNY: "We'll still have problems with the equipment. It's not very high quality. Production may have to be stopped during a repair, depending on which piece of machinery is out of use."

I was starting to see the production push before my very eyes. Everyone had massive capacity but no need for it. They just produced for the hell of it, as far as I could tell.

Company value = zero.

FRIDAYS AT PIZZA TAXI: COMMUNIST ACCOUNTING

JUNE 1994
PRAGUE

I'D USED MY TONE DIALER to check my voicemail back home. We'd taken to calling each other's U.S. office numbers and leaving messages that we would then check from Prague. It was more efficient than leaving notes on everyone's desk. Jamie had left me a message saying we were all going to U Medvídků that night instead of the usual Pizza Taxi. We wanted pivo and pork for a change from the usual Frankovka and pizza. Oh wow. Now I was craving pork, dumplings, and cabbage. I'd been converted.

The conversation started the same way it always did.

ME: "Is anyone starting to feel insane?"

Everyone blurted out at once. Yeses all around.

I'd been here for a year and a half and yet every day still possessed a little of the surreal.

ME: "Half the questions I ask people elicit a response that's nonsensical to me."

JAMIE: "Well, that's an improvement. It used to be 100 percent."

I snorted a laugh.

HENRY: "Why is that?"

Henry was new. An expat from Seattle had joined the Prague office. He was just starting to experience this world.

ME: "It's better than it used to be. I used to get really frustrated by it, but now I expect it."

JAMIE: "True. And I never ask 'why' anymore. That's just foolish."

MIKE: "The key is to avoid 'why' and also 'yes or no' questions. You'll just get a yes or a no with zero explanation."

ME: "I honestly don't think I've ever heard a Czech ask 'why' about anything."

JAMIE: "It would have been pointless under the communists, so maybe they just abandoned it altogether."

ME: "True. I must be adapting. Now when the answer doesn't make sense to me, I wonder if my question even made sense."

JAMIE: "I know the feeling. I question my own sanity on a regular basis."

ME: "I don't think it's just us. Have you ever spoken to Irena? She's from here and told me she took some college courses that were impossible to understand."

Irena was a new Czech statutory auditor in the office, but she was young like us and had been hanging out with the expats and staff.

HENRY: "Like what?"

ME: "Honestly, they all sound like words that don't go together to me: Dialectical Materialism, Scientific Communism, Political Economy of Socialism."

HENRY: "Whoa."

MIKE: "Is science different under communism? I don't think it should be . . ."

ME: "My personal favorite, though, is Accounting of Capitalism."

HENRY: "I assume we just call that Accounting . . ."

We all laughed. He was probably right.

ME: "She also said that she took a class she was told was very important, but after an entire year, she still wasn't sure what it was about."

HENRY: "Whaaa??? How does that work? Or make sense?"

ME: "She said it was called Economic Information and Control."

Lots of laughter. Lots of shrugs.

It warmed my heart to know that the Czechs also encountered things that made no sense. They just shrugged them off; we were starting to.

MIKE: "I heard that some of the classes were basically the same as others— they just changed the order of the words in the course name."

We couldn't stop laughing. How was this education?

Decades later, Irena would tell me that the Economic Information and Control class turned out to be accounting, auditing, and internal controls. The work she ended up doing her entire career.

MIKE: "Has anyone noticed all the cooperatives around the country?"

JAMIE: "I've seen the signs on buildings in the smaller towns. It's amazing but weird that they have co-ops."

We'd all seen them.

MIKE: "Yeah, well that's the thing. They aren't co-ops as we know them. They're state-owned companies."

We laughed. The exact opposites. Communist government–owned companies vs. hippie community–owned co-ops. We shook our heads. Only here would they give a government company a name that sounded like it was some sort of feel-good community organization.

ME: "That seems like another part of the institutional gaslighting they do here. Like the incessant 'It's impossible.'"

JAMIE: "And they have a long way to go before they embrace capitalism."

MIKE: "They don't feel the need to sell a thing."

ME: "Did Stephen tell you about the corn flakes?"

JAMIE: "No . . ."

ME: "His wife, Sharise, discovered that a small shop near their house carried corn flakes."

JAMIE: "They have corn flakes? Let's go!"

ME: "Hold your horses. When she went last week, she couldn't find them.

She went back a few times, but no luck. So she asked the shop owner where they were."

JAMIE: "Oh no . . ."

ME: "Oh yes. He told her he no longer carried them."

MIKE: "Ok . . ."

ME: "After she prompted him further, the owner explained that no sooner could he unpack those corn flakes and get them on the shelf than they were sold. Then he would have to order them all over again, receive the shipment, etc., so he stopped carrying them."

EVERYONE: "Noooooo!!!"

We all started repeating, "They stopped carrying them," like it was the best punchline of a joke we'd ever heard.

ME: "Suddenly, I understand Kafka."

Everyone laughed, and they agreed. Kafka wasn't writing about the absurd. He was writing about the communist system.

ME: "And the accounting—which I affectionally call 'communist accounting'—is mind-boggling."

Everyone started talking at once. Accounting might be boring to others, but it was our livelihood.

ME: "My client has transactions going through numerous accounts temporarily for no reason—and I mean for a few hours or minutes—I can discern. And, of course, nobody can explain it to me. Honestly, I sometimes wonder if this is what money laundering looks like."

EVA: "You know that under communism nothing could be reserved for or written off because nothing was allowed to fail."

ME: "Ahh yes. Everyone paid their debts, everything always worked perfectly, and there were NEVER any mistakes."

MIKE: "The government just moved goods and money around from one bucket to another. That was the plan in planned economy."

Were we finally getting it?

LAURENT: "Accruals didn't exist—everything was cash based. Nobody had ever thought about the fact that perhaps we should record December's electricity charges in December when we used the electricity instead of January when we paid the bill."

ME: "Maybe that's because there was no electricity in some of the buildings."

We laughed. Most of us had had that "trying to work in the dark" experience. And that was true in more ways than one. Every audit or review we did revealed new and unusual issues that nobody had ever tried to understand before.

MIKE: "Did you see the quote by a KPMG partner in the paper the other day?"

KPMG was another big accounting firm setting up shop in the Eastern Bloc.

JAMIE: "No, what was it?"

MIKE: "The partner compared the 'opaque local accounting legislation to the famous Czech black light theater,' saying, 'You see what is up front, but the people who move the objects are in the dark.'"[12]

That was the perfect description. We toasted that partner for saying it out loud.

ME: "I've been working on that big project comparing every section of international accounting standards to Czech accounting standards. Almost everything was different."

BRENDA: "I've written memos describing every Czech accounting gimmick we've uncovered and have been able to decipher."

Each assignment was a dive into the unknown.

ME: "I had a few clients with no customers. I mean . . ."

JAMIE: "But they've expanded their production capacity!"

Everyone laughed a knowing laugh and began chatting animatedly.

This work was extremely difficult and mentally exhausting. We were often winging it, trying to get to a good answer.

ME: "My cement client invested in some smaller construction companies, and we had a hell of a time getting information. One day, Markéta left me a note about the inventory that said 'Some not precise inventory count is done every month, and the guessed quantity is multiplied by a selling price based on estimation of specialists.'"

JAMIE: "Oh lord. Was she joking? Or serious?"

ME: "Honestly, I'm not sure. It's funny, but it's also probably about as accurate as we're going to get."

BRENDA: "Have you seen the actual audit opinion issued by another firm that said 'We are of the opinion that the findings specified above are not of such nature and extent so as to substantially distort the financial statement of the company'?"

MIKE: "What? Is that a bad translation or have we really lowered the bar so far that we're just hoping not to distort things now?"

Nobody knew.

JAMIE: "I love the Model Auditors' Report that's been floating around. Someone stuck it in my mail file anonymously. Have you seen it?"

He pulled out a piece of paper and shared it with all of us.

Dear Shareholders:

We have eyeballed the ballpark figures on the balance sheet of December 31, 1992, and the statements of lies, retained deficits and source and application of executive petty cash for the year then ended. Our examination included a general rationalization of the so-called accounting procedures and such tests of accounting records and other unsupported entries as we considered unavoidable subject to the constraints of our time budget and audit fee.

Our gut feeling is that these ballpark figures are good solid numbers and we feel fit to roll with them as the financial position of the company as at December 31, 1992, having been prepared in accordance with generally accepted corporate memos applied randomly on a basis consistent with that of producing a satisfactory profit for the year.

Yours in haste,

Author Unknown

JAMIE: "To summarize: 'Screw it. We can't make heads or tails of what we're seeing, so we're just gonna guess that these numbers are ok, and we can't be bothered to fix them if they aren't.'"

MIKE: "Or . . . 'Nothing makes sense, so we'll just wing it.'"

We laughed until our sides hurt. The audit opinions issued at home had standard, set language that we'd had to memorize to pass the CPA exam. But here, all bets were off. We made up new procedures because the standard steps couldn't be performed. We drafted memos explaining accounting treatments none of us had ever seen or imagined before. And we wrote crazy new audit opinions to reflect the reality of the work we had performed and what we had found. Or not been able to find.

ME: "I don't know about you guys, but as hard as this has been, I'm certain that I am much better at my job now that I've had to figure it out from scratch."

"Na zdraví! Nádraží!"

BRICKS MÉLNÍK

APRIL 1994
MÉLNÍK

MARTIN AND I HEADED TO BRNO to visit the brick production plant. We needed to figure out whether this investment was worth anything and whether they would be able to repay a loan they got from Cement Hranice.

The company produced bricks made of wood and cement. As we drove up to the plant, we noted that there was no smoke coming from the smoke-stacks. In fact, there seemed to be no activity at all. Was it closed? Was anyone there to meet us? We were anxious to find out what was happen-ing—or not happening—at the plant.

We were in luck. The production manager, pan Němec, met us and gave us a tour. We chatted as we walked around the yard.

NĚMEC: "We're very excited. We've expanded our production capacity from 2,000 bricks a day to more than 6,000 bricks a day."

ME: "Wow. Great . . ."

We walked from section to section noticing that the piles of bricks were not the same. Many of the bricks were clearly disintegrating before our eyes. I asked what I assumed was obvious (but you never knew).

ME: "Is there a problem with these bricks?"

NĚMEC: "Yes. When we first started producing bricks, we didn't quite have the 'recipe' quite right. So we tried different mixes of cement and wood until we got it right."

ME: "Ahh. So each section is from one of those batches?"

NĚMEC: "Yes."

ME: "Can any of them be used?"

NĚMEC: "No."

ME: "Ok . . . so they're still here in the yard . . . are they also in the inventory balance on your books?" Again, it felt like a silly question to me, but I'd learned my lesson.

NĚMEC: "Yes! We plan to write them off slowly."

Oh dear. That would distort the financials and make it look like they had bricks of value that they clearly did not have. *Note to self: Write them all off immediately.* And recommend that they go ahead and throw them away since they're worthless.

ME: "So . . . we noticed there's nobody here, and the plant is quiet today. Why is that?"

NĚMEC: "We expanded last year so we can produce more bricks than ever, but the bricks need to be dried. The previous owner of the building cut off the heat. This means we can't dry the bricks during the winter."

ME: "So, you produce at full capacity the rest of the year?"

NĚMEC: "Well, no. When we make bricks, we also produce a lot of dust. So much dust that the health authorities have said we are creating air pollution. We aren't allowed to produce bricks until we modify the machinery to prevent the air pollution."

ME: "Do you have plans to do that?"

NĚMEC: "No. We can't afford it."

I paused . . . at a total loss about what to ask next. I redirected the conversation.

Factory tour complete—and illuminating—we headed to the small office building. In the office, we spoke with the chief, Niederlová, and looked at the general ledger. It didn't balance.

The general ledger did not balance.

The very first lesson in accounting is that every entry has two equal sides, and everything balances out in the end.

But not here.

After a lot of discussion, we learned that some sort of one-sided entry had been made a long time ago and nobody knew how to fix it. It couldn't be that hard. Right? But they didn't actually keep good records. And what they had were, of course, all handwritten. We discussed it at length but with no resolution. I had absolutely no idea how this could have happened or what we would do about it, but right now, we needed to move on to the next problem . . . the projections for next year.

ME: "In reviewing your projections, we noticed you don't project any sales . . ."

NIEDERLOVÁ: "That's right. We don't have any customers."

I pursed my lips. She seemed completely comfortable with this.

ME: "Ok then. But you just dramatically expanded the factory, right?"

NIEDERLOVÁ: "Yes!" she said proudly. "We took a loan from Cement Hranice and tripled our production capacity."

Their capacity was more than one million bricks a year. In 1993, they sold 25,000 bricks.

I was non-plussed.

ME: "But it's our understanding that you aren't able to produce because of the air pollution and you don't have plans to renovate the plant to fix that. Is that right?"

NIEDERLOVÁ: "Yes, that's right."

I rubbed my temples and looked at Martin. I was completely dumb-founded.

ME: "Did she really just say that? Did she really just say that it's totally cool that they have no customers because they can't make any bricks anyway and it's all good because this means they can keep their jobs???"

Martin nodded sheepishly.

ME: "So let me make sure I've got this. They've expanded capacity but don't have any customers. And they can't run the machinery because they can't afford to fix the pollution problem. But it doesn't matter since they have no customers anyway. Is that right?"

Martin translated between us.

NIEDERLOVÁ: "Yes. As long as we don't produce anything, the health authorities will let us stay in business and we can keep our jobs."

It had finally happened. Holy sh*t. The light bulb went on in my head. All the things that had happened over the past year suddenly clicked and fell into place. It all made sense even though it didn't make any sense at all. My mind was blown.

Pani Niederlová wasn't wrong. She could sit in the office eating lunch and doing crossword puzzles every day. Not a bad life. As long as the company didn't get shut down by the health authorities, the company stayed open. And as long as they didn't produce bricks, there was no pollution. Nobody gave a hoot if they sold anything or made any money. They were all set. Absolutely genius.

Our work here was done.

Company value = zero.

GOODBYE, MIKE

APRIL 1994

ANOTHER DEPARTURE. Another going away party. I would be one of the only expats left in the office.

For: Everyone
Subject: Mike's leaving celebration

As most of you know, Mike has spent the last year and a half flying to New York City every other week (a "weekend" being anywhere from 3 to 5 days long) to visit a reportedly amazing woman named Sheila. Next Tuesday, he is again leaving for New York but unfortunately, this time he won't be coming back. So everyone who will miss Mike or his queso and wants to say good-bye (and even those who still have never seen Mike and aren't really sure he ever worked here), please join us Friday night as we take Mike out to his favorite places in Prague one last time.

We'll meet at U Cedru, in Prague 6, Friday, April 22nd at 8 p.m. for some kung pao and mezze. After that we'll head into town for drinking, dancing and celebrating (Ed is threatening to go to some club recommended by a taxi driver but I'm sure we can think of something better).

THE GRIFT

MAY 1994

JAMIE AND I WERE DRIVING TO KUTNA HORA for the day. Kutna Hora was about an hour from Prague, and we were jazzed. It was a small town known for one thing. The bone church. Officially known as the Sedlec Ossuary, it would soon be designated a UNESCO World Heritage Site and become a major tourist attraction. But in 1993, it was more of a weird rumor amongst the expats, all of us trying understand what the Czechs meant when they told us it was decorated with human bones. We had to go see it!

It was a beautiful day; the sun was bright. The road was lined with fields and only the occasional building. There were no other cars in sight. Suddenly, the policie appeared behind us on a curving country road. They turned on their flashing lights, so we pulled over onto the gravel. I was sure I hadn't done anything wrong. I didn't even have the blue foreigner plates! We thought we would avoid this. But I rolled down the window and waited to find out what kind of trouble I was in. One policeman stayed in the car; the other approached my window.

POLICIE: "Dokumenty."

I handed him my international driver's license and the car registration papers.

ME: "Why did you pull me over?"

POLICIE: "You made an illegal turn."

I was pretty sure I hadn't.

ME: "Where?"

POLICIE: "Back there." He pointed to the direction we'd come from.

ME: "What was wrong with my turn?"

He didn't respond. I have no idea if he really understood me.

ME: "Can you show me where? Where is the sign?"

He handed my documents back.

POLICIE: "You will have to pay a fine."

ME: "But what did I do?"

POLICIE: "You made an illegal turn."

I resigned myself to paying a fine just to make this end.

ME: "How much is it?"

POLICIE: "How much do you have?"

Whoa. The shakedown.

I breathed deeply. We had been warned about carrying too much money while driving around the countryside, so we had spread our money out between our wallets, pockets, and shoes.

I pulled out my wallet and showed him what was in it . . . not much. A few hundred crowns—the equivalent of about $10. His expressionless expression changed. His eyes tightened. He was NOT happy.

I apologized repeatedly for having so little. I held my empty wallet up to the open window to show him it was empty. Jamie showed his empty wallet as well. We played dumb.

They left unsatisfied. Maybe even angry. They'd expected so much more. They'd pulled over a foreigner and only gotten a few hundred crowns for their trouble. Strangely enough, neither Jamie nor I were outraged. Indignant. Mad. We were used to it. It was the price to be paid for being a "rich" foreigner.

CONCRETE BRNO

MAY 1994
BRNO

NOW THAT I WAS GETTING THE HANG OF the economic model, this should be easier, right?

Ne.

Vašek and I headed to the last investment company we needed to value, Concrete Brno. On the way there, we passed a bright blue luxury tour bus with the Concrete Brno name and logo on the side. This seemed odd. Why would a concrete company have a luxury bus? I turned to Vašek with a quizzical look on my face. We understood each other now so I didn't even need to ask my question out loud. Vašek had no idea either. He sat back in his seat staring out the car window again. We couldn't wait to get there.

Vašek and I spoke with the four main clients at Concrete Brno:

The general director, pan Čejka.

The chief accountant, paní Čejková (the general director's wife).

The economic director, paní Kubyová.

The production manager, pan Čejka (the general director and chief accountant's son). Nothing to see here ...

In addition to assessing the value of this investment, we needed to evaluate whether or not Concrete Brno could pay Cement Hranice the 25 million Kč they had borrowed for . . . something. Nobody had told us what.

We went to the general director, the elder Čejka, for a company overview.

ČEJKA: "Concrete Brno used to have four sites. We now only have two. One lease was cancelled because a foreign competitor bribed the state. The other was cancelled because of pressure from Greenpeace. Thankfully, the other two sites were leased from different governing bodies that have not given in to these environmental groups."

Conspiracy nut? This was a lot for our first conversation. I was trying to process all this. Why would someone bribe the government to cancel their lease? Why would environmental groups want their leases canceled? What environmental issue was Concrete Brno causing? I had many questions that I knew would never be answered to my satisfaction.

ME: "So what is Concrete Brno's plan for handling the two site closures?"

ČEJKA: "We found a new site nearby and signed an 'agreement about a future agreement' with the future owner."

I asked Vašek if I understood correctly.

ME: "So, they've signed an agreement to lease the site from someone who doesn't own the land yet?"

VAŠEK: "Yes."

ME: "Can we ask for more details?"

Vašek spoke with him for a few minutes and then turned to me.

VAŠEK: "The title has not yet been transferred from the state to the new 'owner' who wants to lease the land to Concrete Brno. In addition to leasing the land to Concrete Brno, the new 'owner' wants to produce panels at the site with concrete purchased from Concrete Brno."

ME: "So let me see if I understand this . . . the person doesn't own the land they plan to lease to Concrete Brno. And once they own it and Concrete Brno leases it, the new 'owner' plans to make their own products at the plant instead of Concrete Brno's?"

VAŠEK: "Yes."

Got it. Perfect. Why the hell would they lease the land under these circumstances?

ME: "And Concrete Brno is ok with this? What else can he tell us about the planned move?"

ČEJKA: "It will cost a lot of money to move production to new sites. I would like to get the money from Cement Hranice, but since they refuse to lend it to me, I will go to a bank. I don't think I'll have any problem."

ME: "What? He thinks they'll get a loan from a third party because the owner of his very own company doesn't want to loan it to him?"

My question was rhetorical. I was bracing myself for even more crazy, so I was delighted to learn that this company had actual customers. Almost 200 of them! This was a nice change. We left pan Čejka and went to accounting.

We wanted to speak to paní Kubyová, the economic director. Also in the accounting department was the chief accountant, paní Čejková.

We had a few questions.

ME: "Pan Čejka said he plans to take out a loan for the move to a new site. Can you tell us about that?"

KUBYOVÁ: "This will be a problem when the banks see how much money pan Čejka owes Concrete Brno and how much Concrete Brno owes Cement Hranice."

Wait, what? Pan Čejka owed money to Concrete Brno? The plot thickened. Who was planning to get this loan? Pan Čejka? Or Concrete Brno? It was starting to feel like pan Čejka believed he and Concrete Brno were the same thing; he didn't understand that he was an employee.

With zero clarity on this topic, we moved on to our biggest question. We had reviewed the bank statements earlier and seen something unusual. A very large cash withdrawal. An even four million Kč (or about $130K).

ME: "What is this four million Kč withdrawal by pan Čejka?"

KUBYOVÁ: "I do not know. It was withdrawn without my knowledge. Cash management is very difficult since one bank statement comes directly to me but the other goes to pan Čejka. I don't receive it from him for days."

Well, that must make it a little easier to just randomly withdraw large sums of cash since there's a company bank account that accounting doesn't have any information about. We made a note to discuss this large withdrawal with pan Čejka.

ME: "Is there anything else you think we should take a look at?"

KUBYOVÁ: "Concrete Brno bought 9.7 million Kč of machinery and equipment from pan Čejka, but I'm not sure this transaction was properly recorded."

Fantastic. The intermingling of pan Čejka and Concrete Brno continued. Why was Concrete Brno, run by pan Čejka, buying equipment directly from its general director, pan Čejka? What equipment was it? Why did he have it to begin with? Where did he get it? Did he buy it just to sell it to Concrete Brno at a profit? Did Cement Hranice know about this? Or was profit irrelevant here like it was everywhere else? Was there some other, more communist motivation? We didn't have any idea what to make of the whole thing. But it all seemed like a hornet's nest of conflicts.

Off we went to ask pan Čejka about the withdrawal. He spoke not a word of English, so Vašek translated.

ME: "Vašek, please ask pan Čejka about this 4M Kč withdrawal. What did he use this money for?"

Vašek and Pan Čejka held a conversation in Czech for several minutes. Then, Vašek turned to me.

VAŠEK (nonchalantly): "Pan Čejka told me to tell you he bought equipment for the company."

I thought he *sold* equipment to the company . . . but I digressed. Back to the issue at hand.

Vašek narrowed his eyes when he looked into mine. I knew something was up. I kept my face as neutral as I could.

ME: "Ok. He told you to tell me that? So really, it's something else. Can you ask him what kind of equipment he purchased."

VAŠEK asked him and then told me: "He said to tell you it was several trac-
tors and a truck."

I took notes furiously so pan Čejka would think I was buying it.

ME: "Ok, great. What did pan Čejka actually do with the money?"

VAŠEK: "I'll try to find out."

Vašek asked him. The pair chatted for several minutes. Vašek finally turned
to me.

VAŠEK: "He told me not to tell you, but he bought a house."

Keeping a poker face wasn't my strength—I'd been told that in my first
performance review and had been working on it—but now was the time
to really put my practice into action. *Keep calm, Melanie. Keep calm.* I took
some more notes about fake equipment.

ME: "Ok. Got it. A house for himself and his family?"

VAŠEK: "Yes."

ME: "Do you think you can find out where the house is?"

VAŠEK: "I think so."

I was beginning to see why Vašek was known by the other Czechs for being
"very good" in the Czech language. I never quite understood what it meant
until this moment.

They spoke in Czech for several minutes. I didn't interrupt. I feigned bore-
dom while Vašek worked his magic.

In a few short minutes, Vašek had pan Čejka on record admitting he'd
taken money from the company and bought a house for his family. I think
being "good in Czech" meant he was a really good suck-up. But I must say
I was impressed. When Vašek explained it to me later, I learned the conversation had gone something like this:

VAŠEK: "Ok. She thinks the money was for equipment. I want to congrat-
ulate you. Well done on getting the money for a house! Tell me about
it? Is it big? New?"

ČEJKA: "Oh, yes. It is brand-new construction and big enough for the
whole family."

VAŠEK: "Very impressive. You are clearly a smart and powerful man. Is it in a good location?"

ČEJKA: "Oh, yes. It's on a hill with an amazingly beautiful view."

VAŠEK: "Incredible! I wish I were as savvy as you are. Where is this house?"

ČEJKA: "Here is the address. You should come for dinner."

VAŠEK: "I'd love to. I can't wait to learn more from such a wise and wily businessman."

Genius. But we had even more sketchy things to ask about. The bus. Again, Vašek worked his magic and told me about the conversation later:

VAŠEK: "Pan Čejka, on the way here, we saw a luxury bus with the Concrete Brno name and logo on the side. Is this the company's bus?"

ČEJKA: "Oh, no. I started my own company that produces tiles and pavement."

VAŠEK: "But the bus says Concrete Brno on the side."

ČEJKA: "Yes, my company is also called Concrete Brno."

VAŠEK: "Interesting. Why does a tile and pavement company need a tour bus?"

ČEJKA: "We sponsor a football team that uses the bus. And sometimes we give tours around the Czech republic."

VAŠEK: "I love football! So, the bus belongs to your company that has the same name as Cement Hranice's company? And uses the bus to give tours and transport a football team?"

ČEJKA: "Yes, and once, I used it to take some friends on a ski trip."

VAŠEK: "Great! Sounds fun."

I was flummoxed. There wasn't a chance in hell the costs had all been charged to the correct company or that these were legit business activities.

In summary, pan Čejka co-opted the company's name and used the same address, telephone, and fax numbers. On top of that, he used the bus for personal reasons too. He was shameless.

It turned out he felt he had been short-changed in the sale of Concrete Brno to Cement Hranice. He was merely rectifying the situation. After

Vašek and I submitted our report, pan Čejka, his wife, and his son were all fired. I never found out if he had to pay the money back. I'm sure in the end it was hard for Cement Hranice to pick just one reason to fire them.

And now I'd seen firsthand the famous communist Czechoslovak adage, "If you aren't stealing from the state, you're stealing from your family."

WE HAVE MUSIC!

MAY 1994

FOR A YEAR AND A HALF the only way we'd been able to get new music was by buying CDs when we traveled to other countries. One of my favorite things was spending time at the Virgin Megastores in Germany. We could put on earphones and listen to almost any music we wanted. We spent hours there and always came home with stacks of new CDs. But now we had a music store in Prague! Popron had just opened near Národní třída and just a few blocks from Jamie's client site. I swung by to get him so we could check out Popron.

I hadn't been to this office building before, but I had the floor and office number where Jamie was working. I entered the lobby and looked for the elevator. There was a group of people gathered in front of it. I walked up behind them and tried to figure out what I was looking at. It was like the elevator had an audience. Then I saw it.

I spotted another expat (easily identifiable by his boring dark suit) and moved beside him.

ME: "Is that . . ."

HIM: "Yeah . . . it is."

ME: "But how . . ."

HIM: "I'm not sure . . ."

ME: "I'm gonna need to watch for a minute . . ."

HIM: "Same here."

The elevator had two doorframes but no doors. Really, it looked like two elevators. One that only went up and one that only went down. And they never stopped moving! It can only be described as sort of like a ferris wheel that you have to get on and off of while it's moving. The platforms moved up and down in synchronicity.

The locals were queued up taking turns getting onto the elevator while people were simultaneously getting off. It was like the escalator of elevators. They all seemed perfectly comfortable stepping on and off at just the right moment—when the floor of the box was at the same level as the floor we were standing on. They made it look easy.

But I had a lot of questions. Where did the box go at the top and bottom of the building? Did it flip over? Or did it somehow go over the top in the same position, like a Ferris wheel seat? What happened if someone didn't get off at the top floor? Would they safely start coming down the other side? What if I didn't time my step on or off perfectly? Would I fall to the ground? Get trapped between the elevator floor and the ceiling when it got that high? Nothing about this elevator seemed like a good idea to me.

ME: "You gonna try it?"

HIM: "I guess I have to."

We were at the front of the line now. He told me I could go first. Great. I approached the moving box and tried to get the timing right so I could just step on gracefully. I wasn't feeling confident. I had a few false starts where I knew my timing was off so I let a few go past me. People behind me started getting antsy and I knew I was about to be yelled at. So I held my breath and did a slightly mistimed step onto it. I had to step up a bit like I was climbing a stair. But I was on!

Now I had to figure out how to get off.

I eventually got the hang of it and it became a fun tourist attraction whenever people came to visit.

The crazy escalator-elevator of my nightmares. "The Elevator of Death," otherwise known as a Paternoster lift.

WHERE ARE ALL THE COWS?

MAY 1994

ONE WEEKEND, FIVE OF US PILED INTO my Škoda to drive to Šumava, a favorite Czech vacation spot. As we drove along the country road, we smelled what was surely cow manure. Yet there were no cows in sight.

Jamie and I gave each other knowing quizzical looks. We knew what the other person was thinking, and we were completely baffled. The question was almost becoming metaphysical. I nodded for him to ask.

JAMIE: "What is that smell?"

MARKÉTA: "Cows."

Ok, good. We weren't totally crazy.

ME: "That's what I thought. But I don't see any cows."

MARKÉTA: "Yo, yo, yo."

JAMIE: "So . . . where are they?"

MARKÉTA: "They're in the house."

Stop. Pause. Deep breath.

ME: "They're in a house?"

MARKÉTA: "Yes, they're in that white house over there."

Stop. Pause. Another deep breath.

JAMIE: "Which house?"

Markéta pointed to what looked like a long white house.

ME: "What else is in the house?"

MARKÉTA: "Pigs."

Ohmigod.

ME: "So pigs live in houses too?"

JAMIE: "Come to think of it, I've never seen a cow or a pig in this country."

ME: "Good point. Pork is the national dish. But there is not a pig to be seen."

There must be pigs, right?

MARKÉTA: "They live in the houses."

To say we were baffled would be an understatement.

JAMIE: "Is this a summer thing?"

MARKÉTA: "No. They always live indoors. Sheep too."

Inquiring minds had to know more.

JAMIE: "So how do they eat?"

MARKÉTA: "People bring them the food."

ME: "Don't the cows eat grass?"

MARKÉTA: "Yes, people bring it to them."

JAMIE: "Do they ever let the cows out?"

MARKÉTA: "I don't think so."

Was she kidding? People gathered the grass and delivered it to the cows in the houses? We were aghast. Wouldn't it be more efficient to let the cows roam? Wouldn't it help them build muscle and stay healthy? Perhaps this was an attempt to make all their beef veal. But why the pigs? Why couldn't the pigs go outside? Does low muscle tone make bacon better?

The Czechs were perplexed by our questions. Had it never occurred to them that cows and pigs could roam in the many beautiful, green pastures throughout the Czech republic? To be fair, the "houses" were actually barns, but they looked just like people's houses. Still, we tried to convince them they should LET THE COWS OUT!

In the end, we decided it had to be some communist scheme to create jobs. Didn't it? That's what the expats thought, anyway. The Czechs just shrugged at the suggestion.

MOSCOW

MOSCOW. The very heart of Soviet Communism. The capital of *Das Kapital*.

I had been living in Prague for more than a year, and I was comfortable in Eastern Europe now. My friends and I had traveled to Hungary, Slovakia, and Poland. We wanted to do something a little more adventurous. Jamie and I decided to go to Moscow for a long weekend.

It was 1994, and Americans needed a formal invitation from someone in Russia in order to be allowed into the country. We secured an invitation letter from the expats at our fellow Arthur Andersen office in Moscow. And we booked our flight . . . on the infamous Aeroflot.

ME: "Are we sure we want to do this?"

JAMIE: "It's concerning . . . but maybe the stories are exaggerated."

Chickens in the aisles, cabins crammed with carry-ons, horrible food, a cobblestone through a window, and rude service. Russian-made aircraft with names that sounded like Russian spies: Tupolev, Antonov, and Ilyushin. Someone told us about their trip where the plane drove down a runway where someone had left construction equipment. The wing was clipped by the equipment and the side of the plane was punctured. Gas leaked from the plane and ran onto the runway. The plane was evacuated and the passengers spent 24 hours in Sheremetyevo International Airport waiting for another plane. Good times.

ME: "Did you see the *USA TODAY* article about it?"

JAMIE: "The one called 'The Pilot Has Turned On the No-Chickens Sign'?"[13]

I laughed nervously.

ME: "That's the one. It said the flight attendant spat on the pilot and called him a drunk. And also that the company told their people not to steal luggage anymore!"

JAMIE: "We'll carry our bags on with us."

ME: "For sure."

JAMIE: "I loved the part where the pilot refused to depart until he got an apology and then the passengers said they were going to kill the pilot."

Funny, not funny.

ME: "Wait, wait. Didn't someone's dog throw up?"

JAMIE: "Yes, and chickens fell out of an overhead compartment."

We laughed at the thought of these things happening on a plane.

JAMIE: "More importantly, the Aeroflot staff are now taking politeness classes. Because for a long time they 'didn't pay attention to passengers.'"

We grinned. Sounded right. You couldn't make this stuff up.

JAMIE: "Sadly, I think a few months ago, a pilot let his son into the cockpit to sit at the controls. The plane crashed in Siberia, killing everyone on board."

Sigh.

Jamie and I were adventurous, but that was alarming. Why, oh why, hadn't we booked on Czech Airlines?

We boarded the flight and were pleasantly surprised. It seemed normal. Except for the part where they had us all put our carry-on bags in a pile at the back of the plane. In front of the bathroom door. Nothing was secured, and everyone was going to need to hold it for the two- to three-hour flight.

The service wasn't what I would call friendly, but I didn't feel we were in danger. A low bar but the only bar we had. Then we landed.

The backrest of every seat on the plane lurched forward. The seat next to me slammed shut like a clam. I hit my head on the seat in front of me. It was more of a shock than anything else. But then I heard a rumble. All the bags piled at the back were rolling down the aisle. I looked around. Others seemed to take it in stride. I didn't know if this was standard on Aeroflot flights. Were the seats on this plane broken? Were the baggage handlers on strike? If any of this had happened in the U.S., it would have made national news. Nobody in Moscow said a word. Incredibly, we arrived in one piece with our luggage largely undamaged, and I was grateful.

The hotel recommended by the office was one of the nicest hotels I'd ever stayed at. Some high-end Western chain that catered to every international traveler in Moscow. The breakfast buffet was a world tour of breakfast foods. They had the typical American fare of eggs, bacon, and toast; a European-style breakfast with rolls, salami, cheese, and tomatoes; an Asian congee bar with all the fixings; an omelet station; pastries; both cold and hot cereal; an incredible array of world fruits—bananas, dragonfruit, kiwi, and many we didn't recognize; and coffee, tea, champagne, and at least a dozen freshly squeezed juices. It was absolute heaven.

Why didn't this exist in Prague? Or did it and we just didn't know about it? There were a few big hotel chains opening up in Prague. Maybe we should have checked them out.

We lingered over breakfast—honestly, we could have stayed all day—reading the latest happenings from the selection of newspapers from around the world. Finally, we pulled ourselves away from the smorgasbord. Off to see Moscow.

We hired a driver for the day—someone recommended by the office and who spoke some English. It was ridiculously cheap and our best bet at getting around town. Navigating the metro, Russian, and the Cyrillic alphabet at the same time seemed dicey. A lot of Czechs spoke English, but that didn't seem to hold true in Russia—most Russians spoke Russian.

Our driver took us to the sites we'd requested: Red Square, St. Basil's

Cathedral, the Kremlin, the extraordinary churches within its walls, and Lenin's tomb.

We waited in a long line to see Lenin, embalmed for eternity. Why the Russians wanted to see him like that, I didn't know. As far as I was concerned, he'd created this communist mess. But since this seemed to be the thing to do, we did it too.

The line wound past the headstones of people buried along the wall bordering the mausoleum—the Kremlin Wall Necropolis—including the headstone of Joseph Stalin. I was stunned that the leader of the Great Terror, who was responsible for millions of deaths, would still be honored this way.

Entering the mausoleum was eerie. Black walls and red décor. Lenin wore a black suit. Only his embalmed face and hands were visible in the spotlight. The line of people shuffled past. In awe or in horror—I couldn't tell. We wound around his glass-encased resting place so we could see him from all sides. Surreal to realize he'd been dead for 70 years and still looked like himself.

Later that afternoon, we were ready to head back to our hotel, but our driver asked if we were interested in seeing . . . something. We weren't sure what he was trying to say, but since he'd offered, we were curious. We nodded "Yes, let's go see whatever this completely random Russian cab driver thinks we should see."

He drove for 20 minutes until we came to a small park behind a tall building. It looked like a junkyard.

ME: "Is that Lenin's head?"

JAMIE: "I don't think so, but look, here's somebody's ear . . . "

There were the old statues of Stalin, Dzerzhinsky (the founder of the Soviet secret police), Kalinin (the former head of the Soviet state), and somebody's head. Some were upright, but Stalin and others were sprawled across the ground. The great leaders of Communism were lying in a vacant lot near the river. Abandoned to the animals and elements. Some of them were enormous, but they lost their impressiveness lying in disrepair in a field. We wandered between them slowly, not sure whether to show respect or disregard.

ME: "Ooh. There's Stalin."

JAMIE: "Someone bashed in his nose."

ME: "Seems reasonable. And I think these are his feet."

I couldn't help but feel the anger and despair of the Russians who'd torn these monuments down. Their former leaders had not done right by the people. Now those leaders had been discarded like garbage.

Eventually, this would become Fallen Monument Park. The first statue was dumped there in 1991. Over time, even more were taken down and left here. The statues accumulated until it became a tourist attraction. A junkyard of communism. The ash heap of history.

Our driver dropped us off at a restaurant he recommended. The menu was only in Russian. Russian is actually somewhat similar to Czech, but the Cyrillic alphabet made it impossible for us to read the menu at all. Our waitress didn't speak any of the languages we knew anything about: English, Spanish, Portuguese, French, German, or Czech. We eventually pointed to the board out front announcing the specials and hoped for the best. We were excited to try the local food. And the vodka. Vodka was universal.

The waitress returned with two plates of food. There were chicken-like corpses on our plates. Thankfully, they didn't have feathers, but they also seemed far too small to be chickens. I mean, would they serve us each an entire chicken? We just weren't sure. But we could do this. We shot some vodka and dug in. Ok, not exactly. We took a tentative bite. It TASTED like chicken. Either Russians couldn't feed their chickens much, or we were eating some other animal; a lot of things taste like chicken. Whatever they were, they were skinny. Maybe the skinniest chickens on Earth.

In the morning, we went to the big open-air market for souvenirs. We wanted something Russian. Ruské! We were not disappointed. No tacky, "China-made" souvenirs here. No magnets. No key chains. No "I love Moscow" T-shirts. What we found was even better.

We roamed through stalls full of old Soviet propaganda posters, hand-made Russian dolls, hand-painted Matrioshka dolls, old Soviet lapel pins celebrating government anniversaries or sports events, and people's junk. It was an enormous communism garage sale. Finally, the Russian people were making a buck off communism.

We browsed for hours, mesmerized by the relics of a once powerful and now non-existent country. The posters of Lenin were eerie. They were clearly ripped from the walls by enterprising vandals. We bought a little of everything. As much as we thought we could take back in our suitcases. I couldn't wait to put them on display in my flat. Now, my décor would be some weird combination of 1970s colors, IKEA furniture, and Soviet memorabilia. Like a phantasmagoric dream. I was stoked.

That night, we decided to try to find a restaurant someone had told us about a few weeks ago. We had been in a Czech pub—as usual—talking about our upcoming trip to Moscow when someone overheard us and asked if we liked Mexican food.

ME: "Do we like Mexican food???"

JAMIE: "We would kill for good Mexican food!"

ME: "But we're going to Moscow, not Mexico."

GUY: "The best Mexican food in all of Eastern Europe is in Moscow."

JAMIE: "Seriously? How is that possible?"

I mean, the bar was low and we were skeptical. But we were always on the lookout for a good chimichanga. The man told us everything he knew about the place. We took copious notes on the back of a beer coaster.

Now in Moscow, as Jamie and I stepped out of our hotel, we pulled out the coaster and read the instructions.

1. Go to the Hotel Intourist. (This was the enormous, Soviet-style high-rise just off Red Square. The only place foreigners had been allowed to stay if they visited between 1970 and the country's collapse in 1991.)
2. Walk through the lobby past the hookers and black-market money changers.
3. Go to the 20th floor.
4. Find room 2011.
5. Knock.

This sounded a little sketchy to us. More than a little. *Insanely* sketchy. A restaurant in a hotel room? But the guy seemed sincere, so it was worth a shot. We craved anything made with meat, beans, tomatoes, and cheese.

We easily found the Hotel Intourist. It was tall, gray, and starkly ugly. Especially when compared to the beautiful buildings on nearby Red Square. The lobby was, indeed, full of scantily clad women standing around waiting for men to approach them and skeevy-looking men getting ready to pull cold, hard cash out of their trench coat pockets. Tourists were the prime target of their services, so this was clearly the place to be. We navigated our way to the elevators, turning down their help with every other step. We didn't want their kind of help.

We hopped off the elevator at the 20th floor and walked down a long, dreary hallway until we found room 2011. We paused in front of the door, worried we were about to disturb some unsuspecting tourists in their hotel room. How would we explain why we were there? Would we be able to communicate with them? How would we explain why we were knocking on their door? Finally, we decided to go for it and find out what was behind door number 2011.

Knock, knock, knock.

A man opened the door with a lively smile. He had deep olive skin and a colorful short-sleeved shirt. He welcomed us in. We were immediately thrown off. There were almost no people of color in the former Soviet Bloc—except at the Chinese restaurants. What was common at home was simply not common here. It was all white. All Slavic.

The bed and other furniture in this room had been removed. In their place were two round tables with a few chairs. Both tables were empty. There was a tiny kitchenette in which two men were cooking food. There was a Mexican serape hanging in the kitchen doorway to obscure our view a little. Like a Mexican izakaya.

The man who answered the door introduced himself as Juan and his cooks as Raul and Elian. They were Cuban. Viva la revolución! *Mexican food, here we come.*

Juan seated us at the table by the window and asked us what we wanted. The menu was sparse, but we were salivating. We ordered the tacos with beans and guacamole. While we waited, we peered out the grimy window. We could see the Red Square from where we sat. Another surreal moment.

Soon, the food arrived, and the waiter refilled our waters. Definitely the best customer service we'd experienced in the past year and a half. We dug in.

It. Was. Heaven.

Original ingredients. Perfectly prepared. I could have eaten five platefuls.

The food at this nameless Mexican restaurant in a Moscow hotel room was infinitely better than our sad attempt at Jamie's place. Clearly, they knew how to make tortillas better than we did. And I amused myself imagining them flying back from Cuba with suitcases full of cheddar, Oaxaca, and cotija cheese. Their food-stuffed luggage was surely no different than mine. I would tell everyone I knew that if they went to Moscow, they needed to go find our new Cuban friends.

Quarterly News

of the

WEIRD AND WONDERFUL

APRIL–JUNE 1994

I LOVED SPRING IN PRAGUE. The weather was warming up, the air was easier to breathe, and the tourists had not yet descended on the city.

(HN/1) The cabinet passed an amendment to the clean-air law yesterday that would require all motor vehicles to be subjected regularly to technical and emissions inspection.

Fantastic news!

Nuclear safety = good. They "agreed" that everything's safe? That doesn't seem valid to me . . .

(HN/1) The Czech cabinet yesterday approved a report on nuclear safety for the year 1993 and agreed that all nuclear-power operations, as well as waste disposal, are completely safe.

(RK/6) A poll by GfK shows that 47% of Czechs agree that only products that are not produced domestically should be allowed into the CR as imports; 33% disagree with this.

I didn't even understand this . . . what other products would be imports?

I couldn't decide if I thought this was reasonable or harsh. It reminded me that all I saw of communism was the economic and cultural impacts. I had no insight into the much worse aspects people had faced. Prison, punishment, and death.

(MFD/3) Vladimír Koronthály (KDS) and others proposed in Parliament that wearing socialist-era medals of honor should be outlawed. Koronthály said that wearing the medals propagates communism and is the same as someone's wearing a swastika flag.

(MFD/1) The Czech army confirmed yesterday that researchers experimented with the smallpox virus in the 1960s and '70s. Sources say that the virus was probably never destroyed, despite an international recommendation that all reserves of the virus be eliminated or transferred to labs in the U.S. and U.S.S.R. A former researcher said the recommendation went unheeded not because of evil intention, but rather because of laziness.

Probably???

(MFD/3) Prague will seek to limit prostitution, sex shops, erotic salons and sales of porno magazines to an area near Florenc bus station, Mayor Koukal said. This is an area where many businesses already exist, so the public should not object to the noise, he said.

Hahaha. GREAT.

(MFD/III) Ordering pizza out remains an option of last resort, MFD says. Few pizzerias deliver, the paper notes, and a good cook can whip up some Italian at home for one-tenth the price.

Wait. Where was this mythical delivery pizza?!

(MFD/3) The world record for relay-race beer drinking fell Sat. when a group of 100 people downed 100 beers in just over 12 minutes at a contest in Velké Zboží. The old record was 13 minutes 34 seconds. The fastest participant gulped down a half-liter of 12° brew in three seconds.

Pretty sure the Czechs were world record holders in drinking their beloved "liquid bread."

(MFD/3) Psychologists say the rise in entrepreneurship has played a part in destroying the family. Many business-people no longer have time to join their family on vacations, they say, and stress and anxiety resulting from the desire to succeed disturb home life.

Ok then.

GOODBYE, JAMIE
(OR JAMIE AND THE RIBS)

JULY 1994
PRAGUE

JAMIE WAS LEAVING PRAGUE. Mike and Peter were already gone. I was going to be alone. Not *alone* but kind of lonely. I had Tereza, Jason, and Therese. And my Czech friends. Markéta, Josef, Martin, and so many more. But it was the end of the Fridays at Pizza Taxi crowd.

I was trying to plan a going-away party for him. All he really wanted was to have an American-style BBQ to share his love of ribs with the Czechs. Jamie was from Nebraska. He loved a good steak, but BBQ was his favorite thing. So, we set out to try to make that happen—or at least come as close as possible.

We had never seen ribs served anywhere in Prague and none of our Czech friends even knew what we meant. Every time I thought someone was trying to describe ribs on a menu, it turned out they were talking about kidneys or liver. We made the rounds to every butcher in town. If they were carving up cows and pigs, they had to have ribs, we reasoned. Every animal must come with them. Right?

But every conversation was the same:

JAMIE: "Do you sell ribs?"

BUTCHER: "Co?" (What?)

JAMIE: "Ribs?"

He pointed to his own ribs.

The butcher gave him a puzzled look.

Jamie outlined his ribs with his hands.

BUTCHER: "Játra?"

JAMIE: "No. Not liver."

BUTCHER: "Ledviny?"

JAMIE: "No . . . not kidneys. Žebra?"

Žebra was the Czech word for ribs. But since this wasn't something served here, the butchers didn't seem to understand that we were asking for that. "Deli" was difficult. "Žebra" was impossible.

We asked Markéta to go with us.

MARKÉTA: "Chtěli bychom koupit žebra." (We would like to buy ribs.)

BUTCHER: "Co myslíte žebry?" (What do you mean by ribs?)

MARKÉTA: "Žebra, kosti s masem na nich." (The rib bones with meat on them.)

More Czech. Lots more Czech. Even more Czech.

On her fourth attempt, she finally got through.

MARKÉTA: "Ok. He will save that part for us tomorrow. We need to come back at 2 p.m."

Success. Jamie was thrilled.

The next day, we came back to the butcher and—in some sort of Prague miracle—picked up four racks of ribs. Thank goodness because we didn't have a backup plan. My Škoda came in handy for this special occasion since we had to haul charcoal, lighter fluid, matches, four racks of ribs, 12 bottles of barbecue sauce Jamie had brought back in a suitcase at some point, and several cases of beer. We headed to the park on Kampa Island where we were holding this get-together.

We had done advance work and found outdoor, public grills on Kampa

Island in the middle of the Vltava. Who knew? It wasn't glamorous, but it would work. We put the ribs into large aluminum pots of water and boiled them.

After an hour, Jamie checked the ribs. They were tough. Two hours passed. Still tough. As more people arrived, we played frisbee, drank beer, and talked. Three hours later. Ugh, *still* tough. They seemed to be as tough as they had been when we picked them up. Was this caused by keeping the cows in houses? Was there something different about Czech cows? We had no idea, but a decision had to be made. We pulled them out of the water and put them on the grill. Jamie slathered them with BBQ sauce. With bottle after bottle of BBQ sauce.

Jamie didn't say much; he was a man of few words. But I could see him tear up as the Czechs gave him going-away gifts. A HUGE wall calendar from his cement factory client. A Plzen pivo hat. Marketing was new here, and he got some of the first attempts by our clients.

Jamie was glowing. He was sharing his favorite food from home with his Czech friends. Objectively, they weren't the best ribs in the world, but on that day, they were special. At the end of the meal, everyone dipped their hands into the Vltava to wash all the BBQ sauce off their fingers.

Mission accomplished.

CAULIFLOWER

AUGUST 1994

> *The land that vegetables forgot.*
>
> ANTHONY BOURDAIN, *NO RESERVATIONS*, PRAGUE VISIT

ANDREA AND I WERE HAVING OUR COFFEE with Baileys one morning when she invited me to dinner at her parents' house. My friendship with Andrea had clearly grown—it was BIG to be invited to someone's home. I was excited to have a home-cooked Czech meal instead of the usual restaurant fare.

I looked forward to it all day.

I arrived at her parents' house around 7 p.m. I'd made sure to get the address and proper directions so I didn't have another house number debacle. Andrea's parents didn't speak English, so we spoke in hand gestures and facial expressions. We "chatted" in the kitchen while her mother started preparing dinner. My sheer joy must have been obvious when her mother pulled out an ENTIRE HEAD OF CAULIFLOWER! I sat up straight and grinned from ear to ear.

I was psyched! An actual vegetable. Now I didn't particularly love cauliflower, but my entire body felt healthier just looking at it. I hadn't had a fresh vegetable in months except šopský saláts. (I loved šopský salát. Sometimes I ordered two. I knew the country had tomatoes and cucumbers because they showed up in šopský saláts, but somehow, they were never served in any other way.) And as we stood in the kitchen talking and laughing while her mother chopped up the cauliflower, I was wondering how she would prepare it. Steamed? Roasted? Au gratin? I didn't think I cared.

And then it happened. The unthinkable.

My shoulders slumped and I felt my eyes start to water as she dropped all the pieces of cauliflower into a vat of oil. She deep-fried the entire thing! I was holding back a gasp and trying not to show my disappointment. I asked where the toilet was so I could leave the room for a minute and pull myself together.

I told myself it was ok. I would still get to eat a vegetable. Right? But it was not ok. I've never been so excited to eat a vegetable in all my life. To her credit, the deep-fried cauliflower was delicious. But now I was craving fresh vegetables more than ever.

WINE CAVES

AUGUST 1994
MIKULOV

TEREZA INVITED ME TO JOIN HER and two other friends to go to the wine cellars. The four of us piled into a rental car and drove to South Moravia. As usual, we saw no livestock for the entire two- to three-hour trip. Not a horse. Not a cow. Not a pig. We remained baffled.

When we arrived in the town of Mikulov, we were blown away. There were rows and rows of small cellars, most with quaint facades that looked like gingerbread houses. We were in another fairy tale. Some were brick while others were painted white with colorful Czech designs. The doors were almost uniformly arch-topped. They looked like hobbit houses built into the hillsides. We couldn't wait to raise a glass.

We knocked on doors until we found one that welcomed us in. We'd been told that this was how it worked. No reservations, no calling ahead, just knocking on doors. It was hard to believe it would really work.

Franta and Pepa looked to be in their 70s but could have been in their 40s. This was their home and wine cellar, but they were happy to have us join them. They charged us each a few hundred crowns—a lot to them but only about $7 for each of us—to tour the cellar, drink, eat, and spend the night. They spoke no English, but Tereza spoke Czech, so we actually learned a lot. Pepa showed us where they made and stored the wine. It was dark and cavernous with barrels lining the walls. Plus, a rounded ceiling and a small area to do tastings.

We learned that these family wineries had been—of course—taken over by the communist government and forced to grow subpar grapes for decades. Under the communist government, the focus had been on the grapes that ripened fastest, not on complexity or depth of flavor. The state-run restaurants were only allowed to buy wine made from state-grown grapes. Those grapes became the Czech wines we knew that were available in most restaurants: Frankovka, Svatovavřinecké, and rulandské modré. There were others, but these were everywhere we went.

Pepa poured us tastings straight from the barrels. Absolutely the best Czech wine I'd had. Or would ever have. We were astounded and asked Tereza to find out how it could be so much better than what we usually got.

TEREZA: "This wine is so good! It seems very different from the Frankovka we get in Prague."

PEPA: "Yes. It is not the same grapes."

TEREZA: "What do you mean? We thought you all had to grow the grapes the government dictated."

PEPA: "We did. But sometimes we were allowed to keep some production for ourselves."

TEREZA: "Ok..."

We were confused. Just because they kept it didn't make it better. Did it?

Tereza tried one more time.

TEREZA: "So is this wine like the wine you saved for yourselves?"

PEPA: "Yes. We grew better grapes secretly and made better wines to keep at home or sell on the black market."

THIS was why we had come. For the good stuff.

We sat crowded around a small table while Franta served us glass after glass. When we got hungry, they brought out food. Fried pork cutlets, potato salad, and the ever-dreaded tlačenka. There was a lot of food to be feared in the Czech republic, but tlačenka was at the top of my list.

Tlačenka looked awful, and the explanation wasn't any better. It's like the Czechs said, "Let's take the most disgusting parts of a pig and make some food out of it. Bits of a pig's feet, head, organs, skin, and something called podhrdlina (under throat) boiled in a bag. Once soft, they removed the bones and put the rest through a meat grinder. I always thought it was served in aspic, but it was actually gelatin made by boiling the entire head. There were spices and things, but you could literally see the "parts" when it was sliced. Served with onions.

But enough wine can conquer your fear of anything. We tried the tlačenka. Lived to tell. And never tried it again.

I dug into the pork cutlets and potato salad (which was mercifully low on mayo). Especially since Franta insisted that the active ingredients in the pork cutlets and potato salad were a sure cure for a hangover. Grease and acid. Lovely. But she swore by it. Said this magic combo had kept her partying hearty for years now. We couldn't really argue with her, but then she started a strip poker game as some sort of bizarre homage to the meal. I really had no idea what was going on, but the Moravian wine helped. This continued until it was time to exit the game and crash out on the small cots set up for our stay.

The next morning, we woke with raging hangovers. For breakfast, we ate rohliky and cheese and just hoped the bread would soak up the wine before the drive back to Prague.

A truly frightening and fascinating weekend with Franta and Pepa. Strip poker and tlačenka with an elderly couple in their wine cellar wasn't on my bingo card.

FRIDAYS AT PIZZA TAXI: ŠKODA REDUX

SEPTEMBER 1994
PRAGUE

I GRABBED A TAXI FROM THE OFFICE to meet my friends at a pub in Malá Strana. I couldn't be bothered with several tram changes or walking through the crowds in the freezing cold. I tried to show the cab driver that I was a local by using my stellar Czech language skills to tell him to go straight, turn right, or turn left. "Rovně." "Vprava." "Doleva." Mercifully, this driver didn't have a special meter with which to overcharge and rip off tourists.

ME: "Ahoj!"

MARCELA: "Ahoj, Melanie. Chceš pivo?"

ME: "Yes, I'd love a beer."

Marcela signaled to the waitress for one more pivo. I plopped myself onto the wooden bench between Martin and Josef and took a long drink of Pilsner Urquell. My favorite.

ME: "Guess what I did!"

Lots of quizzical looks and shrugs.

ME: "I sold my Škoda."

MARKÉTA: "Yo, yo, yo, Mel. That was probably a good idea."

ME: "For sure. I can't believe someone would pay money for that pile of scrap metal. Hard currency too! But guess who bought it."

MARTINA: "Who, Mel?"

ME: "Roman paid me $800 for it. Half of what I originally paid for it."

MARTIN: "Oh wow. Was it worth that much?"

ME: "Well, it might have been but . . ."

I regaled them with the demise of my "beloved" Škoda.

Roman had been looking for a car to buy for his real estate business finding flats for expats. His wife worked in our office and told him I had a Škoda I might be interested in selling. So one day, I got an unsolicited call from him. Needless to say, I was flabbergasted—but not speechless! Without a second thought, I said, "Well, yes I do." Of course, I thought the dream of selling the car had ended when I told him that I'd recently ditched the car at the side of the road. But I said that if he picked up the keys, he could go look at it. Incredibly, he offered and paid the $800 after seeing and trying to drive the car. Problem solved. For me anyway.

JOSEF: "You ditched the car?"

ME: "It was useless. Constantly having issues. Randomly not starting one day but starting the next. I gave up and left her to fend for herself."

MARKÉTA: "Oh, Mel. That is too bad."

ME: "Hey. I'm just glad I was able to sell it instead of having to flee the country with my car abandoned here forever."

MARTIN: "So now Roman has a car he can use. Good news for everyone."

ME: "Well . . . not really."

They all looked at me quizzically. They were actually curious about what I would tell them next.

ME: "Roman paid to have the dent removed and all the other problems fixed. But on the very first drive in the car, his employee skidded on a puddle, rolled the car, and smashed into a parked BMW."

MARTIN: "No! Was he ok?"

ME: "Yes. Totally fine. But that's not all. They fixed her again, although it hardly seemed worth it to me."

JOSEF: "So it works now?"

ME: "Yes, but it must be haunted. It drives, but those weird *Twilight Zone* things keep happening. The most recent being that for no reason known to man, the headlights have shifted and now one points up and the other points down."

Everyone laughed along with me.

ME: "I don't miss her."

VAŠEK AND THE WEDDING

SEPTEMBER 1994
LIBEREC

VAŠEK, THE MACHO PIG, was getting married.

Most of our expat friends had gone home after the end of their secondment, but Laurent and I were still here. We were the only foreigners invited. We went to Liberec for the wedding weekend. We couldn't wait to see what a Czech wedding was all about.

On the day of the wedding, the bride, Regina, looked beautiful, and Vašek looked happy.

Before the ceremony, at 10 a.m., we drank Becherovka and ate liver dumpling soup to the dulcet tones of Vašek's father playing the accordion. I was getting used to having shots before lunchtime, and the Becherovka helped me stomach the soup.

ME: "Is this how all Czech weddings start?"

LAURENT: "I don't know."

ME: "Is it just me, or does the accordion make this feel a little like a circus?"

Laurent just laughed and did another shot of Becherovka.

The ceremony was brief and nonreligious despite being held in a church.

And it was quick. Bing bang boom, and they were married. As we exited, the mother of the bride handed each of us a shot of vodka.

Third shot of the day and it wasn't even lunchtime. Bottoms up!

We followed the crowd to a Czech pub for the reception. We were seated at long, communal tables and served boiled pork and hranolky (french fries), a variation on pork and dumplings. We were served Fernet (the liquor of the devil due to the small amount required to give me the most splitting hangover imaginable). And more Becherovka.

After we ate, it was time to dance. This was going to be easy considering all the alcohol we'd already consumed. The band consisted of eight denim-clad, beer-guzzling guitar players, including the bride's father, and several women who looked like they'd lived very hard lives, all in jeans. Everyone looked like they had just walked in from the street. No wedding planners or dress code here.

ME: "Suddenly. I feel overdressed."

LAURENT: "Look."

Laurent chuckled and pointed to the ceiling.

LAURENT: "There's a disco ball."

Come on. In a Czech pub? But sure enough, there it was.

It was all such a stark contrast to weddings in America. Bridezillas. Invitations. Matching bridesmaid dresses. Receptions. Honeymoons. It was weirdly refreshing to think a wedding could be more chill than all that. Here, people danced and drank for hours. I mostly looked at the smiles and laughing faces and tried to avoid the Fernet. I'd never had more fun at a wedding reception.

The day after the wedding, a big group of Vašek and his friends went for a bike ride. I was all in. But as I met up with the group, I realized I was wildly unprepared. To me, going on a bike ride is a leisurely activity done in shorts and a t-shirt. The SoCal girl in me was not prepared for biking in Liberec. It was arctic cold and mostly uphill. Not my personal idea of a great time. I walked much of the way and chatted with the bride, the groom, and Laurent all day. The ride, of course, ended at a pub, where I warmed up with my favorite Czech liqueur, Becherovka. It tastes like Christmas. Delicious.

The entire weekend was a blast. It was genuinely joyous, and the bride and groom spent so much time with their guests. Somehow, someway, this wedding felt a little more real to me than any other I'd attended back home.

Quarterly News

of the

WEIRD AND WONDERFUL

JULY–SEPTEMBER 1994

I WAS STARTING TO THINK I was the only person worried about poisonous mushrooms and nuclear disaster. But I was encouraged that there was more than one political party now. Too bad the place was overrun with foreigners, especially Americans.

(LN/2) Budvar and other South Bohemian breweries moved to nonstop production of beer in recent days to meet the increased demand brought on by the hot weather. Samson has gone so far as to double production.

Oh my word. How much more beer could they drink?

This said so much. Capitalism was supposed to be fair . . . but somehow it was still unfair.

(MS/6) A cartoon by Renčín pictures a wealthy cigar-smoking Czech explaining his success to his grandchildren, as servants work busily in the mansion. "Capitalism started with a bang," he says, "and we all rushed headlong into it. Everyone had an equal chance. Especially, of course, those of us who knew where the starting line was."

(LN/2) Nova said it might sue the pro-motion company 10:15 for reneging on a promise of an exclusive interview with Bob Dylan and the chance to film part of the rock star's recent concert. 10:15 admitted that it put the items in the contract without knowing whether it would be possible to fulfill them.

Ummmm . . . this was not how contracts worked . . .

How was this an actual event?

(MFD/Sat/3) The Bolek Polívka The-ater and the theater agency Echo will sponsor the world's first fly-catching championships Sat. in Olšany. Partic-ipants will compete in two events: catching flies at rest and in midair.

(RP/3) Chairman Richard Falbr of the Chamber of Trade Unions (ČMKOS) said yesterday that under the commu-nist regime, women earned only 60% of what men earned for comparable work. Things are not much better now, he argued. But unions alone are not to blame for this. Women who face dis-crimination must stand up for them-selves, he said.

Right. Cuz we haven't tried that for decades.

Ahhh. The negatives of the new system.

(MFD/4) An Olomouc business that ordered a computer from Oáza found only a brick and a piece of wood in the box. Police have not yet been able to uncover where the switch was made.

Well, we couldn't have that.
Ha. The whole "Let's go pick
mushrooms in the forest and
make lunch with them" thing
terrified me.

(MFD/3) Some experts fear that the
long heat wave might lead to a poor
mushroom-hunting season this year.

Well, thank goodness. Still
wasn't planning to eat any.

(MFD/3) Fears that this summer's long
heat wave would lead to a poor mushroom-hunting season were unfounded,
MFD says. Some species are actually
more abundant than in years past. The
best hunting will reportedly be in Sept.

(MFD/2) The government's legislative
council passed a proposed law that
requires car owners to submit their vehicles to a regular technical inspection.
Inspections must now be performed
only when an owner is summoned for
one. Passage of the bill in Parliament
is expected by the end of the year.

It was about time.

Too funny. A different
entry said there were
1,180 Americans in Prague
legally and almost 29,000
illegally. Seemed nobody
was sure at all. To be
fair, there were a lot of
Americans here . . .

(LN/Sat/N1) In a humorous article on
YAPs (Young Americans in Prague),
Hana Lešenarová of Prognosis Weekly writes that no one has been sure
how large the American community
here is. But now a joint census by
Prognosis and Lidové noviny has
come up with a precise number, she
says: 17,692, plus or minus 20,000.

(MFD/2) Czech Television's Council expects the public station to discontinue broadcasting erotic programs as of the end of the year. Programs such as Playboy had their place on public television when private television did not exist, Council Chairman Jiří Grygar said, but not any longer.

Uhhh, they showed that on public television???

They went from one to 74 parties? Total chaos.

(HN/3) Seventy-four political parties and movements are qualified to run in this fall's local elections without needing to canvass for enough signatures to gain approval. (HN lists them all.)

(RP/1) Klaus said yesterday on television that his famous quote from Forbes magazine - "Journalists are mankind's biggest enemy" - was uttered on the way out the door with the microphones turned off. The fact that this made its way into print is an example of bad journalism, he said, not of a politician's making a bad mistake.

Wow. Just wow.

(MFD/3) The mayors of several towns located within a 5km radius of the Dukovany nuclear facility said they will ask that the plant's warning system be cut off because there are too many false alarms. They said that a handcranked siren would be better than the expensive alarm system now in place. If officials do not disconnect the system within two weeks, they added, they will cut it off themselves.

And THIS was not a good idea!

GOSSIP

I WAS DONE. I couldn't bring myself to audit for another year. It was like beating my head against a brick wall. I loved Prague and the Czech republic and wanted to stay even though so many of my friends had left already, but I had to do something different. Anything.

Incredibly, there was another job for me to do in the Prague office. No more traveling at God-awful hours on Monday mornings to reach some obscure Czech hamlet to audit some dysfunctional company. Hallelujah. I would stay another six months.

I missed the gang, so I wrote Jamie, Mike, and Peter a letter about all the happenings in Prague and faxed it to each of them.

Dear Jamie, Mike, and Peter,

Hi everyone! How is everything going? To start with, I am no longer auditing. YEAH!!! I can't tell you how much happier I am. (But of course, most of you already quit auditing, so

you understand.) I am in charge of the internal accounting
system conversion for the Prague, Bratislava, and Sofia
offices. This involves 1) learning everything there is to know
about the new system, 2) teaching the managers, seniors,
and staff how to use all the new forms, 3) teaching the
partners and managers how to read and use the new
reports, and 4) teaching the accounting department how
to do all the input. Believe it or not, the Prague office is
actually going to be on-line and we'll be doing all the input
and reporting for the three offices. The best bit is that
learning how to use the new system involves three or four
business trips to London. The first one is for four or five
days at the end of November.

The cement season has started, and I have to say, I'm
really annoyed. I worked my backside off at Cemos Ostrava
and Cement Hranice for two years, preparing my own PBC
schedules, sleeping at the Cementář, taking the 6 a.m. train
and driving a Škoda. This year, incredibly, because of the new
French management guy from the investing company working
on site in Hranice, the employees drop everything when the
auditors come in, all the PBCs were properly prepared (in
advance, as they're supposed to be), the audit team is staying
at the Růžek (a much nicer hotel than the Cementář),
and they're driving a Western car. It's so unfair. On the
other hand, one of the new staff on the job has a SERIOUS
attitude problem and Ladislav is doing his utmost to make
the expats look stupid in front of the client. That amuses me
greatly. I guess I don't really miss it much after all.

One of our staff has really gone over the edge. It's really sad
and unfortunate and I haven't figured out what to do yet.
According to reliable sources, over the past few weeks and
months, he has been heard or seen 1) gossiping about salary
levels and spreading rumours that Markéta is only ranked
higher than he is because she's friends with Jamie and me,
2) drinking whisky and wine AT WORK, and 3) leaving a rude

note anonymously in Marcela's mail file about the length of her skirts, which upset her so much that she spent her entire paycheck on skirts that hang below her knees. (I'd like to add that her skirts were quite a bit longer than those of most of our secretaries and that even if they had been completely obscene, it is NOT another staff's place to say anything about it anonymously or otherwise!) If anyone has any ideas on how to handle this situation, please let me know. I can't really tell management about this as any direct conversation with him at this point would cause incredible grief for my sources. I am working diligently (and fairly successfully) at convincing my sources that something needs to be done, regardless of the consequences for said sources.

Last night, Barb and Roman were in a terrible car accident. They were in their new (two-week-old) sporty BMW driving home from a day trip to Germany. They were passing a car in the rain when they skidded on an oil slick. They're both alive and have no permanent injuries. Barb has a concussion and other minor injuries and will be hospitalized until tomorrow. Roman, however, has a broken leg, a broken hand, and some major problem with his neck. I've heard both that it's broken and that something's just been dislocated, but he is NOT paralyzed. He does, however, have to remain hospitalized and immobile for four weeks.

The scariest part of the whole thing is that they were on the Czech side when the accident occurred, so they were taken to a Czech hospital. They sat in the emergency/waiting room for SEVEN HOURS and nobody helped them. And Roman speaks Czech! Can you imagine? At that point, they called BMW in Germany (if you own a BMW, you get concierge service), which arranged for them to be transported to a German hospital where they are now. Just thank heavens they weren't driving a Škoda or a Trabant.

Markéta's brother moved back into the family panelák flat after his studies abroad and now Markéta wants to live on her own. She's desperately searching for a flat and a flatmate. Some of the new staff told her that they'd heard how much beer she drinks, and she was so embarrassed that she's been trying to cut back. I told her to be proud of her special ability and to continue drinking her beloved beer. I don't think she'll abstain for very long, really.

Josef was back in his old form last weekend and he's paying for it. He doesn't know why he went to Lavka in the first place. He got home "sometime between 2 and 6 a.m.," and his 10 a.m. jog didn't happen until 1 p.m. (although, incredibly, it did happen). I think he's given up alcohol again . . . he'd forgotten what those hangovers were like.

Ladislav is still telling our clients that we charge too much. Josef is still crazy. Baťa still doesn't have my size in any of the shoes I like and the Czechs still stand in a queue at Kmart waiting for a basket even after I zip past them and go in without one. I'm so happy that communist rule has left the building.

Sorry it's been so long since I've written or spoken with any of you. PLEASE write, call, FAX or e-mail soon. (Oh, who am I kidding? We still don't have email). It's lonely here without you.

Love,

Melanie

P.S. There's been an enormous overproduction of potatoes in the Czech republic (600,000 tons extra)! Wish me luck; I could be rolling in dumplings soon!

TEN TWELFTHS TO 1995

OCTOBER 1994

ANDREA AND I WERE MEETING in front of the office to grab a drink after work. It was a nice night so we decided to walk the tourist route down Karlova and over the Charles Bridge to a new place in Malá Strana near the Prague Castle.

ANDREA: "Ahoj, Kuřátko!"

I smiled. She had taken to calling me 'chick' or 'Little Chicken' after a popular children's book. At least she wasn't calling me Ježek (Hedgehog) or Krtek (Little Mole), two of the most popular characters in the country. They were cute but Little Chicken seemed better.

ME: "Dobrý den! Jak se máš?" (Good day! How are you?)

I said it in my best sing-song voice as the Czechs did.

ANDREA: "Díky, perfektně. Jak se máš?" (Thanks, I'm perfect. How are you?)

ME: "Díky, dobře." (Thanks, I'm good.)

ANDREA: "Nice Czech. Your accent has gotten very good."

I was hardly conversational but my language skills had definitely improved over time.

We were headed to U Krále Brabantského (At the King of Brabant), a medieval pub that had been open almost continuously since 1375 and where Mozart used to drink. Rumor was that Czech kings had gone there via secret passages from the castle. I couldn't wait.

As we strolled Karlova, now the biggest tourist shopping street in the city, we chatted.

ME: "I love all the new galleries and shops. Crystal, leather gloves, garnets, wooden toys, matryoshka dolls. I think that shop sells hand cream made with beer."

ANDREA: "Yes but too many tourists."

ME: "True. This street is terrible during the summer but better now."

ANDREA: "I suppose."

ME: "Honestly, though, I kind of miss what it was like before all this. When the only place to buy souvenirs was from the guy that used to stand on that corner over there, selling old Soviet memorabilia."

ANDREA: "What guy?"

How had she not noticed him?

ME: "He sold Soviet military pins, Olympics and other sports badges, fur hats, dolls, and other things. All authentic. Now we have replicas here. I really wish I'd bought more from him."

Andrea took a drag on her cigarette and just nodded.

ME: "I love all the beautiful colors of the buildings. Pale pink, blue, yellow, peach. It looks like Easter."

ANDREA: "They all used to be brown."

ME: "Really?"

ANDREA: "Yeah. They only painted them these colors after the revolution."

I couldn't even imagine it.

ME: "Why brown?"

ANDREA: "Well some weren't painted at all. But I think the Soviets over-produced brown paint so that's all there was."

I laughed. But of course. Brown suits, brown paint, orange cars. At least they hadn't painted the buildings Škoda orange.

We were approaching the Charles Bridge. It wasn't high tourist season but there were still all sorts of artists selling their wares. Ceramics, drawings, jewelry. As we strolled across the bridge, I stopped and looked at a few things. Some earrings caught my eye so I held a few pairs up to my ears and looked in the vendor's mirror. Andrea shook her head, no. Not right for me. As I put them back and walked away I heard the vendor mutter under his breath.

VENDOR: "Do prdele."

I whipped around. What?! Did he say 'do prdele' to me? Up yours? Or maybe it was just 'damn' because I hadn't bought anything.

ME: "Andrea, did you hear that?"

ANDREA: "Hear what?"

ME: "That man swore at me."

She waved it off and kept walking.

ANDREA: "They swear at everyone."

Well ok then. But now I wondered how often they were swearing at me and I just hadn't noticed. Oh well. We were nearing the end of the bridge and the Devil Man. This man was there every single day, selling his sketches. Of himself, with devil horns. Everyone knew the Devil Man but I didn't know anyone who'd ever purchased one of his sketches. I wondered how he stayed in business but then again, maybe he didn't have any customers. Who knew?

A few more minutes walking and we'd arrived at the pub. It was dark and cavernous, lit by candlelight. The perfect place for sharing secrets, having a tryst, or planning something sinister. I loved it.

We grabbed a few pivos and some seats and chatted in hushed tones. I didn't have anything secret to discuss but I did have a question.

ME: "Can you explain how Czechs talk about time?"

ANDREA: "What do you mean?"

ME: "Sorry. That was wildly unclear. I mean telling someone what time it is. There are a lot of extra words involved."

ANDREA: "Ohhh. It's so simple."

ME: "Well if it's ten minutes after two o'clock we would say 'two ten.' What do you say?"

ANDREA: "Je deset minut po druhé." (It is ten minutes past two.)

ME: "Extra words. Also, since when is 'two' 'druhé?' I thought it was dva. Never mind. Extra words."

We laughed.

ANDREA: "I suppose so, but not SO many extra."

ME: "Fair. But what about this one. If it's is forty-five minutes past four, we would say 'four forty-five' or 'a quarter to five.' And in Czech?"

ANDREA: "Je tři čtvrtě na pět."

ME: "Which translates to what?"

She grinned because she knew this one was the one that kept most of the expats from being able to tell the time in Czech.

ANDREA: "It is three quarters to five."

I burst out laughing. Why? Just why? It was so backwards in my mind. In English it was one quarter to five but in Czech it was three quarters to five. In English that was three quarters past four. I'd never been able to keep it straight.

Andrea kindly ordered another round of pivo.

GAME MEAT

ANOTHER WEEKEND, ANOTHER CHANCE to get out of town. Marcela, Markéta, Martin's wife Monika, and I piled into Martin's car and drove to Český ráj in the Czech countryside for the weekend. Martin told us about a great restaurant on the other side of the mountain. It was known for serving wild game meat, which was an exciting prospect.

As we entered, we were once again reminded that even fancy restaurants here were not like those in the West. It was a sparse room with linoleum floors and cafeteria-style tables topped with Formica. The little décor on the walls had no rhyme or reason. I'm not sure if the place had an actual name or if it was simply "restaurace" like most others.

But the menu was a startling change. They had deer, boar, rabbit, and pheasant! Where were we? It sounded amazing. We each ordered a different dish so we could try everything. My favorite part was the blueberry sauce. I had never had it before, and I was already a fan of meat and fruit. It seemed to be a communist specialty. But it was much better here at this game restaurant than the anemic versions we were served in Prague.

ME: "So what's the deal with meat and fruit?"

MARTIN: "What do you mean? It's delicious."

ME: "Yes! I really love it. I've just never had it at home. Is it a communist thing? A Czech thing? Eastern European?"

MARCELA: "Oh! They've been hunting and serving wild game in the mountains and forests of central Europe since the Middle Ages."

ME: "Well, who knew?! I love it."

MARTIN: "So do I."

Martin also loved fat and organ meat, so that wouldn't have been a ringing endorsement in my mind. Thankfully I had tried it before he tried to sell me on it.

Towards the end of dinner, a waiter came to the table. We ordered another round of pivos. After slashing the paper at the end of the table, the waiter tore four tickets off a big roll and set them on the table. He walked away without saying a word.

ME: "Ummmm, what's this for?"

MARTIN: "I don't know."

Martin didn't seem bothered, but my curiosity was piqued.

ME: "It looks like he has given one to everybody in the room."

ME: "Maybe it's good for a beer? Or maybe there's a raffle. Are there prizes? Does anyone know?"

They didn't. They said "I don't know" to each of my queries and carried on chatting and drinking his beer as if nothing was amiss. I swear the man had zero curiosity about it. The most absurd things happened, and everyone just shrugged their shoulders. Still! In 1994.

We continued drinking our beer, enjoying the end of a truly special dinner. The lights dimmed a little. And then a little more. Soon the room was almost dark. A spotlight flipped on and illuminated a disco ball hanging from the middle of the ceiling. White spots began dancing on the walls and floors of the room.

ME: "Did this just turn into a discotheque?"

We all started laughing. Somehow we had totally missed the big clue: the disco ball! Young people filed in. The tickets seemed to grandfather us into admission since we'd eaten dinner there. I was surprised they hadn't just kicked us out mid-drink. How I missed it after seeing one at Vašek's wedding, I have no idea. It just wasn't on my radar at all.

Soon there was music, dancing, and more beer. The music was retro, just a little out of date, but the beer was fresh. We danced our hearts out. What more did we really need?

ABSINTHE

THROUGH WORD OF MOUTH, we learned that some bar in Vinohrady had absinthe. The office was abuzz. The Czechs were super excited about it; I had never heard of it.

The Czechs told us it was a hallucinogenic liquor that had been very popular in Prague before WWII and had been served at the famous Café Slavia. The drink of authors, artists, bohemians, and dissidents. Absinthe was the legendary drink that was rumored to have driven Vincent Van Gogh to madness. It was the drink of Oscar Wilde, Émile Zola, Henri de Toulouse-Lautrec, and Picasso.

It had been banned for decades in most of Europe and the U.S. It was always legal in the Czech republic but production had dwindled when the Communist Party nationalized industry and eliminated private businesses. I guess it wasn't part of the "plan" in the planned economy. Consequently, our Czech friends had never tried it but had heard legends about its power.

A huge group of us, maybe 15 Czechs and expats, made our way to the bar near the TV tower. The place was filling up but we managed grab a long table for our large group. Everyone ordered absinthe. Also known as the Green Fairy due to its customary neon green color, preparing it was a ritual. A glass fountain with two spouts was filled with ice water. Glasses with a portion of absinthe in each were placed under the spouts. A sugar cube was place on a special spoon that sat atop the glass. Then the spouts were opened and the water dripped slowly, dissolving the sugar as it flowed into the glass. The bright green absinthe turned a cloudy yellow-green.

The anticipation was high. We couldn't wait to try it but we knew this ritual was part of the joy of it. Everyone waited until all the drinks had been prepared. Then we let loose.

ALL: "Na zdraví!"

ME: "Whoa. That tastes like licorice soaked in Becherovka."

MARKÉTA: "Yo, yo, yo, Mel. I love the herbal taste."

PAVEL: "Which part is the wormwood? Isn't that supposed to be the good bit?"

ME: "What does wormwood even taste like?"

Nobody knew.

MARCELA: "I found it bitter. Not bad, just bitter."

There were several conversations happening at once as we continued sipping our absinthe and comparing notes. We spent the evening musing about why it was beloved, why it had disappeared, why it was back, and why the ritual was important to the taste, aroma, and experience. Everyone in the bar was doing the same. And everyone was having a blast. There was laughter, and joking, and teasing. A stranger sent me a drink from another table. I sent a drink back.

Nobody hallucinated. No one had the urge to cut their ear off. That was all just a myth.

It was a memorable evening for many reasons but mostly because I had never seen my Czech friends let loose like that before. They seemed unburdened, free, and—honestly—joyful. Maybe the group was just fun. Maybe they loved absinthe. But maybe it was being free to do something that hadn't been possible before. Something they'd longed to do. I went with that. And I'd never forget their sheer joy that night.

Their smiles of freedom.

FRIDAYS AT PIZZA TAXI: COMMUNISM

NOVEMBER 1994

ME: "I think I'm finally getting it."

EVA: "Getting what, dahling?"

The waitress was passing out a round of pivos and one drink I didn't recognize. We'd abandoned Pizza Taxi for more traditionally Czech places now that most of the expats were gone. That night we went to the pub in Obecní dům (the Municipal House). Still no fancy pub names—it was called Pivnice Obecní dům. Essentially, "the Beerhouse in the Municipal House." We had a big group out tonight.

Na zdravis all around. We toasted to the evening. Everyone had beer but Marcela. I had to ask.

ME: "Marcela, what is that that you're drinking?"

MARCELA: "I got Frankovka with cola."

ME: "I'm sorry, what? Is that red wine with soda?"

MARCELA: "It's so good!"

I will try almost anything, but no. I grabbed my pivo.

ME: "I think I'm finally understanding so many things. When I came here,

I thought everyone would be excited and open to change. You'd waited so long for this. But I think that change was so much harder than anyone had expected. At least harder than I expected."

JOSEF: "Well, it isn't easy to come out of decades of oppression."

ME: "Seriously. This gap between the two economic models is like purgatory."

HENRY: "I often wondered how you could stand having no choices about anything: food, car color, education, beer. But now I think I get it."

MICHAELA: "When those choices are taken away, you adapt. You accept. You stop caring so much because you have no way to fight back."

ME: "It's true. I've been here less than two years, and I've stopped caring about a lot of little things."

MARCELA: "Being angry didn't put more food on the shelves."

And wanting a green car didn't make one available. In fact, I don't think any of my Czech friends ever even imagined a green car. Because cars were orange or white or gray; they were not green. Neither were doors.

MARKÉTA: "It makes me sad. We accepted so much and almost never pushed back."

ME: "But you couldn't have! It doesn't really work now and it sure as hell didn't work before."

Everyone laughed, including Markéta. She knew it was true.

JOSEF: "It was pointless."

EVA: "In theory, it all sounds great. Universal, free healthcare; free education; guaranteed minimum livable income; government job programs; and free food. Fabulous, right?"

JOSEF: "It did SOUND good."

LAURENT: "And Marx wasn't wrong when he said there were inequities in capitalistic society."

PAVEL: "But there were inequities under the communists as well. The communist elite lived far better than the average worker. No different than capitalism."

Even in Karl Marx's vision, the process of transitioning from capitalism through socialism to true communism required a journey through a dictatorial nightmare. That government was supposed to redistribute the wealth according to need and magically make people decide that equality was better than private ownership.

PAVEL: "Theoretically, once a place achieved true communism, there would no longer be a government or even money. Everyone would be equal and there would be no competition."

We refilled the wine. It had clearly been nothing like that at all.

ME: "Has any country has ever made it through the process?"

HENRY: "I don't think so . . ."

PAVEL: "No. They all got stuck. No government has ever given things back."

The path to achieving communism was a conundrum.

ME: "Let me make sure I understand this. In order to get to full, far-left communism, a country must first have a far-right totalitarian government."

PAVEL: "Yes."

ME: "So, a far-right political system is needed to get to a far-left economic system. No wonder nobody ever makes it!"

JOSEF: "Communist officials are never going to give everything back to the people."

MARCELA: "Of course not. Once they're in charge, they stay in charge."

ME: "Maybe it's not a spectrum of right and left. It's a circle. The far-right and far-left meet on the other side. Kind of like love and hate. It's a fine line."

They pondered it. Nobody objected. We were all thinking through it.

HENRY: "Maybe. Bottom line: it doesn't work."

ME: "And it doesn't work because humans don't work that way. Communism goes against basic human nature."

MICHAELA: "You cannot force people to be motivated for the 'rewards' of communism or socialism. Everyone did just enough to keep their job."

PAVEL: "Failure was not permitted. Mistakes were not allowed. Thus,

bureaucracies grew exponentially. Red tape exploded. Rules contradicted rules that contradicted rules."

HENRY: "Look. Capitalism is not perfect. It has its problems."

JOSEF: "But it has to be better than this was."

Everyone nodded in agreement.

Society in the Soviet Bloc was a flower that never bloomed.

HENRY: "I saw a great sign the other day. It said, *'Socialism: Ideas so good
they have to be mandatory.'*"

We all chuckled.

ME: "And have you seen the new Peugeot ad?"

HENRY: "Yes! So good."

> As Lenin wrote, the trick is "not merely a struggle for power but a strug-
> gle against power." A principle that didn't make for a very pleasant
> political system. But does keep you in control of your car.[14]

We rolled laughing. I loved that we were starting to see the Czechs make
fun of the past. It seemed like a healthy part of the transformation.

MERRY CHRISTMAS

ME: "Ve-sel-e Van-ō-se."

MY PARENTS: "She-sell-ee Van-oo-see."

ME: "Ve-sel-e Van-ō-se."

THEM: "Ve-shell-ee Von-ot-see."

ME: "Ve-sel-e Van-ō-se."

THEM: "Vee-shee-ee Vant-oot-she."

Whatever.

My parents came to Prague for Christmas. Somehow, they didn't fly in together, and they wouldn't be flying out together either. They stayed with me since Tereza had gone home for the holidays.

I took them to all the sites any tourist would see visiting Prague. The castle. Charles Bridge. Old Town Square. The Prague Astronomical Clock. Wenceslas Square. The Golden Lane. The Jewish Cemetery. And they bought the things that all normal tourists would buy in Prague. Crystal. Amber jewelry. Marionettes. (Just kidding. Nobody bought a creepy marionette.) Postcards. And, of course, we took the requisite trip to Krakow and Auschwitz-Birkenau. It was not festive, but they were so close it felt mandatory to visit.

We were walking up Wenceslas Square to catch our train to Poland when something caught my eye.

ME: "Ohmigod, look!"

MOM: "What? What are we looking at?"

ME: "I that really a KFC?"

MOM: "I take it that's new?"

ME: "Oh wow. Let's get some for the train ride."

It was true. It was a genuine Kentucky Fried Chicken. I was soooo excited. We didn't have a ton of time before our train left, but it was fast food. Let's go.

We went into its brand spanking new location on Vodičkova Street planning to order our favorites: original recipe chicken, coleslaw, mashed potatoes and gravy, and those mouth-watering biscuits. Yummmm.

We joined the line and looked up at the menu.

ME: "What fresh hell is this?"

MOM: "What's a rohliky?"

I wanted to cry. No biscuits? They were serving the chicken with Czech rohliky. They also didn't have mashed potatoes and gravy. But they had greasy American fried chicken. Good enough for me. The lines were long since this was a new, Western delicacy. The Americans were excited, and the Czechs were curious. We learned from others in line that this KFC used all the chicken breasts to make chicken sandwiches, so all the regular fried chicken was strictly dark meat. No breasts; all legs and thighs. Not ideal, but we decided we could live with that. At least I did, and my family wasn't about to disagree.

We were starting to worry about the time because we had a train to catch, but then it was our turn. The service was not as fast as I thought "fast" food should be. But finally, we got to the front of the line. THEY RAN OUT OF CHICKEN!

KFC ran out of chicken.

No freaking way. Adding insult to injury, the chicken machine broke. So they couldn't make any more even if they'd still had chicken. *Great. We have a KFC that can't make chicken.*

Off to the train we went. Chickenless.

We spent a few days in Krakow and an afternoon visiting Auschwitz-Birkenau, the most notorious concentration and extermination camps of all from the Holocaust. Krakow is delightful. I could go there many times and love it. But this was probably my fourth trip to Auschwitz-Birkenau and that was more than enough for anyone. But I was glad I took my parents to visit it. It was a deeply emotional experience.

We returned to Prague for some more uplifting activities and to get ready for Christmas Day. Tereza and I had gotten a Christmas tree for the apartment. It was beautiful when we decorated it, but it was dead two days later. It was flat on one side when Tereza and I bought it, but we thought that would make it easier to stand it up in front of the window. We were right ... it did make it easier to shove it up against the window, but it also made it easier for the tree to take a dive five minutes before we had friends over for Christmas cocktails. Neat. We'd looped a rope around the trunk and tied it to the living room window handle, where it remained for the holidays. There were spruce needles all over the living room, so everyone had to wear shoes at all times. Incredibly (or not), there didn't seem to be a single store in Prague that sold Christmas tree stands that held water. Not even Kmart. (I saw another untapped market here.) It would be a Charlie Brown Czech Christmas.

Josef had helped us with a longstanding family tradition. I had taken a photo with Santa Claus every year—usually with mall Santa—since I was born and promised my mom I would continue doing so until I had a kid that would take Santa pictures every year. When I traveled, I always found some sort of Santa Claus to take a photo with. This year, Josef came over to house and put on a crazy-long Santa hat, and I sat on his knee in front of the tree for a picture. My mom was delighted.

We were ready. The dead tree was decorated, the Santa pic taken, the presents wrapped, and it was snowy. I had found several Czech Christmas CDs at Popron and we had all the ingredients to mull wine. We were all set for our first (and only) traditional Czech Christmas except for one thing: dinner.

I made the executive decision that we would go out to dinner for Christmas given the options available. I explained it to my parents.

Option one: We could attempt to cook a turkey and the fixings in my kitchen. I mean, my bedroom. Attempting to cook anything substantial in my flat was a frightening thought. The oven was new, but the temperature in the oven never stabilized, so we usually had to sit next to the oven opening and closing the door in order to lower and raise the temperature as necessary (I hadn't been able to find an oven thermometer to help with the task). Doing this for six or seven hours to cook a turkey did NOT sound like my idea of a good time on Christmas. Not to mention how many hours it would have taken us to realize we would likely never find a turkey, cranberries, yams, and green vegetables of any kind.

Option two: We could have the traditional Czech Christmas dinner of smažený kapr, or fried carp. The Czech turkey. The expats affectionately referred to it as "fried crap" because so many menus translated it as such. (Again . . . just one native English speaker could have stopped this.) Made me laugh every time. Worst. Marketing. Ever.

We had three choices for how to have carp for dinner. We could go to a restaurant, buy a live fish to cook at home, or buy a dead fish to cook. Leading up to the holiday, all around Prague, carp were for sale. These three- to seven-pound, bottom-dwelling fish. Outside of supermarkets, huge vats of carp swam around, waiting to be bought. We could buy the fish alive, take it home, and let it live in the bathtub for three days to flush out its insides. When it was time to cook it, we'd have to behead and clean it. That was a no-go. We weren't giving up showers for three days. And we weren't excited about the beheading. Alternatively, we could choose to have it smacked over the head with a stick, beheaded, and cleaned in front of us by the fishmonger. The blood ran down the streets of Prague for weeks at Christmastime. Like a pescatarian horror movie. Regardless of which option we chose, we would then have to risk our lives by eating this extremely boney fish. More than a few Czechs have found themselves in the emergency room after Christmas dinner. Not wanting to see any family members hospitalized, we all agreed not to go the carp route.

We chose option three, and I made reservations at one of my favorite restaurants, Vinárna U Maltézských rytíru (Wine Tavern of the Knights of Malta). Located on a cute street in Malá Strana, the restaurant had a cavernous, below-ground cellar lit by candlelight. It was incredibly charming and known for the quality of the food. I suggested that everyone have what I was having: crispy Czech duck and red cabbage. My favorite dish, by far, in the Czech republic. I loved it and so did my parents.

The next morning, we pulled open Christmas crackers, donned paper crowns and began passing around the "stockings." I'd made "stockings" out of some Easter-themed gift bags I'd found at Kmart. I worked with what I had. Then we opened presents. I gifted them with the most unique new stuff I could find in Prague. Traditional wooden toys, painted eggshells, and wrought iron frames. Shopping had improved dramatically since I'd arrived two years ago.

As we opened gifts, I noticed that the train station across the street was open and a babička was working alone there. I packed up an Easter gift bag with a painted egg, a wooden toy, and some candy. I trudged through the snow to see her. She spoke no English, but I wished her "Veselé vánoce" and gave her the bag of treats. Her surprised, wide smile made my day. I turned for home. She returned to work.

THE NEW YEAR

31 DECEMBER 1994

MY PARENTS LEFT BEFORE NEW YEAR'S EVE so I celebrated with my friends. A few of us went to Markéta's family's chata (summer house) a few hours outside Prague. We drank Fernet and ate chlebíčky with the most garlicky and horseradishy sauce imaginable. I think it took two weeks to get it all off my breath. And Fernet was my hell. I knew that, but I'd fallen for it. It got the best of Brenda too. She spent six hours running around town on New Year's Day before remembering she had cat whiskers painted on her face.

Absolutely hilarious.

Quarterly News

of the
WEIRD AND WONDERFUL

OCTOBER–DECEMBER 1994

WE WERE STARTING TO SEE how many things people had to pay for now that they hadn't had to under the communist system. Dental care, health-care, education. It had to be a huge shock for people. But technology was advancing, Western TV shows and music were coming, and the country was planning for elections. I hoped they would be able to keep looking for the positives to come.

(MFD/7) Dentists in the Ostrava region say that an increase by insurance companies in the amount patients must contribute for certain dental pro-cedures has led to a reduction in the number of people who opt to have their damaged teeth covered with a dental crown. More and more people prefer to have the teeth pulled out, dentists say. If something isn't done, say the doctors, the number of tooth-less people is going to increase.

Holy cow. This change from socialized medicine was going to be bumpy.

So. Many. Questions.

(MFD/3) Unlike in earlier years, sale of alcohol will not be banned in Prague during Nov.'s municipal elections.

(MFD/4) Porno films have saved the Pilsen cinema Eden from an early demise, says 75-year-old owner Mira Hoblíková. The Eden - the first private theater to appear after the revolution - still concentrates on mainstream films, but the porno flicks that show three nights a week keep it in business.

They must have been quite popular given how new this was.

Some cultural advances were outpacing the technology.

(MFD/3) Some TV viewers in Ostrava complain that they often have trouble picking up Nova because users of un-homologated cordless phones operating on the same frequency are interrupting the airwaves. One viewer, Eva Kotová, says she's heard scores of phone conversations on her TV. Some are quite interesting, she admits.

(RP/1) The Academy of Motion Pictures rejected the Czech nomination for the Oscars because the "Life and Extraordinary Adventures of the Soldier Ivan Chonkin" contains no Czechs and no Czech dialog. The "Faust Lesson" will be nominated instead.

Shocker.

And this was why I would never speak or write Czech properly.

(RP/3) TV Nova reported that MP Jan Vik of the Republican Party is carrying out his official duties under a false name. His real name, Nova said, is Jan Vík (with a long-mark over the "i"). Even though the difference is only slight, Nova said, it can make a big difference in terms of such things as checking records in a computer.

(MFD/4) The Prague police will receive Kč 1m from the city to buy more horses for patrolling the streets during demonstrations, etc. Horses often-times command more respect that po-lice officers, Mayor Koukal explained.

Ha. What in the world?

Sigh. Supply and demand still hadn't caught on as an important concept.

(RP/3) Škoda Auto reports that it has completely sold out of Favorits but that Formans are still available. The au-tomaker sees no reason to lower prices to get rid of remaining stock.

(MFD/1) Prague police arrested three people last Wed. for possession of 3kg of enriched uranium 235, which can be used for making a nuclear bomb. Experts say the material likely came from the former Soviet Union.

WHAT THE HELL???

Lines and more lines.

(MFD/3) Thousands of people stood in line for hours yesterday to revalidate their Czechoslovak passport. Old travel documents expire tomorrow.

Carp season! For whatever reason, I was fascinated by the streets flowing with carp scales and blood.

(MFD/3) An inspection in Pilsen of pre-Christmas carp sellers found that near-ly two-thirds of stores and sidewalk stands wished their customers a Merry Christmas by overcharging them for the traditional holiday food.

(MFD/2) The Constitutional Court yesterday abolished the institution of anonymous testimony, effective March 1 of next year. The court sided with those who argued that anonymous testimony violates the rights of the accused. Justice Minister Jiří Novák said that other ways will now be sought for protecting witnesses from those who commit serious crimes.

Wow.

(MFD/2) A Prague judge rejected a request from the city prosecutor's office to allow a search of the home of Republican Party Chairman Miroslav Sládek. Sládek has been wanted for questioning since last week with regard to his behavior in a demonstration on Oct. 28, but police have been unable to find him. They suspect he has been at home the entire time.

Haha. Clever.

PRAGUE
1995

UNIFORMS

JARKA: "Don't you like our uniforms?"

Ohmigod, we're wearing uniforms at work now???

I was enjoying my new role implementing Andersen's new accounting system across the Czech republic, Slovakia, and Bulgaria. Gone were the days of 4 a.m. Monday morning trains to cement factories and cold hotels. No more being banned from restaurants and being gaslit by my clients. I got to stay in Prague, go to the office every day, and head to London for training a few times. I worked with the accounting department personnel in each office to develop new procedures and then trained everyone on how to implement them.

One day, I came into the office, walked into the accounting department, and stopped in my tracks. Every one of them was wearing a green suit with a scarf. Identical suits. Identical scarves. All five of them.

JARKA: "Don't you like our uniforms?"

It had to be a joke. This felt like a setup . . .

ME: "I love the color. But who said you guys need to wear uniforms?"

JARKA: "Oh, we decided to."

ME: "Ummm . . . why?"

I couldn't help myself. I had to ask why.

Jarka looked at me funny. Maybe she thought it was a silly question. Who wouldn't want to wear the same thing as their colleagues?

I tried a different tack.

ME: "Are you planning to wear them every day?"

JARKA: "Of course."

My first thought was, *Have they already bought multiple suits? Or will they wear the same one every day?* My second thought was, *I can never again wear the beautiful green silk suit I just bought in London.* Ugh. I wasn't about to jump on this uniform train.

JARKA: "We think it looks nice."

ME: "Oh, yes. You all look great. I love the scarves."

JARKA: "Don't you want one?" She took her scarf off and offered it to me.

ME: "Nooo. Thank you so much, but I can't take your scarf."

I turned and escaped. *Why, oh why, would they voluntarily choose to dress identically?* I assumed this was a holdover from communist times. To blend in, be one of many, have no individuality, be invisible. Some things I would never fully understand.

Even if I understood.

So they wore their uniforms every day. I did not. But I always regretted not accepting the scarf to remember them all by.

BRIBES

FEBRUARY 1995

ONCE THE NEW ACCOUNTING SYSTEM was up and running in Prague, our office took over the Bulgaria office's accounting. They'd struggled to actually implement the system. So, they just sent us a list of their transactions for us to record. One day, Jarka came to ask me a question.

JARKA: "Boris sent the list of transactions this morning and I'm not sure how to record one of them."

ME: "Let's take a look."

JARKA: "This one, here."

I looked at the transaction log and saw the line item she meant.

"Bribe to parking attendant."

Oh boy. I took a minute to think about it. *Sigh.* I suggested we call Boris, the manager of our Sofia, Bulgaria, office. We got Boris on the line.

ME: "Hi, Boris. Can you help me understand what 'bribe to parking attendant' means?"

BORIS: "We paid the parking attendant a bribe."

ME: "Yeah. I got that part. But why?"

BORIS: "He's in the mafia."

I never learn. I tried again.

ME: "What was the purpose of the bribe?"

BORIS: "I wanted to park in the lot."

ME: "Ok! So, could we say this was this actually a parking expense?"

BORIS: "No, I paid that separately."

ME: "Did this guy actually work at the parking lot?"

BORIS: "No."

I was trying desperately to find an acceptable reason for this payment.

ME: "Ok . . . what was the guy going to do for you in exchange for this money?"

BORIS: "Make sure nobody damaged the car."

Now we were getting somewhere.

ME: "Were you paying him so *he* wouldn't damage the car?"

BORIS: "Him or his mafia friends."

Ugh. A protection racket. We didn't have a "bribe" account to book this to. That wasn't a thing, and I certainly couldn't document that. But I understood that this was a necessary cost of doing business in a city where the Russian mob was running amok. I'd heard this was a huge problem in our Moscow office but hadn't realized it was an issue in Bulgaria too. I thanked my lucky stars the mafia wasn't prominent in Prague.

ME: "So . . . maybe this is a . . . security fee?!"

BORIS: "Sure."

ME: "Great! Thanks so much. From now on, maybe just put these on the log as 'security fees.'"

Whew. I'd found a way to deal with it.

Such were the adventures in accounting in the former Soviet Bloc.

Quarterly News

of the

WEIRD AND WONDERFUL

JANUARY–MARCH 1995

I WAS HEADED HOME SOON. I was excited to see how much progress the country had made during the two years I'd been here. I was continually amused at the humor of the Czech people and their willingness to embrace the craziness of the transition.

(HN/2) Although businesses using single-entry accounting used to be able to choose the year to which they applied expenses and revenues at the beginning of the year, the latest income-tax amendment eliminates this possibility. Those who learned of the change too late are simply out of luck, HN says. A bit of warning would have been nice, the paper notes. Meanwhile, the Chamber of Tax Advisers says the dispute may go all the way to the Constitutional Court.

They were allowed to choose the year? This explained so much about the chaos we found in our clients' records.

As if the dual meters to overcharge foreigners weren't enough.

(MFD/3) Some Prague cabbies have outfitted their vehicles with electrified passenger seats that can be activated if the passenger attempts to rob the driver. Chairman Eduard Šubrt of the Taxi Guild admits that some drivers might also use the electric chairs to punish passengers who refuse to pay an inflated fare.

(MFD/1) MFD says workers, especially those with low wages, are now taking so much sick leave that some companies talk of having a new employment category - the "permanently ill."

Oh, for the love. They definitely didn't need more categories of employees.

Ok, hold up a minute. Škoda, the maker of the golf cart-like cars, was going to help build a nuclear plant?!

(MFD/15) Škoda Praha has put in a bid at the last minute for supplying technology for the completion of the Mochovce nuclear plant in Slovakia.

(MFD/1) Smoke from President Havel's cigarette reportedly set off fire alarms at the Dukovany nuclear plant yesterday. Asked if he did indeed smoke in the highly restricted area, the President responded, "No comment."

OHMIGOD!!!

(MFD/3) Heads of many supermarkets believe that the dramatic rise in the sale of dog food is at least partially explained by the fact that more and more people are buying it for their own consumption. It is considerably less expensive than similar canned foods made for humans, and it is designed to be safe not just for dogs.

Blech. Note to self: keep avoiding the canned goods.

(MFD/3) The police as well as officials of the Ad Council object to a billboard on the Prague-Brno highway that promotes Digital computers using the slogan, "No Speed Limit, but only for users of computers equipped with the Alpha AXP processor." Although the billboard company says it will require the ad to be changed because it confuses drivers, the agency that supplied it, Art Communications, says it sees nothing wrong with it.

Wow.

(MFD/3) Nova was required to pull a new coffee commercial because the voice-over was done by a radio announcer. By law, radio or TV announcers may not appear in TV commercials. Nova protested, saying it cannot possibly keep track of who works for which regional radio station.

Ha. Why would this be a law???

(MFD/3) Labor leaders at the Dukovany nuclear-power plant claim that the risk of an accident is significant because low pay is forcing half of the plant's 600 specialists to moonlight. These people are coming to work tired, labor leaders claim, which increases the chance of an accident.

FINALLY! Someone saw the concern.

(RP/3) František Marek, who weighs 230 kilos (505 lbs.), washed down 24 bacon dumplings with hard liquor and tonic in 15 minutes Sat. to win the first annual dumpling eat-off in Jindřiš.

More blech.

(MFD/Thur/3) The Czech Commercial Inspection advises men to wash their newly bought boxers before wearing them for the first time because a test of a range of men's underwear, both foreign and domestic, found that many contain unsafe levels of formaldehyde.

Uhhhh . . .

(HN/V17) HN says that although many companies have taken steps to prevent employ theft, little is done to prevent the most widespread theft of all - theft of time. Those who are victims of it include customers, suppliers and other employees - anyone who has to wait for a worker who thinks that punctuality is an unnecessary luxury.

This warmed my heart.

(MFD/18) MFD says the language used to subtitle films on the satellite station FilmNet has only a distant relationship to Czech. Martin Smrž of Multichoice, which sells the access cards to FilmNet, says the station will now pay more attention to translations.

A distant relationship to Czech?! I was dying to know what it was.

(MFD/P3) Businessman Petr Maršálek complains that ČSOB refused to exchange money for him at the airport because he had only his passport with him and not his ID card. Does this make sense, he asks, given that Czechs are not allowed to take their ID cards with them when they leave the country? Instead of relenting, ČSOB sent him to a competing private exchange office that was willing to help.

Well, that was a circle of illogical hell.

(MFD/3) MFD says that with the advent of democracy, the lines in Czech stores have disappeared but the lines in front of state offices for such mandatory things as permits or passports have grown out of control.

Lines, lines, lines.

Oh, this made my day. Hilarious.

(MFD/3) Havel's office said it won't take action against a radio commercial for Penthouse in which an impersonator uses Havel's voice to say that the magazine is for men on the rise.

GOODBYE, ME

THE CZECH REPUBLIC WAS CHANGING quickly now. No longer was the country at the top of every capitalist's mind. The voucher privatization had finished at the end of 1994. There was still a lot of work to be done, but the big push was over. The Czech republic was no longer considered risky. Therefore, the potential returns were not as great. It had lost its sexiness. Capitalists were beginning to chase profits further to the East.

It was time to leave. I'd completed the financial system conversion project. And I was ready to go. There were so many people and things I would miss. Most of my close expat friends had left ages ago, but that meant I'd become even better friends with more Czechs. I would miss them all so much. I had learned so much. And I had changed so much.

But I was ready to go home. I was emotionally and mentally drained from the effort of trying to get work done here. Ready for my questions to be understood and for answers to make sense to me. Ready for life and work to be easier. Ready to eat familiar food. Ready to figure out what I would do next.

My friends threw a going away party for me at a new Western restaurant. All the expats and Czechs came out to say goodbye. I was elated, sad, and confused all at the same time. I was ready to go but didn't want to leave. I couldn't wait to start working in the U.S. but was already missing my Czech friends. They gave me lovely cards and weird but wonderful gifts. I'd grown to love unwrapping a surprise every time. Cement factory memorabilia, a lovely gold thread necklace, a T-shirt with a Czech children's book (*Polámal se mraveneček*) printed onto it. Blanka had it made for me. I was beyond touched. I treasured them all.

In return, I gave them the best gift I could think of. I had memorized the very same children's book. It was five verses in a small, foldable cardboard book. I think everyone in the country knew this book. The way everyone in the U.S. knows *The Cat in the Hat*. I stood on a platform at the pub, got everyone's attention, and recited it from memory.

> *Polámal se mraveneček*
> *ví to celá obora,*
> *o půlnoci, zavolali mravenčího doktora.*
>
> *Doktor klepe na srdíčko, potom píše recepis:*
> *třikrát denně prášek cukru, bude chlapík jako rys.*[15]

Translation:

> *The little ant got sick,*
> *the whole forest knows,*
> *at midnight, they call the ant doctor.*
>
> *The doctor taps his little heart, then writes a prescription:*
> *Three times a day, take powdered sugar; he will be like a lynx.*

Three more verses and I'd made it to the very end. They loved it. They clapped and laughed and cried. Gaby's eyes always filled with tears—of laughter or joy, I wasn't sure. Andrea laughed out loud. I got huge hugs. It was the best Czech I'd ever spoken, but I didn't understand the emotional reaction I got from the Czechs. It was not the norm. I wanted to know why they had reacted that way. I went to find Markéta.

ME: "Why did everyone laugh and tear up when I recited *mraveneček*?"

MARKÉTA: "Oh Mel. It's because you read it with such emotion."

ME: "Is that weird? Should I not have done that?"

MARKÉTA: "Oh no, Mel. You should. It's perfect. But Czechs don't read it like that. Gaby loved your facial expressions. Andrea loved the sing-song of your voice. I loved that you looked us all in the eyes and read with feeling."

ME: "Wouldn't everyone do that?"

MARKÉTA: "No, Mel. Czechs would just read it."

Did Czechs read it in some sort of deadpan or monotone voice? Is that how they read everything? Maybe. I could understand that now. And I think they knew that learning to say all these words properly and memorizing this story was my personal gift to them.

As I was pondering this, Vašek, the Macho Pig, walked over and sheepishly gave me a card. He stood there while I read it. My eyes welled with tears.

"I have never learned as much from anyone as I learned from you."

This from the most chauvinistic man I'd ever met. Who carried my bags because I was "a weak woman." Who nicknamed me "matróna" before I'd even arrived. Who always thought he was the smartest one in the room. Who eventually worked with me instead of against me. As we came together to help this place move forward, weed out corruption, and find a path to a new model.

In that moment, it hit me that it had all been worth it. Every meal of pork and dumplings that I'd eaten. Every pound I'd gained. Every bit of black coal dust on my face. Every hair I'd pulled out with frustration. Every terrifying and ridiculous situation I'd been in. Maybe I did make a little difference.

CHARLES BRIDGE

MARCH 1995

AND SUDDENLY, I WAS PACKING UP all my belongings and getting ready to go home. Well, not *home*. Not California. I was moving to Washington, D.C. to work in Arthur Andersen's Office of Government Services. My dearest friends planned to spend my last evening with me.

What:	Dinner, drinks and tons of fun.
Who:	Melanie and a handful of her closest friends.
Why:	#1: To mourn Melanie's departure from Prague.
	#2: To celebrate Melanie's impending adventure in Washington, D.C.
	#3: To keep Melanie from spending her last evening in Prague at home, in tears, or on Karlův most (Charles Bridge) drinking beer (all three of which are distinct possibilities).
Where:	Avalon Bar and Grill, Malostranské náměstí 12

When:	Monday, March 27th at 7:30 p.m.
How:	Please R.S.V.P. to Andrea by this Friday.
	Hope to see you there!

We had dinner, laughs, and tears at Avalon. I told Therese I would leave her my peanut butter and told Tereza that she could have everything else I left in the flat. Having Markéta, Martin, and Andrea there made the evening so special. I was thrilled that I'd ended my time here with Czech friends, not just expats. We spent the evening reminiscing about the two years I'd been here. All the cement factory stories, the culture clashes, the office gossip. Somehow, we'd all learned about each other and where we'd come from. We could understand each other's perspective and found a common ground laughing at the absurdities of both.

When the night was over, we planned to walk back over the Charles Bridge to New Town before catching our metros, trams, and buses home. It would be my last time on the bridge.

As we approached from the Malá Strana side, we could see that someone was putting up barriers at the end of the bridge. We walked up to him and asked if we could pass. Neh.

They were about to film a movie scene. Andrea pleaded with him, Czech-to-Czech. She explained the moment. He relented. He said we could go if we hurried. We would be the last people over the bridge that night. Amazing accomplishment in the world of "it's impossible." Ironically, they were about to film a big scene for the very first *Mission: Impossible*.

We walked across the bridge, and there wasn't another soul in sight. We stood at the edge and looked at the Prague skyline. Café Slavia. The National Theatre. Prague Castle. Malá Strana. All the statues. The towers at both ends of the bridge. And the spires. Everywhere. The city of golden spires. I breathed it in.

I found the statue of St. John of Nepomuk, the patron saint of Czechs.

The panel below was dark with pollution and age. It was the depiction of St. John being thrown overboard from a ship. Headfirst to his death. But his golden belly shone brightly in the spotlight. As was tradition, I rubbed the belly, 'ensuring' that I would return to Prague one day.

It began to snow. Flurries—light at first but then a little harder. Enough that we could see them as they gently landed on the bridge and created a thin coat of white flakes. The movie crew had placed a huge spotlight on the bridge that illuminated everything. We watched the snowflakes pass through its light. It couldn't have been a more perfect final memory of Prague. Here with my closest friends in the most beautiful place in the world in the snowy silence. We hugged silently as the snow fell into the water. It was magical.

Finally, we knew we needed to leave. They were rolling cameras out onto the bridge.

SWEATY SOCKS

APRIL 1995

I PROBABLY SHOULDN'T HAVE put my sweaty socks on the armrest.

I'd arisen early and the office driver had picked me up. The firm paid for business class for my trip home. The lap of luxury. But then, I got bumped up to first class. Even better. I would fly home in luxury. I was looking forward to it.

Dragging my luggage to the airport had left me hot and sweaty. I plopped into my first class seat. I was sticky and clammy—a truly hot mess—but otherwise I was in good spirits. I was certain I smelled as bad as I felt. I took off my shoes and my sweaty, damp socks, putting them on the armrest next to me to dry. They smelled too. I didn't care. I took the champagne offered to me and thought cool thoughts. I really just wanted to watch Prague out the window as we took off.

And as soon as I felt the plane lose touch with the ground and lift into the air, I burst into tears. All the frustration, fun, anger, insanity, disappointments, small triumphs, and love I'd felt in the last two years came over me all at once. The stewardess approached me, glanced awkwardly at my socks, and asked if I was ok. I couldn't speak so I nodded, turned my head, and waved her away. I was overwhelmed with emotion. She returned later to see if I needed anything, and I think she knew that mentioning the socks might put me over the edge.

I stared out the window at distant clouds, melancholic, motionless, and barefoot. Always the auditor, I was already doing the calculations for when I could return.

USA
1995

THE KETTLE

MARCH 1995

I WAS PREPARED. I really was. I had heard stories from people who, after living in Prague for any significant length of time, had gone home and had serious reverse culture shock. A manager who'd left not long after I arrived, Mark, had sent a letter warning us. He had moved home to San Francisco and gone to the grocery store to buy a bar of soap. He stared at the fully stocked shelves with hundreds of different brands and became so overwhelmed that he'd had to leave the store. He had broken down in tears outside the sliding doors. It sounded crazy to me, but I believed him. I was no stranger to crazy.

I was home in California for a week before I moved to D.C. I met my friend Kris for brunch at a favorite restaurant in Manhattan Beach, The Kettle. I was excited for an American breakfast. I prepared myself for all the choices I had to make so I would be ready when the waitress came. I was going to get coffee, not tea or juice. A muffin, not toast or a bagel. Fruit instead of potatoes. And I knew how I wanted my eggs. I could do this. I was ready.

WAITRESS: "What can I get for you?"

ME: "I'd like the Kettle breakfast with coffee, fruit, eggs over easy, and a muffin."

WAITRESS: "What kind of muffin would you like? We have blueberry, bran, apple cinnamon, orange cranberry ..."

I hadn't prepared for this. I was quickly overwhelmed. I panicked.

ME: "I don't care! Please just bring me breakfast!"

She looked a little stunned but walked away.

I couldn't believe that even with warning and preparation—even at a place in my hometown I'd gone to all my life—I was overwhelmed by simply ordering a muffin. Even more strangely, I had never ordered any kind of muffin at The Kettle except a bran muffin. They were absolutely one of my favorite things. And yet I still couldn't answer the question. It should have been a no-brainer.

But I'd panicked. Or maybe it wasn't panic as much as it was disorientation. I needed to exercise my decision-making muscle again. I hadn't needed it for a few years. It would take some getting used to again.

EXULANSIS

APRIL 1995

Exulansis *(n.)*: the tendency to give up trying to talk about an experience because people are unable to relate to it—whether through envy or pity or simple foreignness—which allows it to drift away from the rest of your life story, until the memory itself feels out of place, almost mythical, wandering restlessly in the fog, no longer even looking for a place to land

—*The Dictionary of Obscure Sorrows*

ON MY THIRD DAY WORKING IN D.C. at Arthur Andersen's government practice, Timothy McVeigh bombed a federal building in Oklahoma City. I immediately wondered if I'd made an enormous mistake joining the government practice. I would be working with clients in government buildings, and he had just bombed one! It was a terrifying start. And, of course, when I got home from work, I watched the news about it on CNN for hours. Two years of no TV except CNN had turned me into a news junkie. To this day, I can watch the news for hours on end.

I was given a cube at the office next to a woman named Karen. She had worked in this office for a while and was helping me meet people and get my bearings. I missed Prague and my friends desperately and was only now beginning to even process all my experiences there. I did a lot of processing out loud to poor Karen.

ME: "When I was in Prague . . ."

KAREN: "Yes?"

ME: "When I was in Prague, we had a little old lady working in the kitchen. She used to mend all my clothes when she found safety pins holding things together."

KAREN: "Wow. Really? Nobody works in the breakroom here."

ME: "Oh. Right. That makes sense. I miss her. I may need to learn how to sew on a button now."

KAREN: "Ok. Good luck with that. I need to run. I'll be back in a bit."

Every other sentence I said started with "When I was in Prague . . ." Karen listened patiently for weeks, but I could sense that she was growing weary of my stories. She had things to do and places to go. Maybe just to get out of my story trap. I was driving everyone crazy, and I could practically hear their eyes roll whenever I left the room.

One day, I went to lunch with two colleagues from the office. James and Andrew.

WAITER: "What would you like?"

ME: "I'll have the cheeseburger and a beer."

My coworkers quickly glanced at me. Quizzically. It took me a moment to realize what I'd done. I laughed.

ME: "Oops. Sorry. Forgot where I was for a minute. I'll have a Diet Coke."

A few minutes later, I was wondering about James, as he would be working for me on a project.

ME: "So Andrew, is James a solid performer? How are his analytical skills?"

Again, they both stared. Intensely. Here I was, asking about a coworker in front of that very coworker. I was quicker on the uptake this time.

ME: "Ohmigod. I am so sorry. I completely forgot that everyone at the table speaks English."

It was soooooo awkward.

I could no longer have private conversations directly in front of other people. A given back in Prague.

I was struggling to re-acclimate. I felt isolated. Alone. I couldn't share. I couldn't explain. I withdrew into myself at work.

PRAGUE REVISITED

AUGUST 1995

EVA SENT ME AN EMAIL THAT MADE ME laugh out loud in the office.

From today's *Fleet Sheet*:

"(MFD/4) A České Budějovice man used a kitchen knife to cut off his own penis and then threw it into a wastebasket before seeking medical help. Doctors were able to sew the organ back on but were unable to say why the man cut it off in the first place."

They are still mad.

I missed the madness. I had been so ready to go home, but then I missed my friends more than I ever imagined I would. I'd only been back in the U.S. for a few months, but I needed my friends.

SEPTEMBER 1995

Just six months after leaving, I was missing Prague and my friends desperately, so I went back for a week-long visit. Vašek was out of town but said I could stay at his flat. I went to my favorite haunts and ate my favorite foods. I explored new restaurants, shops, and bars. Prague was still changing weekly.

Late one night when I got back to the apartment building, the key wouldn't turn. I pulled it and tried again. Made sure it was the right way up. No luck. It wouldn't turn. I was stranded. But I knew this place well, so I figured out the way to the main road and started walking. Twenty minutes later, I came up a busy street and headed towards the center of Prague, looking for a hotel. When I found one, I went in and asked if they spoke English. Nope. I would have to try to muster up some of my Czech skills.

I managed to explain to them that I didn't have any cash, and I didn't have my passport on me. Neither of these things went over well, but somehow, I convinced them to rent me a room regardless. I decided my powers of persuasion must be excellent because I was sure my Czech was not.

But the best part of the trip was vacationing with Markéta, Pavel, Martin, Monika, and Marcela in Český Krumlov and Šumava. It was a wonderful, relaxing reunion. I felt like I was home. And it was just the quick fix I needed to keep me going back in D.C.

NOVEMBER 1995

My new friend, Karen, invited me to join her and her group of friends for Thanksgiving at her friend Jeff's house. As I walked into the host's home, my jaw dropped. I just stood there. On Jeff's mantel were picture frames made of wrought iron, just like I had bought in Prague. In the corner was a large birdcage wine rack, just like I had shipped home. He had Czech crystal and a sketch of the castle. It was like I'd walked into my own apartment.

ME: "Hi. Jeff?"

JEFF: "Hey. Melanie, right? It's nice to meet you."

ME: "You too. So . . . how is it that you have that wine rack and those picture frames?"

JEFF: "Oh! They're from Prague."

ME: "Yes . . . I have the same ones." Jeff looked at me skeptically.

ME: "I just came from living there for two years."

JEFF: "No. Way. I came back six months ago after living in Prague working for PriceWaterhouse."

ME: "Seriously? I worked for Arthur Andersen. I audited cement factories!"

JEFF: "I was in tax so spent most of my time in Prague."

Our minds: blown. We swapped stories over dinner.

ME: "Did you ever go to the James Joyce? Or Pizza Taxi? Or U Vejvodu?"

JEFF: "Yes! But we mostly went to Molly Malone's."

ME: "Did you know Brenda?"

JEFF: "Of course! Did you know Roman?"

ME: "Yes! And I worked with his wife, Barb."

We marveled at what a small world it was, including the fact that there truly was so little to buy in the Czech republic that we had purchased the exact same furnishings and souvenirs. I know we bored everyone else to tears. But I finally felt like maybe I wasn't totally invisible. I felt like my experience had actually happened.

SUMMER 1996

Andrea came to visit from Prague. One night, we went out for dinner with a group of my friends and colleagues. Lawyers, CPAs, government executives. All women. Power women. We were all chatting animatedly about our careers, our goals, and where we saw our lives taking us. They made a point of including Andrea in the conversation.

FRIEND: "So, Andrea, what are your hopes for the future?"

ANDREA: "I'm hoping to get married and raise a family."

The silence. Was. *Deafening.* Some women stared at Andrea. Others' jaws dropped. I don't think my American friends had ever heard a woman say such a thing out loud before. At least not as the first statement. Most of us also hoped to marry and have kids, but our answers to my friend's question would have been career-oriented. To us, it felt very 1950s to lead with the marriage and kids answer. But Andrea was totally comfortable with her statement. She was a family-oriented woman. She didn't bother mentioning that she worked at Arthur Andersen. I think she enjoyed shocking them.

I just laughed and told Andrea I was sure her dream would come true.

And it did.

SUMMER 1997

I couldn't wait. That summer, I went to Prague for Markéta's wedding. She was marrying Pavel. It was a beautiful event. They married at city hall, and when they got into a carriage to head to the reception at a Czech pub, they picked me up at the side of the road. I hadn't seen them beforehand, so we reunited and hugged in the carriage. The bride was stunning, and they both smiled from ear to ear. We enjoyed an afternoon of pivo and Czech food, including the traditional liver dumpling soup, at a wonderful, traditional Czech pub. There is nothing more wonderfully Czech than that.

JANUARY 1999

I took my new fiancé, Todd, to Prague for Andrea's wedding to the love of her life, Doug. On the way to Prague, we had stopped in London—where Todd proposed. He had wanted to wait until we went to my favorite restaurant in the world, U Šatlavy in Český Krumlov, but he decided he'd rather be engaged when he met my friends.

Andrea and Doug's wedding was a candlelit Western-style affair. The reception was held in a former palace in Prague. The ceremony was in a nearby church, which surprised me since the Czechs were generally not religious. But Doug was British. It was the perfect blend of Western and Czech weddings. Candles lit the stairwell up to the reception in Palffy Palace.

After the wedding, I took Todd to visit Český Krumlov on a bus with no heat. Ok, there *was* heat but barely. I spent the entire three-hour trip (each way) with my toes on the tiny heating strip near the floor of the bus. We never removed our hats or gloves. It was kind of miserable, but I just laughed. Of *course*, there was no heat. I couldn't wait to take him to U Šatlavy. After we'd visited the old center and the castle, I took him around the winding roads to find it. I was super excited as we rounded the corner. As I started to say, "There it is!" I came to a halt. I was speechless. The building had caved in and was covered in snow. Did the snow take it out? Or was the building just too old? I had no idea, but I was devastated. Todd, however, was relieved that he hadn't waited until this moment to propose.

I also took Todd to Karlovy Vary. Mercifully, this was a much shorter trip—90 minutes each way—and this bus was luxurious and warm. Too warm, in fact. We removed our hats, coats, and gloves and settled in. We had brought our own snacks for the trip: oranges. I was from California. Oranges? No big deal. But eating oranges in Prague was a huge deal. I leapt at the chance when I saw some on sale. We happily ate our oranges sitting side-by-side, putting the peels into a plastic bag to throw away later. About half an hour into the trip, we were overcome by a familiar smell. Sudden. Shocking. Todd looked at me with a "WTF?" look. I couldn't help but laugh back. A woman had taken off her coat several rows in front of us. We breathed into the bags of orange peels for the last thirty minutes of the trip.

The moment was weirdly nostalgic for me.

A few days later, my Czech friends gathered at Martina's house. She had a new baby I wanted to meet. It was winter, and I arrived by taxi. I was so excited to see everyone. We went into the house and settled in with coffee and chlebíčky (of course).

ME: "So!? How old is the baby?"

MARTINA: "Six months."

ME: "Awww. And what is her name?"

MARTINA: "Barbora."

ME: "I can't wait to meet her. Where is she?"

MARTINA: "Outside."

ME: "Outside? Is someone taking her for a walk?"

MARTINA: "No. She's on the porch."

I looked to the porch. Outside?! It was the dead of winter and there was snow on the ground. It was soooo c-o-o-o-old.

I felt like it was 1993 again and that I had to have been asking the wrong question. But I was out of practice, and I couldn't think of what to ask next. So I stayed silent.

MARTINA: "Do you want to see her?"

ME: "Yes—very much."

We got up, and Martina led me to the back door. Outside, on the back porch, the baby was asleep in her stroller. Bundled up, with pink cheeks, sleeping soundly.

ME: "Ohmigod. She really is outside. Why is she outside?"

MARTINA: "For the fresh air. It's good for them."

ME: "But it's so cold! It's 28 degrees out here! And it might snow more!"

MARTINA: "But she's under the covering and it's so healthy for them to get fresh air."

She wasn't wrong—fresh air is good for everyone. But I also knew that nobody back home was leaving their baby outside, alone, in the freezing cold. Still, it was weirdly grounding to encounter such a cultural contradiction again.

EARLY 2000s

Martin and Monika came to visit Todd and me in D.C. I was excited to show them a little of the U.S. I planned dinner at a local Mexican restaurant, knowing that Mexican food in Prague wasn't great. I mean, D.C. didn't have great Mexican food either, but it was better than Prague. As they opened the trifold menu, I could see a concerned look come upon their faces. Martin closed his menu shut.

MARTIN: "Just tell me what I should order."

ME: "It's a lot, isn't it? Look on the left at the enchilada section."

MARTIN: "Ok."

Martin reopened his menu.

ME: "You can get a platter with three enchiladas and try one of each: beef, chicken, and cheese."

MARTIN: "Perfect."

MONIKA: "I'll do the same."

ME: "You'll also need to choose rice or beans."

MARTIN: "Ok. I'll have rice."

MONIKA: "I'll try the beans."

They were ready.

The waitress came and asked for their order.

MARTIN: "We'll each have the enchilada platter with one of each kind of enchilada."

WAITRESS: "Great. Would you like Spanish rice or refried beans with that?"

MARTIN: "I'll have rice. She'll have the beans."

WAITRESS: "And would you like a creamy white sauce, a tangy red sauce, or a zesty green sauce with that?"

Oh no. Martin and Monika whipped their heads in synchronicity and stared at me, speechless. I jumped in.

ME: "They'll have the red sauce."

They slid back into their chairs, relieved.

MARTIN: "Can I get a beer?"

WAITRESS: "We have Budweiser and Coors on tap; in bottles, we have Corona, Dos Equis, Tecate, Sol, Bud Light, Miller Lite, and Michelob. Oh, Heineken too."

We all laughed.

ME: "We'll have four margaritas, on the rocks, with salt."

SPRING 2012

I had the chance to go to Prague again. Markéta and I grabbed a quick coffee. We hadn't seen each other for more than a decade. I'd been married and divorced. We each had two small children. Life had moved forward. When we got together it was as if no time had passed. We were the same people.

MARKÉTA: "Mel. I was worried what you would be like. But you are still Špagetka."

I laughed at the old nickname.

ME: "And you haven't changed a bit, big spaghetti."

She smiled

MARKÉTA: "But I need to tell you something."

ME: "Ok. What's up?"

MARKÉTA: "We had another nickname for you back then."

ME: "Oh no. If it's matróna, I already know."

She chuckled.

MARKÉTA: "We called you smršť."

ME: "Smršť? What in the world does that mean?"

She looked a sheepish.

MARKÉTA: "Whirlwhind. Really, storm or typhoon."

I could not stop laughing.

ME: "No way. That's amazing. When I worked in L.A., before moving to Prague, my colleagues nicknamed me Hurricane Melanie. I've been given the same nickname in two countries and two languages!"

She shrugged with a smile. Clearly, there was something to it.

It was a beautiful reunion. We talked about the years I had lived there and the ways Prague had changed. More stores and restaurants. Entrepreneurs everywhere. Artists flourishing. I even went into some galleries that had opened when I lived there almost 20 years before. And I recalled learning that Josef's father had once gone to jail because he visited an art gallery while he was on an approved trip out of the country. I was so happy to see the artists and galleries flooding the market.

She took me to a new restaurant that served traditional Czech food in a modern setting and we talked some more.

ME: "So I've been telling stories about my time here for years. People always get a good laugh when I tell them about the absurdity and inefficiency of late stage 'communism.' About how crazy and illogical things seemed from a Western perspective. But now I'm really curious about something."

MARKÉTA: "What is it, Mel?"

ME: "How did you guys view us? What did the expats do that you found strange or funny?"

She thought about it for a moment.

MARKÉTA: "Well, I always thought it was odd that you and Jamie brought coffee to work in those cups. I mean, I get it NOW."

I laughed aloud at the idea that she thought it was weird then but really understood now that there was such better coffee available in the world than we had then.

MARKÉTA: "Mel, you understand this place because you experienced the impact of communism. My children don't understand at all."

ME: "Neither do mine."

MARKÉTA: "They have no idea what it was like to only have one kind of yogurt."

I spit out my coffee, and we laughed. Communism had been so much worse than that. The fear, the pollution, the lack of freedom, the cruelty and suffering. But the little piece I'd experienced was the tail end of an economic system that had nothing to do with producing what people wanted and needed. And yogurt was one small example.

And she was right. I *did* know what that was like. *Will my children ever understand? Will hers?* Markéta and I were part of a dwindling group of people who had experienced that world. I had only been in it for a few years. Markéta for 25. Others for 40 years. Who would ever believe what an authoritarian government and a planned economy could do to a country and a people?

SUMMER 2014

When I returned to Prague with three friends in 2014, I thought, *Prague has finally arrived!* It was truly wonderful, amazing, and what we had always dreamed of for the Czechs. There were tourists in vintage cars, on bicycles, in horse-drawn carriages, and in futuristic, pedaled vehicles. People were parachuting over the city. There were numerous new art galleries, restaurants serving such a wonderfully diverse selection of food, and a lot more information about the history, the buildings, and the sites.

On the other hand, our hotel room had some odd features like a staircase up to the bathroom and then a large step down into it. It was a hazard that almost sent more than one of us to the hospital, but we managed to survive it. And the menus all over town could still use a review by just one native English speaker. No menu should have the word "gastric" on it.

But now I'm careful what I wish for. I saw things I never thought I would see in Prague. Just like the Czechs couldn't have imagined a green Škoda, I could never have imagined being almost run down by a Segway on the cobblestones of Old Town Square. I always dreamed of outdoor seating on Prague's squares. Now I'm kind of sorry they have so much outdoor seating. The square was packed, and we could barely navigate through the chaos.

CHRISTMAS 2018

I took my teenage children to the Czech republic for Christmas. I was excited to share this place with them. And I was excited to see my friends. Markéta arranged for us to go to the Kouzelný cirkus with her and her daughter. She said it was her favorite thing as a child, and she couldn't wait to share it with us.

We sat down in the theater, excited to experience this nostalgic show. As it began, I was confused but I reserved judgment. It was in Czech, of course, but I figured the kids and I would still enjoy the costumes and acts. But . . . the show was *crazy*. All capitals CRAZY.

I glanced at the kids. They were whispering to each other. I looked back at the stage. Marionettes with GIANT heads, strange stalky clowns, bizarre dances, and no cohesive story that I could discern. I looked to my left at Markéta. She was giving me the side-eye, trying to gauge my reaction. I gave her my best "what in the world?" look. She just shook her head.

I stifled my laugh. Clearly, she couldn't explain what we were seeing. I sat back and enjoyed the chaos.

As I watched, it reminded me of the one and only black light theater show I'd gone to when I lived in Prague. Black light theater is a Prague specialty where the stage is blacked out but there are UV lights and the performers wear fluorescent costumes or light bulbs. It was called The Garden of Earthly Delights and was based on its namesake painting by Hieronymus Bosch. The painting is wild. Fantastical. It's somehow religious and hedonistic at the same time. It has humans and animals but is also fantastical. Watching a bunch of people act out the painting in that setting was the craziest thing I'd ever seen. Kouzelný cirkus was a close second.

After the show, she closed her eyes, hung her head, and said only one thing.

MARKÉTA: "I don't know how to explain that."

Thirty years on from the Velvet Revolution, Markéta was chagrined that this used to seem normal to her, that she had loved it, and that she had brought us to it. She was seeing it through new eyes and was embarrassed. I loved the whole experience. For me, Markéta, and our kids.

Over the next few days, I took the kids around town. We went to some obvious places like the Charles Bridge and the castle. We went to some offbeat places too.

I took the kids to Café Slavia. Not because I thought it would mean something to them right then, but because I hoped one day when they were older they would appreciate the history of that place. It had been renovated in a beautiful art deco style with wood, mirrors, and round café tables.

We went to see two sites that I'd just learned about. In 1942, the Czechs had assassinated Reinhard Heydrich. A Nazi leader, known as The Butcher of Prague, and main architect of "the final solution." We went to the church—which I'd passed many times—where the Waffen-SS (Hitler's police) had trapped and killed the Czech soldiers who took down Heydrich. There are still visible bullet holes on the street above the crypt and there is a museum honoring these men. Somehow this had never come up when I lived in Prague, so this was my first visit.

We also went to the National Monument at Vítkov. It is a MASSIVE structure, up on a hill. And somehow not only had I never noticed it enough to ask what it was, nobody had ever talked about it. It had been built in the 1930s but then used for various purposes throughout the Communist regime. It had reopened to the public in 2000. Wild.

Then I took the kids to Prague City Hall to see The Elevator of Death, which they nicknamed the "escalator-elevator." They were as horrified as I'd been the first time I saw one. But they quickly rallied and had a great time figuring it out. I took videos of them getting on and off gracefully, not so gracefully, together, and separately. They even stayed on it all the way over the top and around the bottom—something I'd never been brave enough to try. I'm such a bad mom.

When we finished, we took the metro to Náměstí Míru to find some lunch. I wanted to take them on the longest escalator I'd ever been on. The metro was insanely deep and the escalator was terrifying. It took more than two minutes to ascend the escalator and if you weren't careful, you could tumble down 285 feet—almost as long as a football field. We held on tight and emerged onto the square—blinking like moles that had inadvertently come up from their burrow.

We were hungry, and there was a new pizza place here that I wanted to try.

CZECH WAITRESS: "What would you like to drink?"

MY DAUGHTER: "Coca-Cola."

MY SON: "Me too!"

The Coca-Cola came out in the old-school, curved bottles. My kids loved it.

The pizza was good, and the service wasn't half bad.

Several days later, we were in the same neighborhood. We decided to go back to the same pizza place because it had been so good. Everyone ordered their pizzas, and then the waitress asked us what we wanted to drink.

MY DAUGHTER: "I'd like a Coke."

WAITRESS: "We don't have Coke."

ME: "Coca-Cola? Are you out today?"

WAITRESS: "No. We never had Coca-Cola."

MY DAUGHTER: "But you had Coke three days ago."

WAITRESS: "No, we didn't."

MY SON: "But we had Cokes here the other day."

WAITRESS: "It's impossible. We only serve Czech cola."

My daughter furrowed her brow in confusion and looked at her brother. He furrowed his brow back at her. This wasn't right. They'd definitely had Coca-Cola here. They both turned to me and waited for my response.

ME: "Can you bring them two Kofolas, please?"

My kids frowned. The waitress scratched our drink order on her pad, looked at us nonplussed, and walked away.

I slid back in my seat and smiled to myself.

I kind of hoped the Chinese restaurant was still serving "chicken in a strange way."

THE END

EPILOGUE

*Both communism and socialism have the same effect
upon the individual—a loss of personal liberty.*

EZRA TAFT BENSON,
FORMER U.S. SECRETARY OF AGRICULTURE

I HAD SEVERAL LIGHT BULB MOMENTS throughout my time in the
Czech republic. Moments when I saw how some small part of the communist system had worked, when the illogical situations suddenly made
complete sense, and when I realized how that had impacted the people living in its long shadow.

In his New Year's address speech on January 1, 1990, the newly elected president Václav Havel had described it perfectly:

> "The previous regime—armed with its arrogant and intolerant ideol-
> ogy—reduced man to a force of production, and nature to a tool of
> production. In this it attacked both their very substance and their
> mutual relationships. It reduced gifted and autonomous people, skill-
> fully working in their own country, to the nuts and bolts of some
> monstrously huge, noisy and stinking machine, whose real meaning
> was not clear to anyone. It could not do more than slowly but inex-
> orably wear out itself and all its nuts and bolts."[16]

Jamie mailed me a *Washington Post* article that summed it up perfectly:
". . . for four decades the factories of Eastern Europe specialized in producing one thing: junk. Quality control was nonexistent. Social accounting
didn't factor in profits, and it didn't care about losses. A culture flourished,
the old saw goes, in which the state pretended to pay the workers, and the
workers pretended to work."[17]

As surprising, maddening, and occasionally ridiculous as my encounters
were to me, every situation and interaction was probably just as strange
and silly to the Czechs. It was simply the contrast between what made
sense under the communist system and what made sense under the capitalist system. Eventually, we all managed to understand each other and
learn more about the different worlds.

Humans can and will adapt to their environment and survive. The Czech
people did. I did. And it happened so quickly. I was only there for two
years. I adapted quickly and then struggled to adapt back. The Czechs
lived under the Communist government for decades, not even remembering a world that cared about their wants or needs. People stopped pushing
back or asking questions because it was futile. They saved their energy for
other things.

Everything depends on your perspective and environment. People believe
what they've been told. If someone has been told something their entire
life and then some foreigner comes and says they've been lied to the whole

time, it's not like flipping a switch. Even in the face of evidence, it's not a quick process to change someone's mind.

Logic is in the eye of the beholder. I always thought logic was pretty black and white, but it turns out that logic is a result of the environment. In communist Czech republic, it was completely logical to expand production capacity for an inferior product that nobody wanted to buy. Or for a store to stop carrying an item that was popular and sold well. In our capitalist world, those things are incomprehensible.

In the spring of 1995, I was ready to leave Prague. I had mentally exhausted myself trying to get Western work done in a post-communist environment. But the experience was unmatchable, and the impact on me was immeasurable. I am more patient, my expectations are more realistic, and my ability to ask the right questions is finely honed. I have always been one to find the humor in things, but now I revel in the absurd. Kafka is known for being an absurdist, but I think he was a realist; almost everything he wrote about seems plausible. My travel mantra is that the worst and craziest things that happen make the best stories later. I'll remember running out of deodorant and renting cars to go get Dunkin' Donuts more than I'll recall seeing the Eiffel Tower for the first time.

The entire experience comes flooding back to me as I watch the political happenings in the U.S. There are politicians and their supporters trying to move us in the direction of both things I encountered: far right authoritarianism or fascism and far left socialism or communism. Whatever words they use or things they do to move us closer to either of those extremes, they make me nervous. Russia invading Ukraine and flying drones over European countries makes me nervous. It makes the Czechs and other people who lived in the Soviet Bloc extremely nervous. Loss of freedom is much closer than most people know. Most Americans have no concept of what it would be like to lose that. It's the crux of the First Amendment to the U.S. Constitution that guarantees freedom of speech, the press, religion, and peaceful assembly. But now I see those guarantees fading before my eyes. I've learned what it's like to live without freedom, and I never want to lose mine.

My time in Prague feels a little like a dream now. Time has clearly moved on and the place has changed dramatically. It's a European country like any other. Part of me is sad that the hidden world we found in 1993 is no longer secret, but the nostalgia exists in pockets, and the changes are for the better. My time there was a once-in-a-lifetime experience. For a brief moment, capitalism and communism came face-to-face—literally—through the lives of the young Western expats and Czechs who worked, lived, and laughed together.

In 2020, the country renamed itself Czechia. But I don't know a single Czech who uses that term.

—Melanie Thomas
(*aka* Melanie Thomasová)

"Are you a communist?"
"No I am an anti-fascist."
"For a long time?"
"Since I have understood fascism."

ERNEST HEMINGWAY,
FOR WHOM THE BELL TOLLS

Those who fail to learn from history
are doomed to repeat it.

SIR. WINSTON CHURCHILL,
PRIME MINISTER OF THE U.K.

History repeats itself,
but in such cunning disguise that
we never detect the resemblance
until the damage is done.

SYDNEY J. HARRIS,
AMERICAN JOURNALIST

Freedom is the freedom to say
that two plus two makes four.
If that is granted, all else follows.

GEORGE ORWELL, 1984

When and if fascism comes to America it will not
be labeled "made in Germany"; it will not be marked
with a swastika; it will not even be called fascism;
it will be called, of course, "Americanism."

HAROLD LUCCOCK,
YALE DIVINITY SCHOOL PROFESSOR

NOTES

1   Harvard Student Agencies Inc., *Let's Go 1987: The Budget Guide to Europe*, St. Martin's Press, 1987.

2   Václav Havel, "New Year's Address to the Nation," January 1, 1990, Speakola.com.

3   Marcel Ludvík and Otakar Mohyla, *Olympia Guide Czechoslovakia Prague*, Olympia Publishing House, 1989.

4   Erik Best, *Fleet Sheet*, 1992–present.

5   Key: ČD (Český deník), E (Economist), EK (Ekonom), HN (Hospodářské noviny), EJSNF (English Journal of Slovak Nationalistic Feeling), LN (Lidové noviny), MFD (Mlada Front Dnes), MRCR (Market research in the Czech republic), MS (Mladý svět), RK (Respekt), RP (Rudé právo). Page number follows code.

6   Paul M. Sherer, *Communist cookbook a Confusing Recipe*, The Prague Post, 1993–1995, exact date unknown.

7   Matt Reynolds, "Still Standing," *The Prague Post*, 10 March 2005.

8   Steve Fisher, "Top 10 Possible Ad Slogans for the New Czech Republic," *Prognosis*, April 16–April 29, 1993.

9   Maggie Ledford Lawon, *McDonald's Teaching Czech Farmers How to Grow Crops*, The Prague Post, December 8–14, 1993.

10 J.S. Newton, "Career Opportunities," *Prognosis*, November 12–November 25, 1993.

11 *Pollution from past nags Czechs*, The Associated Press, March 1993, exact date unknown.

12 Lubomír Sedlák, *Czech accountancy practices still giving 'fuzzy' picture to investors*, The Prague Post, 1993-1995, exact date unknown.

13 Jack Kelley, *The pilot has turned on the no-chickens sign*, USA Today, 1993–1995, exact date unknown.

14 The Sunday Times magazine, July 25, 1993.

15 Josef Kožíšek, *Polámal se mraveneček*, Athos publishing house, 1993.

16 Václav Havel, "New Year's Address to the Nation," January 1, 1990, Speakola.com.

17 John Pomfret, "The Big Leap Into Capitalism: Nations' Road to Free Economy Uneven, Unmarked," *Washington Post*, October 24, 1994.

ACKNOWLEDGMENTS

FOR MORE THAN THIRTY YEARS, I've shared these stories with friends and colleagues—sometimes over coffee, sometimes over wine, always with laughter and curiosity. I remember many of these incidents vividly, not just because they were unforgettable but because I've retold them so often. People were amazed, amused, and enlightened. Their reactions reminded me how extraordinary it was to live in the former Soviet Bloc—and how important it is to share that experience.

Over the years, many friends encouraged me to write these stories down before time blurred the details. Their support and enthusiasm were the spark that got this book started—and the fuel that kept it going.

When I began writing, I worried: Would my stories make sense on paper? Would they still be funny? Would they offend? Could I express my shock and wonder without hurting anyone's feelings? I believe I've managed to strike that balance (fingers crossed), and I have many people to thank for helping me get there.

First and foremost, my children. When I started writing, I told myself I didn't need to publish, but I did need to write all of this down for my kids. So that one day, they might read about my experiences and learn a little bit about authoritarianism, socialism, and their mom through a firsthand account. It was the idea that they would read this that got me going.

Next, to **Rollie Quinn** whose regular asides—"you really should write this down" or "let me introduce Melanie . . . she really needs to write a book"—nudged me from storytelling into writing.

To my memoir emotional support team, **Ellen Goldstein** and **Susan Quinn**—thank you for your unwavering belief in all our books since our memoir class. Sharing our progress, doubts, and triumphs has been a gift. I may be the last to publish, but I got here because of your encouragement and your honest, invaluable feedback.

A heartfelt thank-you to **Emily Gindlesparger**, the first person to read one of my stories. You didn't know what to expect, but your reaction—your laughter, your insight, your insistence that I *had* to publish—gave me the confidence to keep going. You helped me see that my stories could be funny, clear, and educational all at once. You also reminded me that this memoir is something unique.

I'm grateful to **Ballast Books** for your patience with my timeline and for navigating the challenges with me. To all my beta readers and reviewers, thank you for your thoughtful feedback at every stage. A special thanks to **Maxim Naumenko,** a Ukrainian friend who lived in the Soviet Bloc until the mid-'90s. When you told me the book resonated deeply with you, I knew I had accomplished something meaningful.

There is no way to express my thanks to **Markéta Čejková** (née Nechvátalová) properly. For being my friend for more than 30 years, for giving me feedback on an early draft of this book, and for helping me with the Czech language and punctuation, which elude me still. Our shared experience, seen from opposite sides, only brought us closer.

To my Czech friends—**Markéta, the other Markéta, Andrea, Josef, Vašek, Martin, Honza, Běla, Jana, Iva, Marcela, Monika, Martina, Michaela, Irena, Ladislav,** and so many others—for your resilience, perseverance, kindness, and sense of humor, and for tolerating our confusion and naivete.

To the expats who went through the looking glass with me—**Jamie, Mike, Peter, Eva, Anna, Stephen, Tereza, Mitch, Laurent, Thierry, Henry, Jervis, Doug, Jason, Therese,** and the rest. We may all remember things a little differently, and the conversations may not be exact, but I hope you enjoy the spirit of the stories I've shared. And to those whose stories are reflected in the "Fridays at Pizza Taxi" chapters—thank you for letting me include your experiences. They enriched mine.

Finally, a huge thank you to **Philip Pendleton Wilson Jr.** Without you, this book, the website, the Facebook page—none of it would exist. You captured my voice, helped me rediscover forgotten moments, and pushed me when I needed it most. Your creativity helped me create an immersive experience for readers and for myself. Your enthusiasm for this book was, at times, stronger than mine, and that kept me moving forward.

This book is for anyone who's ever felt like a fish out of water. I hope you find laughter, insight, and connection in these pages. Enjoy.